TEACH... ...IO OF
L... ...S
LES... ...TIES

Hilda K. Weisburg and Ruth Toor

The Center for Applied Research in Education, Inc.
West Nyack, New York 10995

To our always supportive husbands, Marvin and Jay

Library of Congress Cataloging in Publication Data

Weisburg, Hilda K.
    Teacher's portfolio of library skills lessons & activities.

    Includes index.
    1. School children—Library orientation.   2. School libraries—Activity programs.   I. Toor, Ruth
II. Title.
Z675.S3W443   1985   025.5'678   85-14921

ISBN 0-87628-799-2

Printed in the United States of America

ABOUT THE AUTHORS

Hilda K. Weisburg earned her M.L.S. from Columbia University as a specialist in Children's and Young Adult's Services. At present, she is the library media specialist at Sayreville War Memorial High School in Sayreville, New Jersey, having been at the elementary level for many years. She has given inservice programs for several school districts, served on the State Task Force on Standards, and is listed in the 14th edition of *Who's Who of American Women*.

Ruth Toor earned her B.A. from the University of Delaware and her M.L.S. from Rutgers University. She is the library media specialist at Chatham Township Elementary School in Chatham, New Jersey, is a consultant for media center programs and facilities, and served as head of the State Intellectual Freedom Committee. She is the past president of the Educational Media Association of New Jersey, is active in the American Library Association as chairperson of the ALSC Scholarship Committee of the Association for Library Service to Children, and is delegate to the American Association of School Librarians' Affiliate Assembly.

Hilda K. Weisburg and Ruth Toor are coauthors of the *Elementary School Librarian's Almanac* (The Center, 1979), *The Complete Book of Forms for Managing the School Library Media Center* (The Center, 1982), *Media Skills Puzzlers* (Library Learning Resources, 1984), and coeditors of *The School Librarian's Workshop*, a newsletter published ten times a year (Library Learning Resources, Inc.). They have been featured panelists and speakers at national, state, county, and local conferences and workshops for library media specialists and teachers.

ABOUT THIS PORTFOLIO

The *Teacher's Portfolio of Library Skills Lessons & Activities*, written by two practicing library media specialists with a combined total of nearly thirty years of on-the-job experience, will make you confident that any instruction you give in grades K–9 will be accurate, extensive, and relevant. As you prepare these lessons and activities you will feel as though a library consultant is at your side giving you help and advice.

Although library instruction should always be the responsibility of a library media specialist with the certification and background necessary to develop a coherent program of skills and experiences to expand student competencies throughout the grades, many schools do not have one or else share a specialist among several schools. It is, therefore, difficult to provide instruction in the full range of information-gathering techniques needed by today's students.

Conscientious teachers who try to fill the gap with mass-produced ditto materials find these often incorrect, too generalized, and assuming knowledge on the part of the user without providing the necessary background information. Often, the library skills imparted to students through these materials have no final objective and do not follow through in a logical sequence or allow for the continuous reinforcement necessary in becoming both comfortable and adept in using library skills. Thus, the *Portfolio* was written to make your job easier by providing your students with the necessary library skills they will need throughout their lifetimes.

The *Portfolio* is divided into four parts. Part One consists of ten chapters covering all of the subject areas that make up a basic library skills program. Each chapter contains background to provide you with the knowledge you need before you begin to teach the unit. Unlike other such books, it does not assume you have extensive knowledge and builds from the basics to help you reach a level of understanding beyond that provided in most teacher training programs, although below the level of expertise achieved by a professional library media specialist. Subjects of interest solely to the librarian, such as the selection, acquisition, and processing of print and nonprint media are not included in this book.

Several lessons in the skill areas are given in each chapter and new words and terms that have been introduced are also listed in the Glossary. Included in each chapter, too, are teaching units and learning center ideas.

In Parts Two, Three, and Four, you are directed to a series of activities that provide opportunities for students to reinforce and master what you have just taught. For example, you can distribute puzzles, games, and reference questions from Part Two to students at the opportune time, knowing exactly which skill will be practiced. At the same time, you can decorate your room with a bulletin board from Part Three to reinforce the skills from the lesson and supplement your instruction. You can then encourage further individual exploration of library skills with book reports from Part Four that not only provide a check on what the students have read, but also help develop their creativity.

As a teacher, you know how important it is for everyone to be able to find information efficiently and without frustration. This book provides, in one place, all the help you and your students need to fully employ the resources of a modern media center.

If there is a full-time library media specialist in your school, the knowledge you have gained through the *Teacher's Portfolio of Library Skills Lessons & Activities* will allow you both to work together to develop a comprehensive, interdisciplinary approach to skills that expands the curriculum while enriching each student's education.

Hilda K. Weisburg

Ruth Toor

CONTENTS

PART ONE

Lessons in
Library Skills

Chapter 1

SHELF ARRANGEMENT

BACKGROUND INFORMATION

Libraries are arranged to respond to your needs as a user. For example, public libraries have a section for new books because many patrons want to keep up with the best sellers and special collections, such as mystery or science fiction. School libraries also set up separate areas in order to provide the easiest access to materials based on the abilities and interests of those who use that library.

It is because the organization of the library is tailored to your requirements that you soon become adept at finding what you want without developing much technical knowledge of how and why the books got there. After years of reading for pleasure and doing research papers for college courses, you can now speak confidently of the difference between fiction and nonfiction arrangements and may even have some idea of what the numbers on the spine label mean. Somewhere along the way, you might even have been required to learn the major divisions of the DEWEY DECIMAL CLASSIFICATION SYSTEM, most of which you probably forgot, but some hazy memory may linger.

This experience gives you a good base with which to begin teaching library skills, but if you want students to be comfortable, efficient, and knowledgeable when they work in a library, you need a better understanding of the systems for classifying books, an awareness of the possible variations within the systems, and an opportunity to debunk some of the more popular library myths. In the process, you will acquire a working vocabulary of library terminology. New terms will be explained and a glossary of capitalized terms is provided at the end of the book.

Call Numbers

Every library book has letters or a letter-and-number combination on its spine label, referred to as the book's CALL NUMBER. The call number is the classification that identifies the book and also appears on the left hand corner of the BOOK CARD and BOOK POCKET. Students are often told that it is the book's "address." This is true in the sense that a major function of the call number is to indicate the book's position on the shelves.

Generally, call numbers come in two parts ($\boxed{\begin{array}{l}\text{FIC}\\\text{CLE}\end{array}}$, $\boxed{\begin{array}{l}\text{F}\\\text{CO}\end{array}}$, $\boxed{\begin{array}{l}\text{551.4}\\\text{ADL}\end{array}}$, $\boxed{\begin{array}{l}\text{973}\\\text{C}\end{array}}$). The upper half denotes the location. F or FIC commonly refers to the fiction section, although some libraries have eliminated this designation entirely. Nonfiction books have the classification numbers on the top. The bottom half on all books shows the first one, two, or three letters of the author's last name. (Some libraries may use a CUTTER NUMBER for the author, giving a letter followed by a number sequence ($\boxed{\begin{array}{c} 796 \\ W44 \end{array}}$). Books shelved in special areas may have a three-part call number ($\boxed{\begin{array}{c} \text{PROF} \\ 371.3 \\ \text{FIN} \end{array}}$).

When teaching shelf arrangement to students it is customary to explain that fiction is arranged in alphabetical order by the author's last name. Actually, all books—fiction and nonfiction—are arranged by area and then by author. It is just that fiction is a very large area, while in some nonfiction categories a school library may own only two books within the same classification number.

Classification of Books

The classification used on the call number depends on the type of library you are in. School and public libraries most commonly use the Dewey Decimal System. Academic, technical, and some senior high school libraries use LIBRARY OF CONGRESS CLASSIFICATION.

You are probably most familiar with the Dewey Decimal Classification, the system devised by Melvil Dewey in 1876. According to Dewey's scheme, all subject matter is divided into ten major categories by hundreds. (See Figure 1-1.) These headings are subdivided into large areas by 10s (see Figure 1-2) and each of them is then further broken down into units. Numbers can be expanded to several places beyond the decimal, permitting a very specific description of the subject of a given book. (See Figure 1-3.) The number of places used beyond the decimal depends on the size of the library and the age of the children using it.

Figure 1-1. DEWEY DECIMAL CLASSIFICATION SYSTEM

	THE 10 MAIN CLASSES
000	GENERALITIES
100	PHILOSOPHY & RELATED DISCIPLINES
200	RELIGION
300	THE SOCIAL SCIENCES
400	LANGUAGE
500	PURE SCIENCES
600	TECHNOLOGY (APPLIED SCIENCES)
700	THE ARTS
800	LITERATURE (BELLES-LETTRES)
900	GENERAL GEOGRAPHY & HISTORY

Figure 1-2. SECOND SUMMARY

THE 700 DIVISIONS	
700	ARTS
710	Civic & landscape art
720	Architecture
730	Plastic arts, sculpture
740	Drawing, Decorative & minor arts
750	Painting & Paintings
760	Graphic art, prints
770	Photography & photographs
780	Music
790	Recreational & performing arts

Figure 1-3. SPECIFIC DESCRIPTION

796	ATHLETIC & OUTDOOR SPORTS & GAMES	
796.3	Ball games	
796.31	Ball thrown or hit by hand	
796.32	Inflated ball thrown or hit by hand	
	796.323	Basketball
	796.325	Volleyball
796.33	Inflated ball driven by foot	
	796.332	American football
	796.334	Soccer
796.34	Racket games	
	796.342	Tennis (lawn)
	796.345	Badminton
796.35	Ball driven by club, mallet, bat	
	796.352	Golf
	796.353	Polo
	796.354	Croquet
	796.355	Field hockey
	796.357	Baseball
	796.358	Cricket
796.36 — 796.39	Unassigned	
796.4	Athletic exercises and gymnastics	

If you look at the way the major categories are set up, several points become apparent. Despite what you may have been taught, the Dewey Decimal Classification System is *not* a system for arranging nonfiction books. It is a system for arranging *all* books.

Fiction books could be assigned numbers within the 800 category. Librarians do not do this, however, for several reasons. The classification numbers would separate authors from different countries. Anyone looking for recreational reading would have to look in several places within the 800s. As was noted earlier, shelf arrangement is based on user needs. That is why many elementary collections have a section of easy reader books while other libraries may separate short story collections.

Referring to the Dewey Decimal Classification System as only a nonfiction arrangement makes no sense when you realize that folk and fairy tales are found in 398.2. Surely *Cinderella* or *Paul Bunyan* are not nonfiction—so much for one of the oft-repeated myths!

To sum up, when you teach the Dewey Decimal Classification System you should stress that it is a subject arrangement that uses numbers, not just a numerical arrangement, since the latter obscures the underlying idea. No matter which classification system is used, the arrangement of books is by subject. Library of Congress uses a combination of letters and numbers to organize everything by subject.

Some Special Classifications

The subject arrangement idea helps to explain how libraries handle biographies. At one time, under the Dewey system libraries used 92 rather than a three-digit number, and you will occasionally still find that classification. Most libraries now use "B" to denote a biography. Below the "B" you will not find the letter(s) of the author's last name, but rather either the first three letters or the entire last name of the person that the biography is about. Biographies are therefore arranged alphabetically, but since the person is the subject of a biography the concept of keeping books together by subject is intact. All books

about George Washington are together under
```
B
WASHINGTON
```
.

The 920 classification is reserved for COLLECTIVE BIOGRAPHY—books that contain short histories of the lives of many people sharing a common theme (such as Presidents of the United States or famous women scientists). The letter(s) under the 920 classification are those of the author's last name, since no one subject can be pulled out. Libraries vary greatly as to where they shelve the 920s. Some file them sequentially after 919; others place them immediately before or after the biography section. If you are looking for collective biography, you may have to ask.

The reference collection is identified by "R" or "REF." This material is normally shelved separately and may not be borrowed from the library, although there are several exceptions. Some school libraries permit teacher borrowing and many allow students to borrow reference books overnight. Dictonaries and atlases are frequently stored in special cases because of their unusual dimensions and the frequency and length of use.

One More Myth

Somehow over the years, librarians have given students the impression that those practitioners of the library arts who are intimately acquainted with the Dewey Decimal Classification System can look at a book and immediately assign to it its one true classification and that each book has only one possible number. True, you will never find a book about baseball (796.357) located in the midst of astronomy books (520) unless it has been misshelved. On the other hand, does a book about gypsy moths belong with insects in 595.7 or does it belong in 632 as an agricultural pest? Hamsters can be found in 599 as are other books on mammals, but they can also be found in 636 as a domestic pet. Transportation is in the 380s but automobiles are found in 629.2 under engineering. There are countless similar examples. Sometimes there are three or four places where a book could be correctly classified. Keep this in the back of your mind as you teach Dewey and shelf arrangement. The only way you can be sure to find what you want is to use the card catalog.

TEACHING UNIT 1: BOOK SPINES

The simplest and quickest way to begin teaching shelf arrangement is to set up this learning center. After you have introduced the fiction arrangement (steps 1–5 under "Directions"), two or three students can work with the spines at one time, taking between fifteen and thirty minutes to complete the task. By allowing one hour a day, you can move your entire class through the activity in one week. Have two groups complete fiction spines on the first day. On the second day, explain nonfiction arrangement (steps 6–8). Then move the first two groups into nonfiction spines while two other groups do fiction.

Objectives:

At the conclusion of this unit students should be able to:

1. Explain how nonfiction and fiction books are arranged.
2. Arrange a series of call numbers in correct shelf sequence.

Materials:

acetate for transparencies

water-soluble transparency markers

overhead projector

Preparation:

1. Make the five permanent transparencies if you have the proper equipment.
2. If you do not have the facilities for making permanent transparencies, make poster-size reproductions of the transparencies illustrated. Cover them with clear self-stick vinyl so you can write and wipe off.

Directions:

1. Tell the students that they are about to learn how books are arranged in the media center.
2. Explain that when they look at a library book the call number tells them where the book is shelved.

3. Show the first transparency. (See Figure 1-4.) When you refer to it, use proper library terms. You might say, "The call number is found in three places on a book: on the spine label, the book card, and the book pocket." Some students may know of other places where libraries may record call numbers. There is no need to mention during this unit that the call number is also found on the catalog card unless a student adds this information.

Figure 1-4. FIRST TRANSPARENCY

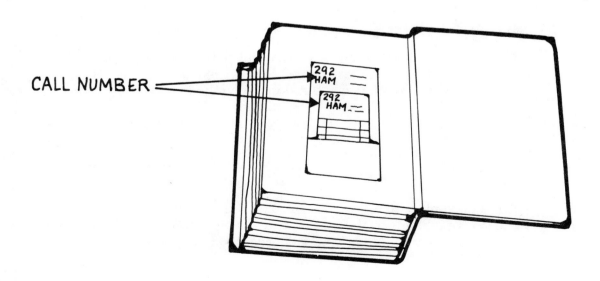

4. Show the second transparency. (See Figure 1-5.)

   - Ask if the call numbers are for fiction or nonfiction. (FIC indicates fiction.)

   - In what order is fiction arranged? (The correct answer is *not* "alphabetical"; it is "alphabetical by author." After all, you can arrange books alphabetically by title or even color. Students find it funny if you suggest that orange books can be filed under "O," then black books could come first, followed by blue, then brown books.)

   - Use a transparency marker to fill in the spine labels. (See the Answer Key for Figure 1-5.)

ANSWER KEY FOR FIGURE 1-5

FIC	FIC	FIC	FIC	FIC	FIC	FIC	
ADK	AND	BEA	BRU	CER	DEL	FIS	
FIC	FIC	FIC	FIC	FIC	FIC	FIC	FIC
FRO	HEN	HIC	HOR	ISH	KAL	KEN	LAM

---

5. Show the third transparency. (See Figure 1-6.)

   - Now you have several call numbers beginning with the same letter. What steps are needed to put these books in order?

   - Fill in the spine labels. (See the Answer Key for Figure 1-6.)

ANSWER KEY FOR FIGURE 1-6

FIC	FIC	FIC	FIC	FIC	FIC	FIC	
SAC	SAI	SAL	SAN	SAU	SAW	SAY	
FIC	FIC	FIC	FIC	FIC	FIC	FIC	FIC
SCH	SCO	SEL	SES	SHA	SHE	SHI	SNY

   - As a next step, ask what students would do with two call numbers that are both FIC/CLE FIC/CLE ? (Remind them that fiction is arranged by author, and the author's name is not Cle. They must look at the cover or title page to find the complete last name.) It may take a while, but students should learn that the sequence for alphabetizing is:

   Last name
   First name
   Middle name (if any)
   Title (omitting "A," "An," and "The" when they come first to facilitate filing since many titles begin that way)

   - This is a good place to end the lesson. You can continue this introduction next time. To add physical movement to a sedentary lesson, ask students to line themselves up in alphabetical order, last name first, of course.

Figure 1-5. SECOND TRANSPARENCY

Put spine labels on books

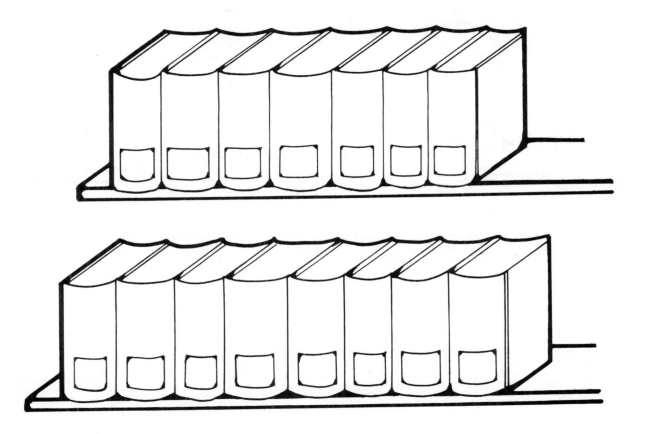

FIC HIC FIC CER FIC FRO FIC KAL FIC AND FIC ISH FIC HEN

FIC BRU FIC LAM FIC DEL FIC HOR FIC ADK FIC KEN FIC BEA FIC FIS

Figure 1-6. THIRD TRANSPARENCY

Put spine labels on books

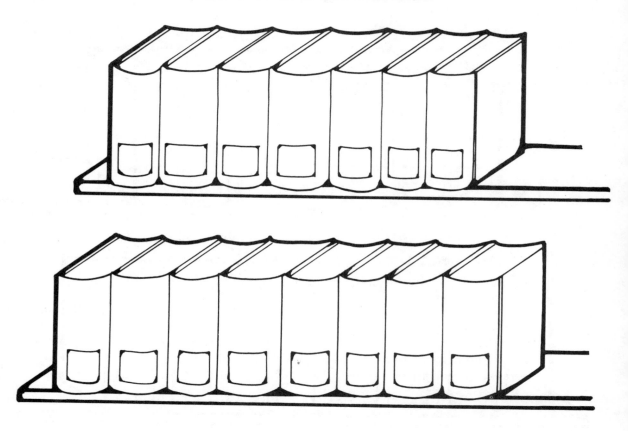

6. Show the fourth transparency. (See Figure 1-7.)

   • Are these fiction books?   (No.)

   • What are they?   (Nonfiction.)

   • How do you know?   (They don't say "FIC.")

   • Ask students if they have any idea what the numbers mean. Some may know the numbers for sports or animal books because they are two popular nonfiction categories. A few may be aware of the Dewey Decimal Classification System but you will have to explain in such a way that all students are aware that the numbers were created by Melvil Dewey, who devised the Dewey Decimal Classification System. In his system all subject matter is divided into ten numerical categories.

   • Use transparency markers to fill in the spine labels. (See the Answer Key for Figure 1-7.)

ANSWER KEY FOR FIGURE 1-7

701	709	725	736	738.3	746.1	746.4	
MAR	RIL	FIS	ALK	BRO	LAS	HOD	
756	770	781.7	784.4	787	791.5	793	793.7
FOR	WEI	BER	NIC	KET	BAD	CAR	ADL

---

7. Show the fifth transparency. (See Figure 1-8.)

   The Dewey numbers can get very complicated, especially if you don't understand decimals. If you learn one simple rule, however, you will have no problems. The rule is: *arrangement is done in column-by-column sequence.*

   Remove the transparency and explain how to implement this rule. Use an overhead projector or chalkboard and write a sequence of numbers such as:

621.09	621.909
621.4	621.97
621.13	621.133
621.2	622.1

   Ask students which number should come first. Do not comment on the answers. Just write the following names in another column next to the numbers:

   HAYNES
   HAYES
   HAYWOOD
   HAYCROFT

   Now ask which name should come first, second, and so forth. Once you receive the correct response, try to make the students explain the reasoning process they used to arrive at the right sequence. Eventually, they will explain that they realized that every word began with an "H," so they looked

Figure 1-7. FOURTH TRANSPARENCY

Put spine labels on books

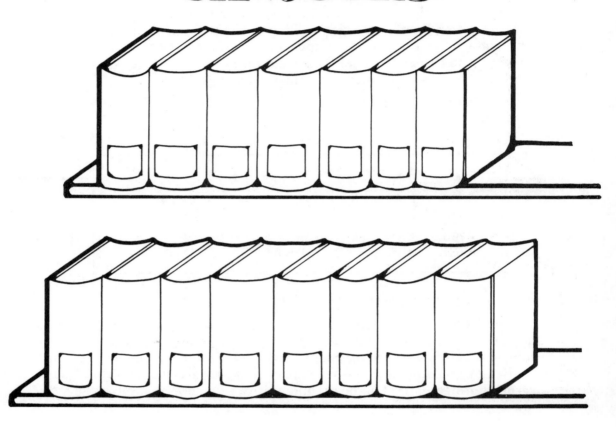

746.4 HOD	793 CAR	738.3 BRO	781.7 BER	709 RIL	787 KET	701 MAR

784.4 NIC	756 FOR	793.7 ADL	746.1 LAS	770 WEI	791.5 BAD	736 ALK	725 FIS

Figure 1-8. FIFTH TRANSPARENCY

Put spine labels on books

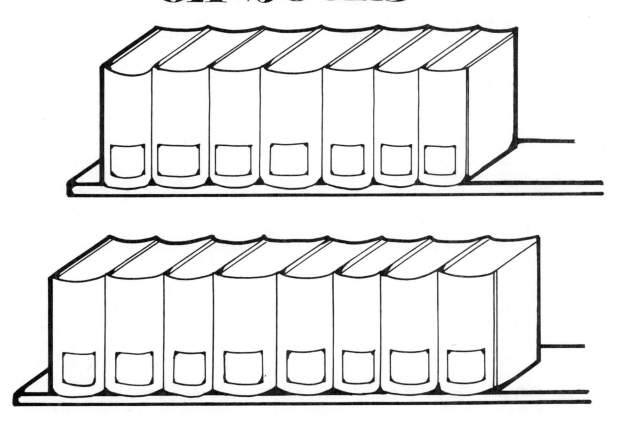

| 914.2 STR | 909.07 FOS | 915.493 SPI | 910.4 HEA | 914.6 BUC | 915.7 ARS | 913.32 FEN |

| 901 MOR | 914.38 ELI | 910.09 RAB | 915.61 GID | 914.15 SAS | 901.9 RES | 915.4 WEI | 913.32 COT |

at the next letter. Since all the second letters were the same, they looked at
the third letter. Finally, they found that the fourth letters were all different,
so they were then able to put the names in sequence.

Draw lines between each of the letters and each of the numbers in the
columns:

H	A	Y	N	E	S		
H	A	Y	E	S			
H	A	Y	W	O	O	D	
H	A	Y	C	R	O	F	T

6	2	1	.0	9		
6	2	1	.4			
6	2	1	.1	3		
6	2	1	.2			
6	2	1	.9	0	9	
6	2	1	.9	7		
6	2	1	.1	3	3	
6	2	2	.1			

Doing this will help the students to realize that they can put books in
numerical order by adapting the technique they used to put books in alphabetical order. To further clarify this concept, tell them that to alphabetize
they must look at the word in a letter-by-letter sequence; to put books in
decimal order they must look at the number in a number-by-number sequence, one column at a time.

To get everyone on the right track, go through the steps by saying,
"The numbers all begin with '6s,' so move to the next column. These are all
'2s,' so move to the next column. These are all '1s,' except the last one.
Because it is a '2,' it will be the last number."

Erase 622.1 and write it outside the column; then return to the drill.
Call students' attention to the fact that the next column, which is the one
after the decimal point, has many different numbers. Ask which is the lowest or which comes first. Students should have no trouble coming up with
the correct answer. But if someone should say that 621.4 is lower than
621.13, bring their attention back to the alphabetical chart. Remind them
that although HAYCROFT has more letters in it than HAYES, it precedes
HAYES because "c" comes before "e." Conclude by saying, "The 1 after
the decimal is lower than 4; therefore, 621.13 comes first. It does not matter
that there is still another digit after the 1."

CAUTION: Do not let students read 621.13 as "six twenty-one point
thirteen." Numbers after the decimal point must be read individually. If
students read the number as "thirteen," they will think of it as thirteen, and
everyone knows that thirteen is more than two!

The effectiveness of teaching this way rests on absolutes. There is no
room for deviation. Although instruction should allow for creativity, inter-
pretation, and more than one approach to a solution, this is *not* the case
with lessons about shelf arrangement. The drill approach succeeds because
there are no exceptions to this rule. It always works.

Repeat the exercise with another series of numbers. Again ask which
number comes first and be sure that the student reads the number correctly. Whether the answer is right or wrong, ask the student to explain how he

or she arrived at it. Vary the procedure by giving two lists of numbers, one properly sequenced and the other randomly sequenced. Both lists should consist of decimals that fall within the same number, such as:

796.09	796.357
796.1	796.33
796.35	796.7
796.4	796.21
	796.9

Have students insert the random numbers in the second column into the first column.

8. Go back to the fifth transparency. Now use a marker to fill in the spine labels. (See the Answer Key for Figure 1-8.)

ANSWER KEY FOR FIGURE 1-8

901	901.9	909.07	910.09
MOR	RES	FOS	RAB
910.4	913.32	913.32	914.15
HEA	COT	FEN	SAS
914.2	914.38	914.6	915.4
STR	ELI	BUC	WEI
915.493	915.61	915.7	
SPI	GID	ARS	

Fiction Book Spines

Materials:

25 strips of 1″ × 6½″ colored posterboard

2 pieces of 6″ × 9″ colored posterboard

1 sheet of 8½″ × 11″ colored construction paper (or another 6″ × 9″ piece of posterboard)

felt marker

1 manila envelope, large enough to hold all of the materials

Preparation:

1. Go to the fiction shelves in your media center and prepare a list of twenty-five authors and titles. Choose several that require alphabetizing by the second or third letter or use the following list:

Alcott, Louisa M.	*Little Women*
Asimov, Isaac	*Fantastic Voyage*

Babbitt, Natalie	*Goody Hall*
Bulla, Clyde	*White Bird*
Cameron, Eleanor	*The Court of the Stone Children*
Carlson, Natalie Savage	*The Empty Schoolhouse*
Cleary, Beverly	*Ramona the Pest*
Dahl, Roald	*James and the Giant Peach*
Dickens, Monica	*The House at World's End*
Edwards, Julie	*Mandy*
Haywood, Carolyn	*Eddie and Gardenia*
Henry, Marguerite	*Brighty of Grand Canyon*
Key, Alexander	*The Golden Enemy*
Lawson, Robert	*Ben and Me*
Lenski, Lois	*Judy's Journey*
Lindgren, Astrid	*Pippi Longstocking*
Mendoza, George	*GWOT!*
Sachs, Marilyn	*Laura's Luck*
Stevenson, Robert L.	*Black Arrow*
Stolz, Mary	*Noonday Friends*
Sutcliff, Rosemary	*Witch's Brat*
Thurber, James	*The 13 Clocks*
Tolkien, J.R.R.	*The Hobbit*
Watson, Sally	*Magic at Wychwood*
White, E.B.	*Charlotte's Web*

2. Use a felt marker to label the spines. Be sure to include the author, title, and call number. Authors' names should be written first name first.

3. Use a 6″ × 9″ piece of posterboard to prepare the alphabetized answer card.

4. Print the directions for using the book spines on construction paper or 6″ × 9″ posterboard.

5. Use a 6″ × 9″ piece of posterboard to prepare a question card with three or four questions. Answers can be written upside down on the card, or the students can check with the teacher. Here are a few sample questions:

   • Who wrote *Mandy*?

   • What is the title of the book by George Mendoza?

   • Who is the author of the book that has $\boxed{\begin{array}{c} \text{FIC} \\ \text{THU} \end{array}}$ as a call number?

Directions:

1. Students are to arrange the spines in correct alphabetical sequence. (Your directions to the students should remind them that fiction is arranged in alphabetical order by author.)

2. After arranging the spines, students are to check their responses with the answer card.

3. Students who successfully alphabetize the spines are to answer the question card.

4. All of the materials should be put back in the manila envelope for storage.

Nonfiction Book Spines

Materials:

50 strips of 1″ × 6½″ posterboard in 4 different colors

4 pieces of 6″ × 9″ posterboard in the same 4 colors

1 sheet of 8½″ × 11″ colored construction paper (or another 6″ × 9″ piece of posterboard)

felt marker

1 manila envelope, large enough to hold all of the materials

Preparation:

1. Go to the nonfiction shelves in your media center and prepare a list of fifty call numbers, preferably in sequence. A suitable sequence might look like the one shown.

620 LAR	620.09 BRA	621 BOU	621 EPS	621 FIN	621.32 RUS	621.381 KLE
621.382 NAT	621.384 GOU	621.386 EVA	621.386 KNI	621.386 SCH	621.388 HAE	621.388 WIL
621.389 MUR	621.389 OLN	621.4 WEI	621.4 ZIM	621.48 COL	621.702 WIL	621.8 ZAF
621.9 MEY	621.9 YAT	621.9 ZIM	621.909 EPS	621.97 EDS	621.97 EPS	622 BUE
623 GRA	623.4 BER	623.4 COL	623.409 NIC	623.7 COO	623.82 BUR	623.82 COO
623.82 GIL	623.82 HAN	623.82 SNY	623.88 GIB	623.89 CHA	624 CAR	624 CUL
624 PEE	624 SUL	624 VEG	625.1 HAR	625.2 KES	625.2 OPP	625.7 PAR	625.7 PAR

2. To keep track of the level of difficulty, use one color posterboard for all spines with a three-digit Dewey decimal number, a second color for spines with one number after the decimal point, a third color for spines with two numbers after the decimal point, and a fourth color for spines with three or more numbers after the decimal point.

3. Use a felt marker to print each call number on the appropriate part of a book spine.

4. Use the 6" × 9" pieces of posterboard to prepare answer cards that are color-coded. For example, if blue posterboard was used for spines with three-digit call numbers, use blue for the answer card. (The blue card should include all the numbers.)

5. Print the following directions for using the book spines on either the construction paper (if the unit is to be mounted on a bulletin board) or the extra 6" × 9" posterboard piece (if it is to be kept as a learning packet).

Directions:

1. Assign the students one color or several colors of book spines, depending on their abilities and knowledge of library skills.

2. The students are to arrange the spines in correct numerical sequence. (Remind the students that nonfiction is arranged in numerical order.)

3. After arranging the spines, the students are to check their responses with the appropriate answer card.

4. Direct students to choose one spine in a given color, to take the spine to the media center, and to check the shelves there. The students are to find the name of the author and the title of the book with that call number.

5. All of the materials should be put back in the manila envelope for storage.

TEACHING UNIT 2: MIXED-UP SHELVES

The best way for students to learn fiction and nonfiction shelf arrangement is by direct, hands-on experience. For this, you need access to a media center or a cooperative public library. The unit may be too difficult without some professional help, but it is included because it is the most effective way to teach this skill.

If your school has a nonprofessionally staffed media center and you decide to attempt teaching the unit, reserve the room for the first period of the day and prepare the shelves before school begins or on the afternoon of the previous day. If your class will go to the public library, be sure all the preparations have been made in advance.

Objectives:

At the conclusion of this unit students will be able to:

1. Use a call number as a guide to arranging shelves.

2. Arrange a series of fiction books in correct author sequence.

3. Arrange fiction titles by a single author in correct sequence.

4. Arrange a series of nonfiction books in correct Dewey decimal sequence.

Materials:

acetate for transparencies

water-soluble transparency markers

overhead projector

filmstrip on library arrangement

Preparation:

1. Preview a filmstrip on library arrangement if one is available. Possible choices include:

    SVE's *The Elementary School Library* (BD 153SATC)
    Spoken Arts' *Quickwick Your Library Guide* (SAC 2018)

2. Make a transparency of fiction shelf arrangement. (See Figure 1-9.)
3. Make a transparency of nonfiction shelf arrangement. (See Figure 1-10.)

Figure 1-9. FICTION SHELF ARRANGEMENT

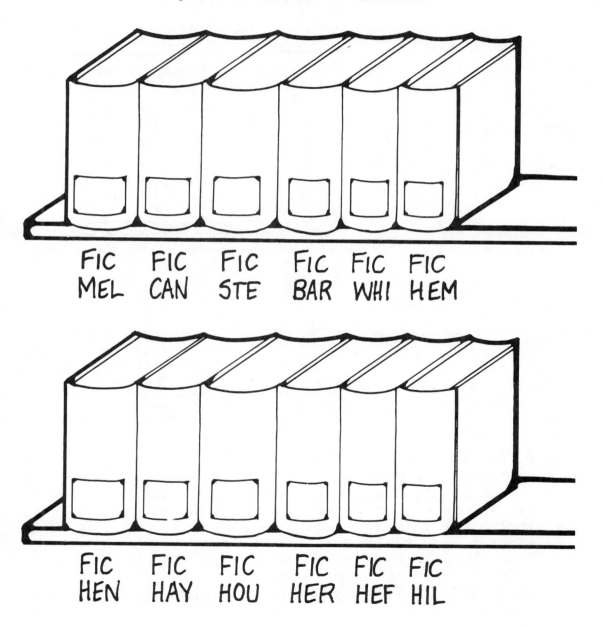

FIC   FIC   FIC   FIC   FIC   FIC
MEL   CAN   STE   BAR   WHI   HEM

FIC   FIC   FIC   FIC   FIC   FIC
HEN   HAY   HOU   HER   HEF   HIL

Figure 1-10. NONFICTION SHELF ARRANGEMENT

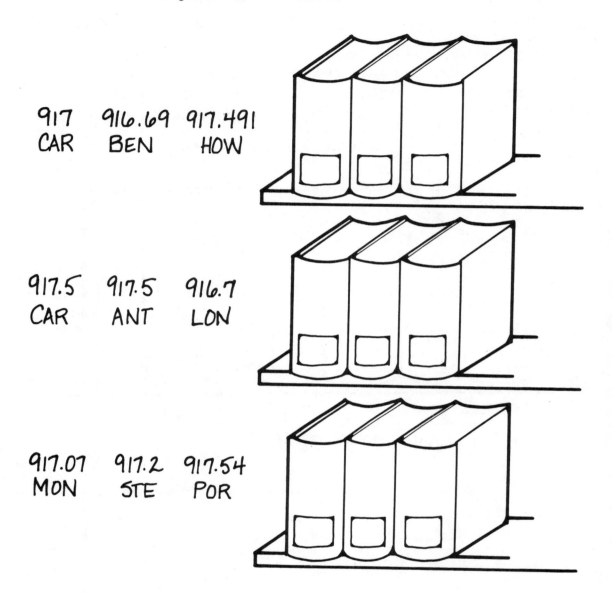

917   916.69   917.491
CAR   BEN   HOW

917.5   917.5   916.7
CAR   ANT   LON

917.07   917.2   917.54
MON   STE   POR

4. *Before the lessons on fiction arrangement:* Select one shelf of books for every two or three students and rearrange the books in a random sequence. If the media center is not large enough to permit students to work at the actual bookstacks, set up the books on tables or the floor. Two groups can work at the same table if the call numbers are widely spaced (for example, one group works with "C" authors, another with "L" authors). Make a list numbering the shelves, then determine the level of difficulty (see NOTE following) and assign students accordingly.

5. Put a card or piece of paper with the group number next to each set of books.

6. *Before lessons on nonfiction arrangement:* Select and rearrange shelves as you did for fiction. For Lesson 3, the most difficult shelves can be long, but

should not have books with call numbers that go more than two numbers beyond the decimal. The easiest shelves should have at most one or two books with one number beyond the decimal.

NOTE: For each of the lessons, the shelves selected should be of varying difficulty. Students are then paired with someone of similar ability, thus avoiding the problem of a brighter student doing all the work while the other one learns nothing. For fiction, the easy shelves are in "I," "J," "O," "Y," and "Z." There are fewer books and most of the alphabetizing is complete by the second letter. The most difficult shelves tend to be in "C," "H," and "S" where there are many books with authors who share the same first three letters of their last names as well as prolific authors requiring students to locate and alphabetize by complete names and titles. For nonfiction books, the shelves in the 510s and 400s tend to be very easy and good to use as simplest shelves in Lesson 3. The 290s will work well for the easiest shelf in Lesson 4. The most difficult shelves are in the 620s and the 910s.

Lesson 1

Fiction arrangement: Begin with the filmstrip on library arrangement if available. In reviewing it with the class or as an introductory discussion if you don't have one, stress the main concepts the students must learn.

- A call number indicates where a book is shelved.
- Fiction books are arranged alphabetically by author: last name, first name, middle name, title (omitting "A," "An," and "The" when they are the first word).
- The Dewey Decimal Classification System is a method of assigning numbers to books according to their subject.
- Nonfiction books are arranged in numerical order. When books have the same number, you arrange them within that number alphabetically by author.
- The Dewey Decimal Classification System is the most generally used system of arranging books. There are others—particularly the Library of Congress System—but students are unlikely to use them unless they have access to college or special libraries. Therefore, what they learn in this unit can be applied to most libraries for the rest of their lives.

Then show students the fiction transparency (Figure 1-9) and have them tell you the proper sequence. Inform them that at the next lesson they will have the chance to demonstrate what they know about fiction arrangement. You may jokingly suggest that for homework they review the alphabet. If you have third or fourth graders you might want to add a little physical activity at this point. Have students line up in alphabetical order (by last name, of course). With an older class, you can save this exercise for just before lunch or dismissal.

Lesson 2

Fiction arrangement: Bring students into the media center. Review the rules for arranging fiction books and assign them to their group number. Do not let them start until you give them some directions. Suggest that they develop a plan of action before they begin to put the books in correct order. For example, when looking at the call numbers students may notice that all begin with the same letter. They must then check to see if all the second letters are the same. If second letters are different students can begin their task by making piles of books with the same first two letters. Thus, all "HA" authors are in one pile, "HE" in another, and "HI" in a third. Temporarily disregarding the "HE" and "HI" piles, the students arrange the "HA" authors by going to the third letter and beyond as necessary. As soon as the "HA"s are done the books should be put on the shelf to avoid cluttering the work area. Continue with "HE" and so forth. This instruction allows you to monitor students' progress while they are working by seeing if they are attacking the problem logically.

Lesson 3

Nonfiction arrangement: Group the students in the same way as during the previous lesson. The rearranged nonfiction shelves should be fairly simple, and only a few call numbers should have more than one numeral after the decimal point. Again, there should be several levels of difficulty. Before the students go to the shelves quickly review nonfiction arrangement and remind them of the column-by-column rule. Also remind them that the Dewey Decimal Classification System keeps books together by subject.

Conclusion: Congratulate the group on a job well done and discuss any problems encountered. Usually several students forget the column-by-column rule when it comes to putting it into practice. If there is time ask several students what kinds of books were on their shelves. This reinforces the subject orientation of the Dewey System. Explain that next time they will again rearrange nonfiction shelves, but that the shelves will be much more difficult.

Lesson 4

Nonfiction arrangement: Students are grouped as before in Lesson 3. Again, give a short review of nonfiction shelf arrangement. This time the students' responses will be quicker because they know what is expected. They will still make errors when they get to the shelves, which is why this hands-on approach is so successful. The shelves should be more difficult, with the hardest shelves having six-digit numbers.

Hands-on Unit Test

To conclude the unit and evaluate the accomplishments of the students, plan a hands-on test. It's more fun than a conventional pencil-and-paper test, and just as accurate as a measuring device.

You need one blank 3″ × 5″ card for each student and some advance preparation. Again, reserve the media center for the first period of the day. Before the class comes in take a random walk along the shelves. On each card, write the call number, author, and title of a different book. Be sure it is in its correct location on the shelf. (Even in a well-staffed media center books can be misshelved.) Choose from a wide variety of locations to reduce traffic during the test. Also choose call numbers of varying levels of difficulty.

When students come in, give each one a card. Instruct them to find the book and bring it and the card to you. When they do so, record their success. (If they bring the wrong book, ask pointed questions and redirect them until they locate the correct one.) As a second part to the test, have another student shelve the book. The original student then checks to be sure the book was correctly returned. Again record the results. There will be more errors in this part of the test. The advantage of this type of exam is that you can correct errors even at the final stage, and the test serves to instruct as well as to evaluate.

TEACHING UNIT 3: A TRIP AROUND THE MEDIA CENTER USING THE DEWEY DECIMAL SYSTEM

This unit, in which children become acquainted with the Dewey Decimal Classification System, can be easily adapted to your own schedule. The material takes approximately seventeen sessions to cover; however, the unit can be stretched over a longer period by periodically reviewing what has been learned, or it can be shortened by covering a block of 100 three-digit numbers at each session. During each session, the children are taught about one area of nonfiction and are able to choose from a group of books that you have preselected from that area. Allow fifteen to twenty minutes for this part of the lesson. During the rest of the period, and if you have access to a media center, allow the children to select additional books from the section that was covered. The unit is designed for third to fifth grade.

Objectives:

At the conclusion of this unit students should:

1. Be familiar with the nonfiction arrangement of the media center.
2. Have read books from every section of the nonfiction shelves.
3. Be able to identify popular Dewey numbers such as 796—sports, 398.2—folk tales, and 568—dinosaurs.

Materials:

sheet of 8½" × 11" white cardboard on which to draw a Dewey Wheel (see Figure 1-11)

felt markers for drawing the Dewey Wheel (use a different color for each block of one hundred)

ditto master on which to draw another copy of the Dewey Wheel

enough paper to run off a copy of the wheel for each student

Abridged Dewey Decimal Classification and Relative Index (Albany, New York: Forest Press) for your use in selecting categories of books; either borrow this from your media center or public library, or check the sections yourself

Figure 1-11. Dewey Decimal Wheel

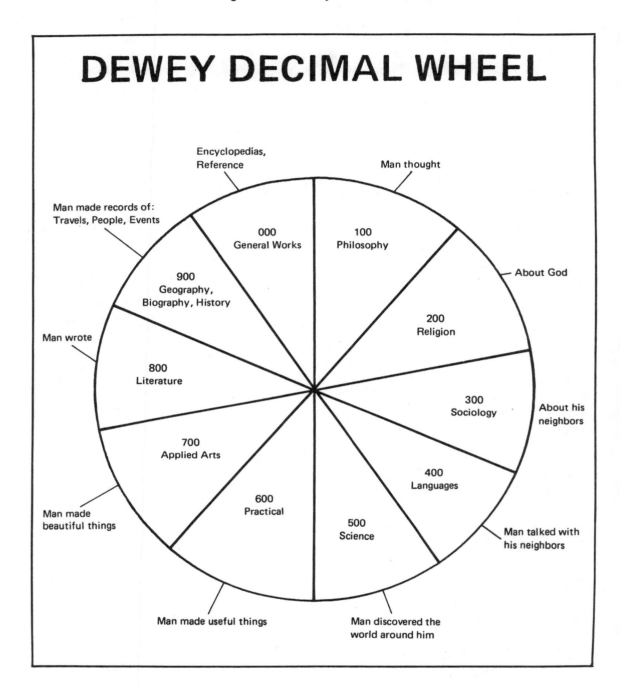

Preparation:

The preparation for each lesson is similar. Decide how large an area you want to cover in your lesson (see the sample schedule). Jot down some of the categories within that area that you feel will be of interest to the students and then go to the shelves and choose a sampling of books from that area which are within the students' ability range. If you do not have access to a media center borrow thirty or more books for each lesson from the public library. Take your Dewey Wheel, and you are ready to teach the lesson.

Suggested schedule for lessons:

1. Biography
2. 000s
3. 100s
4. 200s
5. 300–349
6. 350–398
7. 398.2 to end of 300s
8. 400s
9. 500–549
10. 550–589
11. 590 to end of 500s
12. 600–629.4
13. 630 to end of 600s
14. 700s
15. 800s
16. 900–929
17. 930 to end of 900s

These are flexible guidelines that can be changed according to the needs of your students and the availability of particular categories of books in your media center. For example, there are usually not too many books in the 400s in an elementary school media center, so this lesson would be very brief and books might have to be shared.

Introducing the Unit

Explain to the children that they will be taking a trip around the media center using the Dewey Decimal System. Let them know that by the time this unit is finished they will know where to find books on all different kinds of subjects.

Discuss some terms first. Ask the students if they know what nonfiction means and make sure they are aware that all books in this category contain factual information. Explain that Melvil Dewey invented a system of classifying books that will help them find any book they want, and that if they become familiar with the Dewey Decimal System they will be able to use it in school media centers as well as public libraries. Mention that nonfiction books are arranged on the shelves by numbers and are therefore unlike fiction books which are arranged alphabetically by the author's last name.

Lesson 1: Biographies

In many media centers biographies are labeled with a "B" and shelved in alphabetical order according to the last name of the person that they are about. Since this is an exception to the general rule for nonfiction, this is a good place to begin or end your unit.

Before class, go to the biography section and pull out twenty to twenty-five biographies that you feel are appropriate to the reading and interest levels of that class. With your Dewey Wheel, you are ready to begin.

When the children are seated, ask if anyone knows what a biography is. Explain the term and mention autobiography as well. Some of the children will probably suggest that when they grow up and become famous someone will write biographies about them. If no one does, then suggest it yourself and ask what the call number would be ("B" and the student's last name). You can add that they might even write their own autobiographies. Sometimes the children will mix up the terms "biography" and "bibliography." Be sure to straighten this out before going any further.

Show the students the Dewey Wheel and let them find where biography is located on it. Since biography is the one exception to the Dewey System, explain that in some libraries biographies are filed separately and that you will therefore discuss them first as a special unit. Then point out how biographies are filed on the shelves; if there are five biographies about George Washington and all of them are written by different people, they will all be found together under

| B |
| WASHINGTON |

. Point out that in some libraries they might find biographies filed under 92.

Pull out the books you have chosen. Tell the children that you have selected some biographies that they might want to read and enjoy. Display each one separately, showing the spine label (this reinforces the lesson of how biographies are shelved), the cover, and a few pages of the book. If students want the books, they can have them. Keep doing this until you have gone through all of the books. The children will generally vie for the same books; however if there are any that no one wants just set them aside without comment. Use a sign-out sheet to prevent loss.

When all the books have been shown and discussed, review the rules for shelving biographies. If you use the school media center, take the whole class over to the section where biographies are shelved. Point out the beginning and the end of the biography section so that the students will know this for the future. Each child should take out *at least one* book from the section that you discussed during the session. In this way, he or she will become familiar with books on a variety of subjects during the course of the unit. Let the students spend the remainder of the period browsing among the biography shelves.

Follow the same procedure discussed in the sample lesson for every lesson. Each time you cover a nonfiction section select a variety of books from that section that are at the appropriate reading and interest level and allow the children to choose from them. Look through your Dewey Decimal Classification book in advance to find categories that you might want to mention. During the lesson on 590 to 600, for example, you might pay special attention to 590—general zoology; 591—how animals live, their habits and behavior; 594—mollusks and shells; 597.7—insects; 597—fishes and amphibians; 598.1—reptiles; 598.2—birds; and 599—mammals.

Lesson 2: The 590s

Animals are a popular subject area, and this lesson illustrates how books using standard Dewey numeration can be presented in a slightly different way.

Prepare the transparency (see Figure 1-12) and set up an overhead projector. Before the class arrives, go to the 590 section and pull out several armloads of books that are at the interest and reading levels of the class you will be teaching. Be sure that you have enough books to allow everyone in the class to classify at least one book. A group of students can quickly go through 40 to 50 books.

Figure 1-12.

The 590 s

590   ZOOLOGY

591   HOW ANIMALS LIVE; THEIR HABITS AND BEHAVIOR

594   MOLLUSKS AND SHELLS

595.7   INSECTS

597   FISHES AND AMPHIBIANS

598.1   REPTILES (LIZARDS, SNAKES)

598.2   BIRDS

599   MAMMALS

Explaining the Lesson

When the class arrives, seat them and tell them that today they will be categorizing some animal books. If you have not discussed the Dewey Decimal System with them before, do so now, explaining that Melvil Dewey categorized books according to subjects and that books on animals are classified within the 590s. Explain that different types of animals have different call numbers within that category.

Turn on the overhead projector and show one section of the transparency at a time, blocking out lower portions with a piece of paper or cardboard. Discuss each section and answer questions until the children are familiar with what belongs in each section.

Pick up a book, covering its call number, and ask the class, "In which section does this belong?" For example, if you have chosen a book about birds leave the overheard projector on so that the children can look at the uncovered transparency. Someone will then raise his or her hand and tell you that it should be placed in the 598.2 section. Ask the student why this is so and wait for an explanation to make sure everyone understands.

Follow the same procedure with the other books, choosing books about different kinds of animals each time. Call on different students so that everyone will have a chance to answer. Let the students keep the books that they have "cataloged" if they want to check them out.

By the time you have gone through your stack of books, students will be familiar with the call numbers. Afterwards, allow the class to browse for about ten minutes in that section. Most classes leave carrying huge piles of books from the 590s.

GAME 1: DEWEY SPIN

Before, during, or after any library skills unit on the Dewey Decimal Classification System, give each of your students a guide designed by Sybilla Cook, M.L.S., Glide School Library, Glide, Oregon, that will help them to use the system efficiently. Run off Figures 1-13 and 1-14 on ditto paper and distribute them to the class. The children will have no difficulty in following the directions to create a handy reference.

You can make a larger, sturdier version of it out of oaktag. Mount it on a wall. Ask students to suggest subjects that can be used to fill in some of the blanks on the bottom circle.

GAME 2: UNMARKED MAP OF THE MEDIA CENTER

If students will be using a school media center with little or no professional staff they need to become familiar with where materials are located as soon as possible. Making a map will give them a hands-on experience and provide a permanent record of what they learn.

Figure 1-13. Dewey Spin

Directions: (1) Cut out the two sections on the top circle that have the word "cut" written on them. (2) Cut out both circles. (3) Fill in the blanks in the bottom circle with subjects and call numbers that interest you. (4) Fasten the two circles together with brads.

DEWEY SPIN

CUT   CUT

This Wheel Belongs To:
Name _____
Room _____
School _____

TOP CIRCLE

Figure 1-14.

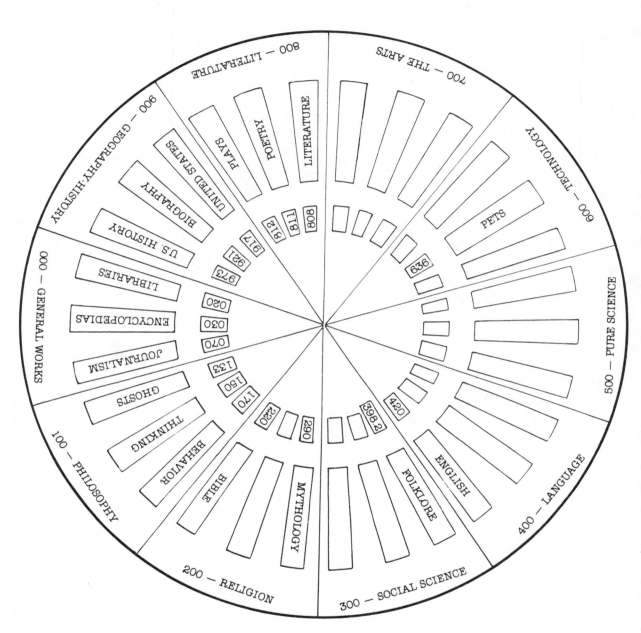

BOTTOM CIRCLE

Materials:

    stencil

    mimeograph paper (enough sheets to run off a copy for each student)

    pencils

Procedure:

1. Before class begins, draw a map of your media center on a stencil. (An example is shown in Figure 1-15.) Include book shelves, the card catalog, the circulation desk, tables and chairs, study carrels, the magazine rack, and other important items. As shown in the sample map, nothing should be labeled.

2. Run off enough copies for all of your students.

3. During the orientation, hand a copy of the unmarked map and a pencil to each child.

4. Make sure that everyone has the map turned the correct way by calling attention to the entrance of the media center and the circulation desk.

5. Tell the students that they should explore the media center with map in hand. They should mark the map to show where fiction books are kept, where nonfiction and biography are shelved, and where the card catalog, the circulation desk, and other landmarks are located.

6. The older students can be more specific and mark where on the shelves certain call numbers are located. (For example: Fiction A-Bu, Nonfiction 540-599.)

7. Tell the students that the maps will be guides for their use throughout the year and that they should keep the completed maps in their notebooks where they can refer to them until they are completely familiar with the location of everything.

8. Allow sufficient time for the students to fill in the labels on their maps. This will depend on the size and complexity of your media center.

Figure 1-15.

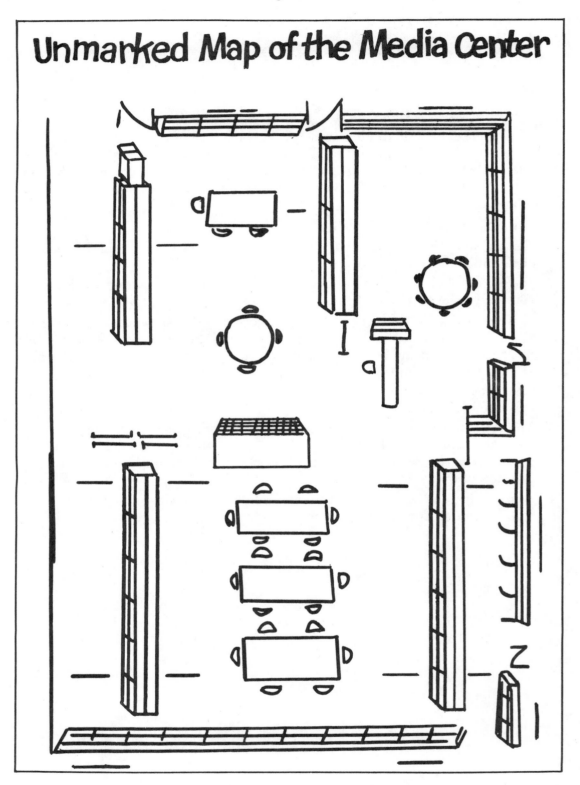

Chapter 2

THE CARD CATALOG

BACKGROUND INFORMATION

Since you use a library you are, of course, familiar with the card catalog. It is generally your first stop whenever you are doing anything more serious than browsing among the shelves. Your success in locating library materials on your own, however, depends on how much you know about the physical structure of the card catalog, the conventions that govern the structure of a catalog card, the way the card catalog is arranged, the various possible alternatives to that arrangement, and the inconsistencies and myths that frustrate even the most conscientious user.

The traditional card catalog is a large piece of furniture containing drawers called TRAYS. These trays have guide letters on the outside and are arranged in vertical rather than horizontal order. In Figure 2-1 the first tray contains cards

Figure 2-1. The Card Catalog

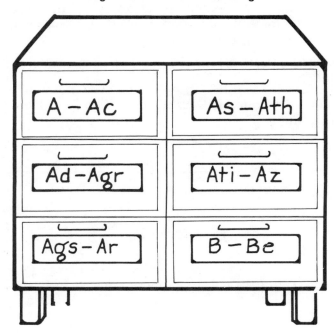

A–Ac. The second tray, Ad–Agr, comes below it. Inside the trays are tabbed cards with guide letters or guide words to speed your search by breaking up the contents of the tray. For the most part, cards are arranged in alphabetical order with the first letter on the top line of the card (after the call number) determining the card's placement in the tray. There is one major exception—if the *first word* is either "A," "An," or "The," filing begins with the *second* word.

At first glance, all catalog cards look similar. On closer inspection, you will notice that there are various types of print as well as computerized and typed cards due to the different ways catalog cards are purchased or prepared. No matter how the cards are obtained they should all follow the same rules for sequence and placement of information. As you use the card catalog keep in mind that it is not and never will be the perfect instrument that it is supposed to be and you will need to make allowances for errors.

TYPES OF CARDS

There are basically three types of cards: the main entry (or author card), the title card, and the subject card. Each book or other cataloged material requires several catalog cards, generally an author, title, and one or more subject cards. Regardless of the number of copies owned by a library, there is only *one* set of catalog cards per title. You can instantly identify the type of card you see because each differs in the information provided on the *top line*.

The Main Entry

The MAIN ENTRY is the card from which all the others are constructed. It indicates who or what has the prime authority for the work. It is often called the AUTHOR CARD because the main entry is generally under the author's name. However, it could also be under an organization, a corporation or government agency, or, where authorship is unknown, it could be the title.

In Figure 2-2, the author is Laurence Pringle. The CALL NUMBER, $\boxed{\begin{array}{c}574.5\\ \text{PRI}\end{array}}$, as explained in Chapter 1, is always found on the left-hand side of the card. All copies of a title have the same call number. The body of the card is organized into several "paragraphs."

Figure 2-2. Author Card

```
574.5        Pringle, Laurence
PRI               Ecology, science of survival. Macmillan,
             c1971.
                  152p  illus  bibliog


                  Shows the relationship between living
             things and their environment, and explains
             the ecological problems of today's world.


                  1 Ecology  2 Man—Influence on nature
             I Title
```

The first "paragraph," under the author's name, begins with the title, *Ecology, science of survival.* The capitalization shown is correct. Library cataloging rules stipulate that only the first letter of the first word and proper nouns of titles be capitalized. Although confusing, this method of capitalization helps you identify the title quickly. If the book was written by more than one person and/or it is illustrated, the complete information as it appears on the title page is given next. Publisher and copyright date follow, with the copyright date often in brackets.

The second "paragraph" is called the COLLATION. It begins with the number of pages in the book. "Unp." means the book is unpaged and often signifies a picture book. The balance of the collation notes if the book is illustrated, has a glossary or index, or is part of a series. (Some cards note the book's dimensions in centimeters at this point.) Catalog cards usually contain a third "paragraph" or ANNOTATION describing the book's contents.

The last part of the card is the TRACINGS. In a sense, this part can be labeled "for office use only" because it gives directions to the typist for making additional cards. It is also used when a book is discarded, since it tells how many cards need to be pulled and where they can be found. For your own knowledge as well as to expand your ability to extract the most possible information from the card catalog, you might be interested in how the tracings work. They use Arabic numerals (1,2,3, and so on) to indicate subject headings and Roman numerals for entries under title, joint author, illustrator, series, and whatever else seems appropriate. In Figure 2-2, the subject headings are ECOLOGY and MAN—INFLUENCE ON NATURE.

The catalog card in this illustration is a typical author card with the author's last name followed by a comma and then the first name and any middle initial or name. The format is so familiar you don't even stop to think that it signals an author entry filed under "P" for Pringle.

The Title Card

Although you know the title of the book in Figure 2-2 (*Ecology, science of survival*), the main entry card is filed under the author's name. To find the location of a book when you know only the title, use the second type of catalog card, the title card. The title is printed above the main entry information (Figure 2-3)

Figure 2-3. Title Card

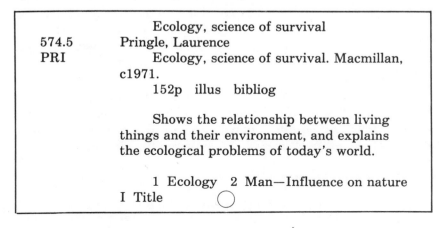

and is capitalized in the same way as when it appears below the author's name. The duplication of lines 1 and 3 is a signal that you are looking at a title card. In the illustration, it is filed under "E."

The Subject Card

Research generally begins when you have a subject to look up, so this type of card is the one most frequently used. Some card catalogs keep subject entries separate from author and title entries but most are integrated. The subject card differs from all other cards because the subject is printed completely in CAPITAL LETTERS (see ECOLOGY in Figure 2-4). In an old library, you may find some cards with typed subject headings in red. This is no longer done.

Figure 2-4. Subject Card

```
                    ECOLOGY
        574.5    Pringle, Laurence
        PRI              Ecology, science of survival. Macmillan,
                 c1971.
                         152p   illus   bibliog

                 Shows the relationship between living
                 things and their environment, and explains
                 the ecological problems of today's world.

                      1 Ecology   2 Man—Influence on nature
                 I Title              ◯
```

Subject headings are *not* invented by individual library media specialists. Most school media centers and public libraries get their entries from the *Sears List of Subject Headings*. College and university libraries most often employ *Library of Congress Subject Headings*. When you use the card catalog frequently you become familiar with the way subject headings are constructed. For example, when possible, the plural form of the noun is used. Entries are under CATS not "CAT"; GHOSTS not "GHOST." Some headings are a bit lengthy, such as MYSTERY AND DETECTIVE STORIES, while others, such as COOKERY rather than "COOKBOOKS," are simply odd. There are rules for building subject headings by adding specified descriptions, such as CATS—FICTION or FOLKLORE—U.S. You can get clues to subject headings by looking up a book on a subject you know under the author or title card and checking the tracings at the bottom.

If you have access to a school media center ask to borrow the library media specialist's copy of *Sears*. If this is not possible, ask to see a copy at the public library. *Sears* is designed to allow marginal handwritten entries showing additional subjects used in a particular library or media center.

Other Types of Catalog Cards

Joint author, illustrator, and series cards are not usually taught. However, students may ask about cards that don't seem to fit the description of any of the three basic types. Since the notation "jt. auth." or "illus." follows the name it is obvious what the card is. In the case of a series title, it appears in the collation statement and when used as an entry helps readers who wish to complete all the titles in a specific series.

THE ARRANGEMENT OF THE CARD CATALOG AND VARIATIONS

People believe the card catalog is arranged in alphabetical order. While this is true, there are many possible ways to alphabetize. Libraries file in word-by-word rather than letter-by-letter order. Library media specialists usually explain the rule as "nothing before something" which doesn't explain anything unless you already understand the rule. What it means is that:

The cat who went to heaven
is filed *before*
CATS—FICTION

The first is a title card (note capitalization) filed under "C" because the first word, "The" is ignored. In this entry, after the "t" in "cat" there is a space indicating the end of a word (or "nothing"), while in the next entry, which is a subject card (note capitalization), there is an "s" (or "something") after the "t." The space, called a "nothing," is filed before any letter, called a "something."

Those media centers following a more traditional system of filing treat the commas and dashes when they are part of a subject heading as a second "nothing." Thus, ART—STUDY AND TEACHING comes before ART AND MYTHOLOGY. (The dash after the "T" comes before the "A" in the second listing. See Figure 2-5) Other media centers use strict alphabetical order, so ART AND MYTHOLOGY would come before ART—STUDY AND TEACHING. Either approach is correct as long as the catalog is consistent. You will have to flip through a few cards before and after an entry to determine which method is being used.

Figure 2-5. A Variation of Alphabetical Order

As noted earlier, some media centers have a "divided catalog." Instead of interfiling all cards, the subject cards are filed separately. Another variation of the divided catalog is to have media (filmstrips, records, kits, games, and so forth) filed separately.

There are other filing conventions that are not widely known. Numbers are alphabetized as though they were spelled out. *The 18th Emergency*, for example, is found under "Eighteenth Emergency." All abbreviations are spelled out. "Dr." is under "Doctor"; "Mr." under "Mister." Most media centers do not spell out "Mrs." any longer since the term "Mistress" has another connotation. People whose last names begin with "Mc" or "M' " are generally filed as though the names were spelled "Mac," although many media centers no longer adhere to this rule. As with other variations, there is no problem if the catalog is consistent and if the user is aware of the possibilities.

Another exception to the alphabetical order arrangement is that some sections of the catalog, such as historical periods of a country or state, are filed in chronological order. Under U.S.—HISTORY, for example, you will find the following sequence:

U.S.—HISTORY—COLONIAL PERIOD, 1600-1775
U.S.—HISTORY—REVOLUTION, 1775-1783
U.S.—HISTORY—WAR OF 1812
U.S.—HISTORY—1815-1861
U.S.—HISTORY, CIVIL WAR, 1861-1865
U.S.—HISTORY, 1865-1898

This arrangement is particularly helpful when you are looking for historical fiction in a certain location within a set time frame. For historical fiction, the word (—FICTION) is added to the heading for the period, as in U.S.—HISTORY—REVOLUTION, 1775-1783—FICTION.

DEBUNKING SOME COMMON MYTHS

Most instructional materials, whether they are books or filmstrips, present the card catalog as though every card were in its proper place and all you have to do is learn the peculiarities of the arrangement. This is simply not so. No card catalog is perfect; some come closer to the standard than others. The degree of perfection depends on the number of people who do the filing and checking and the amount of training they have had, as well as the number of rule changes that have been implemented and whether or not these have been consistently followed. Human error is an added factor. If you can't find what you are looking for and you have allowed for variations try another approach. The book may be on the shelf but one of the entry cards may have been filed incorrectly or not filed at all.

Students are taught that the card catalog is an index to the media center. This is only partially true. Complete media holdings, such as slides, games, or transparencies, may be listed separately. Although cards directing you to materials available in the vertical (pamphlet) file should be included in the catalog, they may not be. Paperback books, which have a short shelf life, are normally not cataloged but there may be a separate author/title list. Periodicals (magazines) are never included. Unless you keep in mind that some resources are not cataloged, you may easily overlook important sources in your search for materials.

Despite its imperfections, the card catalog is the most valuable tool you have for locating library materials. Many systems are now putting their card catalog "on line" so you can use a computer terminal to look up entries. While this sharply reduces filing errors and inconsistencies, you still need to bring an understanding of the organization and structure of the card catalog to your searches.

TEACHING UNIT 1: THE THREE BASIC CARDS

All students need to understand how to use the card catalog. Instruction should begin as early as the second half of third grade; but, when students have not had the benefit of a full-time library media specialist, it is possible for them to be uncertain of the mechanics even when they are in the sixth or seventh grade. Since you will expect your class to find material in the media center or public library, they will need instruction in the basic skills.

Objectives:

At the conclusion of this unit students will be able to:

1. Know the location of a call number on a catalog card.
2. Use the card catalog as a source of information on books in the media center.
3. Distinguish among title, author, and subject cards.

Materials:

transparency of catalog card with 2 overlays

60–90 strips of 11″ × 2″ posterboard (if you prepare 90 strips, evenly divide strips into three colors)

ditto master and copy of test

overhead projector and transparency markers

Preparation:

1. Begin preparing posterboard strips for the catalog card game you will use at the end of the lesson. It is a time-consuming process, so it should be done early.

   a. On each strip write an author, a title, or a subject as it appears on the top line of a catalog card. (See Figure 2-6.)

Figure 2-6.

Cleary, Beverly

Author strip

The Beast of Monsieur Racine

Title strip

DINOSAURS

Subject strip

b. If possible, use entries that are in your school media center's catalog. This will allow you to use the strips for a later enrichment activity. If not, use the following list to prepare your strips:

AUTHORS

1. Carroll, Ruth
2. Coren, Alan
3. Faber, Nancy W.
4. Peare, Catherine Owen
5. Riedman, Sarah B.
6. Rounds, Glen
* 7. St. John, Wylly Folk
8. Van Leeuwen, Jean
9. White, Ann Terry
10. Zion, Gene

TITLES

* 1. And it rained
2. Andy and the runaway horse
* 3. The biggest bear
4. A candle in her room
5. The city and its people
* 6. Dr. Seuss's ABC
* 7. George Washington Carver
8. I and Sproggy
9. Johnny/Bingo
*10. The 13 clocks

SUBJECTS

1. BALLOONS
2. BASKETBALL—FICTION
* 3. CARTIER, JACQUES
4. COMPUTERS
5. MYSTERY AND DETECTIVE STORIES
6. NUTS
7. RAIN AND RAINFALL
8. ST. PATRICK'S DAY
9. U.S.—HISTORY— REVOLUTION
10. WILD FLOWERS

AUTHORS

1. Anderson, Lonzo
2. Butterworth, Oliver
3. Carlson, Dale
4. Pearce, Ann Phillipa
5. Reeder, Red
* 6. St. John, Glory
7. Spier, Peter
8. Wildsmith, Brian
9. Van Stockum, Hilda
10. Zaffo, George J.

TITLES

* 1. And miles to go
* 2. The barn
3. Carl Sandburg, voice of the people
4. Chin music
5. City horse
6. The coming of the Pilgrims
* 7. Dr. Elizabeth
* 8. Johnny Maple-Leaf
* 9. 101 science experiments
10. A weed is a flower

SUBJECTS

1. BASEBALL—FICTION
2. COMMUNITY LIFE— FICTION
3. COOKERY
4. FABLES
5. MOTORCYCLES
6. RARE ANIMALS
* 7. REVELS, HIRAM RHOADES
8. ST. LAWRENCE RIVER
9. U.S.—HISTORY—CIVIL WAR—BIOGRAPHY
10. VISION

AUTHORS

1. Andersen, Doris
2. Carlsen, Ruth Christoffer
3. Childress, Alice
4. Falls, C. B.
5. O'Brien, Robert C.
6. Peck, Robert Newton
7. Rossetti, Christina
8. Schlein, Miriam
9. Wiese, Kurt
10. Zemach, Kaethe

TITLES

1. And so my garden grows
2. Burnish me bright
3. Caspar and his friends
* 4. The city in art
* 5. The 18th emergency
* 6. Mr. Popper's penguins
7. O the red rose tree
8. An orphan for Nebraska
* 9. St. Jerome and the lion
*10. Tom Bombadil

SUBJECTS

1. BUSHMEN
2. CAROLS
* 3. JOHN HENRY
4. PARENT AND CHILD— FICTION
5. PETS
6. POVERTY—FICTION
7. ROME—HISTORY— EMPIRE, 30 BC–476 AD
8. SCIENTIFIC RECREATIONS
9. U.S.—HISTORY—1898- 1919—FICTION
10. WASHINGTON, D.C.— WHITE HOUSE

SPECIAL TIP: You can work with other teachers on this unit. If three of you, each using a different color posterboard, make one set each of 10 authors, 10 titles, and 10 subjects, you will have the 90 strips and can then identify and use the 30 you each made.

2. Make a transparency of a catalog card with two overlays. On a sheet of 8½" × 11" unlined paper draw a 3" × 5" catalog card. Type or write the information that is found on an author card. Choose a card that lists at least two subject headings and an illustrator. Lay a second sheet of 8½" × 11" paper over the first and place the sheets on an overhead projector. Write the title of the book as it would be found on a title card on the top sheet of paper. This will be the first overlay. Lay another sheet of paper over the first and prepare one subject entry. All three sheets should then go through a thermal copier to form permanent transparencies. Mount the author card transparency and hinge on the overlays, one on each side. (See Figure 2-7.)

3. Make copies of the Card Catalog Test shown in Figure 2-8.

Figure 2-7.

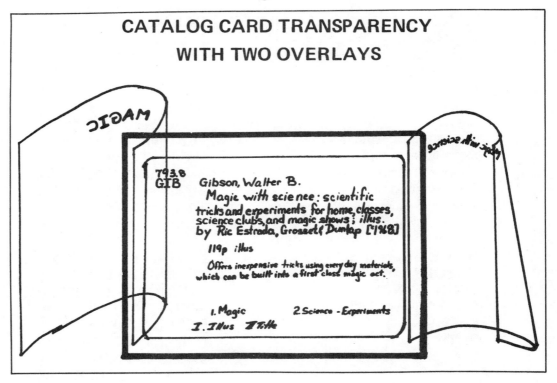

CATALOG CARD TRANSPARENCY
WITH TWO OVERLAYS

MAGIC

Magic with science

793.8
GIB   Gibson, Walter B.
          Magic with science: scientific
       tricks and experiments for home, classes,
       science clubs, and magic shows; illus.
       by Ric Estrada, Grosset & Dunlap ['1968]

          119p illus

          Offers inexpensive tricks using every day materials,
          which can be built into a first class magic act.

             1. Magic   2. Science - Experiments
          I. Illus II. Title

Figure 2-8.

CARD CATALOG TEST

> BRIDGES
> 624   Goldwater, Daniel
> GOL   Bridges and how they are built; illus by
>   Harry Weiss. Young Scott Books
>   c1965
>
>   72p illus maps
>
>   1. Bridges   2. Building, iron and steel
>   I. Illus   II. Title

Use the above catalog card to answer the questions.

1. The call number of this book is [   ]

2. The author is _____

3. The title is _____

4. The illustrator is _____

5. The publisher is _____

6. The copyright date is _____

7. Illus means _____

SUPER TOUGH QUESTIONS

8. The above card is (choose the correct letter) _____, a. a title card b. an author card c. a subject card because _____
   _____

9. Another subject heading for this book is _____
   _____

ANSWER KEY FOR FIGURE 2-8

1.
   | 624 |
   | GOL |
2. Goldwater, Daniel
3. Bridges and how they are built
4. Harry Weiss
5. Young Scott Books
6. 1965
7. Illustrated, which means the book has pictures
8. c, because the top line appears in all capital letters
9. BUILDING, IRON AND STEEL

Directions:

Put the class in a receptive mood by telling them they will be playing a game at the end of the lesson. How well they play depends on how closely they have listened. Highlight the fact that the card catalog is an index to the media center, that media are listed as well as books, and that the arrangement is alphabetical. You can show the catalog card transparency with two overlays so that students see how an author card "magically" becomes a title card or a subject card. Place emphasis on the fact that a top line made up entirely of capital letters indicates a subject card.

Show selected examples of the posterboard strips, explaining that they represent the top line of a catalog card and that by looking at the strip, students should be able to tell whether it illustrates an author, title, or subject card. Students should respond quickly and accurately. Then show them some "problem" strips such as the asterisked titles, authors, and subjects from the list given under "Preparation" on page 39.

Ask students to identify the type of card *and* what letter or letters they would look under to locate it, such as, for "Mr." they must say "M,I". The errors they make will give you the opportunity to correct misconceptions and teach the rules. At the conclusion of the class, play the catalog game to see what students did understand as well as to reinforce the learning.

Catalog Game:

Divide the posterboard strips into three piles, each containing some authors, titles, and subjects. (If you use the 90 color-coded strips each group should have one color only.) Divide students into three groups, have them sit in a circle, and place strips face down in the middle of each group with students taking turns.

The first person turns a strip face up. The next person turns up another one and must decide if it is the same type as the first. If the first strip shows a title and the second, an author, a second column is started. If they are both titles the second is placed below the first and the next person turns over another one. The game is over when all the strips are face up. There should be three columns: one of authors (last name, comma, first name), one of titles (first letter of first word and all proper nouns capitalized), and one of subjects (all capital letters).

Invariably during the course of the game a student will misplace a strip and several group members will try to correct the error. To prevent the game from becoming too rowdy permit students who think a mistake has been made to make one change before they draw.

At the conclusion of the game check the results and see if students can explain their errors. The class will enjoy the activity and you may want to shift the strips around and let everyone play again.

As soon as possible after the lesson give the class the Card Catalog Test (shown on page 42) you prepared.

TEACHING UNIT 2: A LEARNING CENTER

This learning center is a follow-up to the class instruction on the card catalog. It will require a lot of preparation but you can reuse the materials all year, every year. Place it in a corner of the room and cycle students through the activity to be sure everyone has the chance to polish up skills.

Although use of a card catalog is not necessary, you will need to obtain 25 to 30 printed catalog cards as well as an equal number of blank ones. Libraries that order their books processed (complete with plastic cover, book pocket, label, and so forth) normally receive extra cards which are often used for scrap. If your school does not have a library media specialist try the high school or public library.

Objectives:

At the conclusion of this unit students should be able to:

1. Distinguish among author, title, and subject cards.
2. Locate a call number on a catalog card.

3. Look at any type of catalog card and tell the author and title.

   NOTE: Some students may also be able to use the information on the tracing to locate additional subject headings.

Materials:

three pieces of posterboard, as close to 9″ × 15″ as possible

black fine-tip felt markers

25–30 printed catalog cards (these should all be author cards; try to get at least two per book so the duplication will minimize your preparation)

25–30 blank catalog cards

10 6″ × 9″ pieces of posterboard for task cards

yarn

pack of 3″ × 5″ cards for student use

clear self-stick vinyl

Preparation:

1. On the three pieces of posterboard print the information you would find on an author card, a subject card, and a title card for the same book. (See Figure 2-9.)

   • You may use the sample set here or choose a book in your card catalog with more than one subject heading shown in the tracings. But make only one subject card, following the capitalization and paragraph structure as shown.

   • By keeping the book on display at the learning center you will tie the abstraction of the card catalog to the reality of a book.

2. Label each of the three cards as an author card, a title card, and a subject card. List the components (author, title, call number, publisher, and so forth) and then use yarn to connect the word to the appropriate part of the card.

3. Prepare task cards (see Figure 2-10) relating to the oversized cards.

Figure 2-9.

Author Card

793.8
COB
	Cobb, Vicki
	      Bet you can't: science impossibilities by Vicki Cobb and Kathy Darling. Illus. by Martha Weston. Lothrop, 1980.
	      128p. illus
	
	      1. Experiments 2. Scientific recreations I. Darling, Kathy, jt. auth. II. Weston, Martha, illus. III. Title

Figure 2-9, continued.

Title Card

```
                    Bet you can't
      793.8         Cobb, Vicki
      COB               Bet you can't: science
                    impossibilities by Vicki Cobb and
                    Kathy Darling.   Illus. by Martha
                    Weston.   Lothrop,   1980.
                        128p.   illus

                        1. Experiments   2. Scientific
                    recreations  I. Darling, Kathy, jt. auth
                    II. Weston, Martha illus   III. Title
```

Subject Card

```
                    EXPERIMENTS
      793.8         Cobb, Vicki
      COB               Bet you can't: science
                    impossibilities by Vicki Cobb and
                    Kathy Darling.   Illus. by Martha
                    Weston.   Lothrop,   1980.
                        128p.   illus

                        1. Experiments   2. Scientific
                    recreations  I. Darling, Kathy, jt. auth.
                    II. Weston, Martha, illus.   III. Title
```

Figure 2-10.

```
Task Card 1

    1. Card 1 is an author card because
    2. Card 2 is a title card because
    3. Card 3 is a subject card because
```

```
Task Card 2

    4. The call number is
    5. The Dewey number is
    6. COB are the first three letters of
```

```
Task Card 3 (optional)

    7. You know the book has pictures because the catalog card says
    8. How many people wrote this book?
    9. Name them
```

> Task Card 4
>   10. How many pages are in the book?
>   11. Who published the book?
>   12. What is the copyright date?

Task Card 5 (Super tough questions)
  13. How many cards are in the card catalog for this one book? (Hint: don't forget the author card.)
  14. If you wanted to find another book done by the same illustrator, what name would you look under in the card catalog?
  15. Give at least one other subject heading for this book.

If your class is run informally, you can make an answer card (see the Answer Key in Figure 2-11) or have students submit their written answers to you for grading.

Figure 2-11.

ANSWER KEY FOR FIGURE 2-10

  1. the author's name appears on the top line.
  2. the title, with its special capitalization rules, appears on the top line.
  3. the top line is printed in all capital letters.
  4. | 793.8 |
     | COB |
  5. 793.8.
  6. The author's last name.
  7. illus.
  8. two.
  9. Vicki Cobb and Kathy Darling.
 10. 128.
 11. Lothrop, Lee and Shepard.
 12. 1980.
 13. Seven—three subject cards, a joint author card, an illustrator card, a title card, and an author card.
 14. Weston, Martha. illus.
 15. EXPERIMENTS or SCIENTIFIC RECREATION.

Preparation (extra catalog cards):

1. Take the extra cards and type the necessary information on them to make title and subject cards. Remember the proper capitalization for titles and subjects.

   • Reserve some of the cards to use as author cards.

   • Include selections from as many sections of the media center as possible.

   • Make several complete sets; that is, author, title, and at least one subject card. Use the blank cards to fill in where necessary. Type carefully and check your work with a professional. Not all of the cards have to be part of a complete set.

- Try to have two or three cards with the same subject heading.

2. Cover all of the sample cards with the clear self-stick vinyl.

3. Analyze the sets of cards you now have and prepare a set of task cards. Since your catalog cards will be unique, you will need to make up your own questions. The five samples in Figure 2-12 are a guide as to the type of task cards you can prepare. NOTE: To use a question such as the first one, you need several cards with the same subject heading, while Card 2 requires several cards with the same call number. You can use Card 5 as is. Here is the answer to it:

FIC   Snyder, Zilpha Keatley
SNY   And all between; illus by
          Alton Raible. Atheneum; c 1976
               216 p illus

               1. Fantasy   I Raible, Alton illus.
          II Title

Figure 2-12.

Sample Task Cards

Card 1   1. Who are the authors of three mystery books? (Subject heading: MYSTERY AND DETECTIVE STORIES)
              2. What is the title of the book by Leonard Everett Fisher?
              3. What is the call number of the book located in the reference section?
              4. What is the subject heading for the book *Unidentified flying objects* by Gene Gurney?

Card 2   Find three cards with the call number $\boxed{\frac{560}{GRE}}$
              1. What is the author's name?
              2. What is the title?
              3. Why are there three cards for one book?
              4. Give the first letter of the three catalog drawers in which these cards would be found.

Card 3   Note: Catalog cards are filed alphabetically according to the top line.
              1. How many of these cards would be found in the C drawers?
              2. How many in the F drawers?

Card 4   Find the cards with the call number   704.94 FIS
1. Who is the author?
2. Copy the top line of the subject card exactly as it appears on the catalog card.
3. Use the information on the bottom of the card and name
   the other subject heading, which is not included in the
   set but is found in the card catalog in the media center.

Card 5   Bonus Task Card   This book has 216 pages.

It is illustrated by Alton Raible.
The publisher is Atheneum. The
   copyright date is 1976.
A subject heading is FANTASY.
Look at the oversize cards on display. Make an author card, a
   title card, and a subject card for
   this book. Use 3″ × 5″ cards.

TEACHING UNIT 3: FINDING THE RIGHT DRAWER

This Teaching Unit, designed primarily for grades 3 and 4, can also be used as an enrichment activity in grade 2 and as a remedial activity for grades 5 and 6. As is noted in the directions, you can use the 11″ × 2″ posterboard strips you prepared for Teaching Unit 1. The more strips you have, the better the unit will be.

Materials:

   two sheets of 14″ × 11″ oaktag

   two sheets of posterboard in two contrasting colors

   felt markers (black wide-tip marker, black and red fine-tip markers, yellow
      highlight marker)

   rubber cement

   30 to 60 strips of 11″ × 2″ posterboard (optional if cards are used)

   30 to 60 extra catalog cards (optional if strips are used)

Preparation:

1. Draw a replica of your school's card catalog on the oaktag or use Figures
   2-13 and 2-14. If you use your own catalog be sure that the letters and num-
   bers on the drawers match exactly.
   • Draw the outline with the red marker.
   • Use the fine-tip black marker to outline the labels on the drawers.
   • Use the fine-tip black marker to write in numbers and guide letters.
   • Use the yellow highlighter to color the number portion of the drawer
     labels.
2. Cut the lighter shade of posterboard in an interesting pattern.

Figure 2-13.

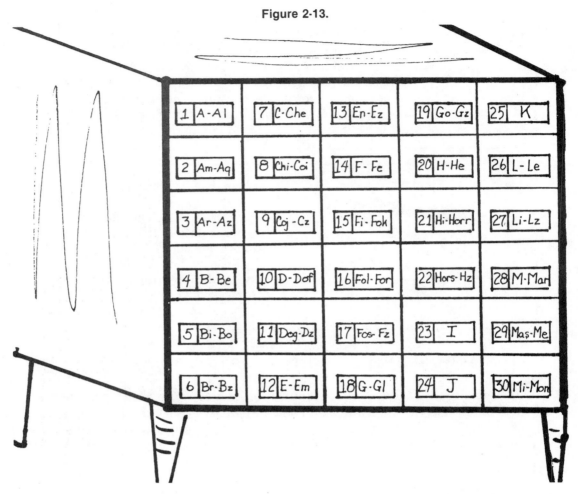

3. Paste the mock-up of the card catalog onto the light-colored posterboard.

4. Paste the catalog and posterboard onto the darker sheet of posterboard.

5. Use the wide-tip black marker to letter "Card Catalog" on the posterboard.

Procedure:

Three different ways of using the strips or cards are given here. The one you choose will depend on the grade level and your preference.

1. Show the strips to the entire class. The students respond by giving the number of the drawer in which the author, title, or subject can be found. You can also have a "spelling bee" with the strips; each student who gives a wrong answer is eliminated from the bee.

2. Show the students the extra catalog cards and direct them to copy the top line on each card and to print the number of the drawer in which the card would be found.

Figure 2-14.

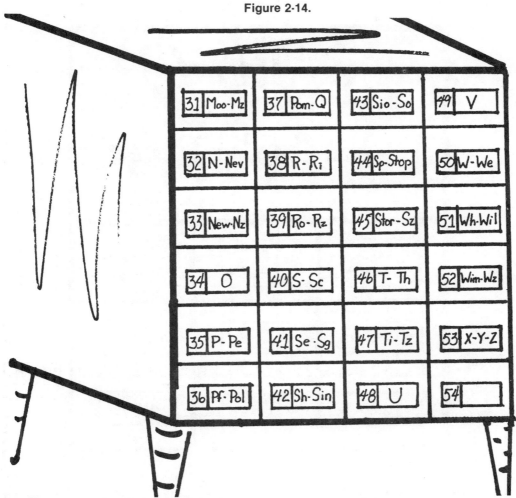

31 Moo-Mz	37 Pom-Q	43 Sio-So	49 V
32 N-Nev	38 R-Ri	44 Sp-Stop	50 W-We
33 New-Nz	39 Ro-Rz	45 Stor-Sz	51 Wh-Wil
34 O	40 S-Sc	46 T-Th	52 Wim-Wz
35 P-Pe	41 Se-Sg	47 Ti-Tz	53 X-Y-Z
36 Pf-Pol	42 Sh-Sin	48 U	54

3. Students work with the extra cards or strips and arrange them in order. When they finish alphabetizing them, have them respond to questions such as, "Which drawer do you need most often?" and "How many drawers are not used at all?" Students can also be asked more advanced questions. For example: "Look at the sample title card for *The cat in art.* Who is the author? In what number drawer will the author card be found?"

GAME 1: CARD-O (CATALOG CARD BINGO)

Card-O is an excellent reinforcement activity as well as a great deal of fun for third to fifth graders. It can be used with small groups or with the entire class if you make enough cards. While playing this game it is helpful to have the card catalog mock-up from Teaching Unit 3 for reference, but it is not required. Start small with five to ten bingo cards with nine squares each. It is best to use posterboard strips, although you can use extra catalog cards.

Figure 2-15.

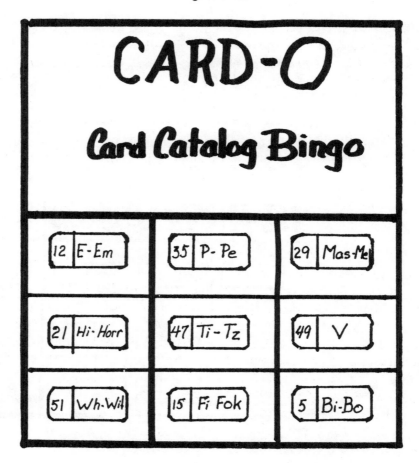

The simplest version of the game is played with bingo cards with nine squares each. (See Figure 2-15.) If you wish to use all of the drawers in the catalog and you want a longer game, make a 25-square card with a free space. For a five-card, nine-square game with each drawer appearing on three cards, 15 strips are needed. This is an ideal number for small groups. For a 15-card, 25-square game with each drawer appearing on six cards, 60 strips are needed. For larger groups, you can increase the number of strips or use each drawer on twelve cards.

Materials:

   posterboard for bingo cards
   - 9 square cards are 6″ × 7″
   - 25 square cards are 7½″ × 8″
   11″ × 2″ strips of posterboard
   black felt markers, wide-tip and fine-tip
   counters or markers for covering squares on cards
   box large enough to hold the strips
   pressure-sensitive labels, ⅝″ × 1¼″
   clear self-stick vinyl

Preparation:

1. Label the strips with authors, titles, and subject headings or use the strips from Teaching Unit 3. If the group is small, it is not necessary to have a strip from every drawer in the catalog, but a variety of strips is imperative. If more than one strip are from the same drawer, a player might have to cover the same square twice, so each strip should be from a different drawer.

   NOTE: You can prepare several sets of cards and strips for the small-group version of the game. By carefully selecting drawers with single guide letters or several guide letters or by choosing easy or difficult headings for the strips, you can regulate the difficulty of the game. If you do make several games on different levels, use a different color for each level. Be sure that the strips and bingo cards for each level are the same color.

2. Write the answer (the correct drawer number) in very small letters in the right-hand corner on the back of each strip.

3. Rule the bingo cards with the wide-tip black marker. Use pressure-sensitive labels to make the drawer fronts. Since the preparation for this game is so time-consuming, you might have a volunteer prepare the cards and then fill in the drawer numbers and letters yourself.

4. Use the fine-tip marker to make lines dividing the drawer numbers from the guide letters.

5. Refer to the posterboard strips before filling in the letters and numbers of the drawer fronts. For example, if a strip reads HORSES, write "22 Hors-Hz" on several cards. If you are making the fifteen-card, 25-square game using 40 strips, the same drawer front appears on nine cards.

6. Cover the bingo cards with clear self-stick vinyl.

Procedure:

1. The strips are placed in a box and shaken up.

2. Each player gets one card and a stack of counters.

3. If there is a free square, it is covered with a counter.

4. The game leader takes a strip out of the box. Being careful not to let the other players see the answer on the back, the leader reads the strip and shows it to all of the players.

5. Players whose cards show the drawer front in which the author, title, or subject on the chosen strip would be located cover the appropriate square with a counter.

6. The strips that have been called are discarded face up.

7. The first player to arrange the counters in a vertical, horizontal, or diagonal row calls out "card-o or "bingo."

8. Counters are removed from the winning card one at a time and checked against the backs of the discarded strips to be sure that the squares were covered correctly.

   Variations: To win at bingo, players need to make an X, L, T, I, or H. The speed at which the strips are called can also affect the difficulty of the game.

GAME 2: LIBRARY LOTTO

Instead of trying to teach library skills in the ordinary way, teach students by using a game. Library lotto is fun and instructs as well as tests a class's knowledge of the link between a book and its catalog card.

Materials:

> extra catalog cards (see your library media specialist or go to the public library)
>
> oaktag
>
> felt markers (thin-tipped)
>
> scissors
>
> paste

Preparation:

1. You will need author, title, and subject cards. Turn some of the cards you obtained into title or subject cards, leaving some as author cards. You need only one author or one title or one subject card per book, rather than complete sets of cards. Be sure the complete call number is given; if not, type it in correctly.

2. You will need one oaktag board per player. To make these, cut sheets of oaktag into 8″ × 10″ pieces. Paste four catalog cards of different entries onto each piece of oaktag so that the oaktag board will have an author, a title, and a subject card, and a card repeating one of the entries in the fourth space. Prepare the remaining pieces of oaktag by repeating this procedure. If you wish to use this game to teach only subject cards, then paste only subject cards onto the pieces of oaktag.

3. Cut book shapes from the oaktag so that there is one "book" for each catalog card. These "books" need to show the spine as well as the front cover and they should be about three inches high. Outline the book shapes with any color marker. Carefully print author, title, and spine labels on each book. You can vary the form by writing the author's name above the title the way many books do.

4. For a game to be played by the entire class, you will need 100 books. To facilitate your task, ask students to help you cut out the books. (It is best, however, if you do the lettering.) If the added hands are not readily available, make only ten boards and 40 books. These quantities are suitable for group fun; yet the cut-and-paste operation will not be intolerable.

Procedure:

1. A leader is chosen and the rest of the players are given one oaktag board. After the players have scanned the catalog cards on their boards, the leader turns the books over one at a time and announces the author, title, and call number written on each book. The players try to identify the books that match the catalog cards on their boards.

2. A student indicates that he or she has a match by raising a hand. The book is then placed over the catalog card. The first student to correctly cover all four cards on a board wins. The game continues until there are three winners.

3. Assign point values to the order of winning; for example, first place equals 5 points, second place equals 3 points, and third place equals 1 point. The game is then played again. This time, the winner is the student who has accumulated the most points by the end of the period.

4. A variation of the game can be made by pasting the books onto the oaktag and calling out the catalog cards. In this version, the caller reads only the top line and the call number of the catalog card; however, he or she must state whether the catalog card is an author, title, or subject card. If more books are placed on one board, the game becomes challenging enough for older students.

5. You can also use the game as a small-group activity with a student leader. Give each oaktag card a roman numeral and each space on the card an arabic numeral. On the back of each book, write its correct place giving roman and arabic numerals. This gives the student leader an answer key.

Chapter 3

THE DICTIONARY

BACKGROUND INFORMATION

In 1828, Noah Webster created the first American dictionary, *An American Dictionary of the English Language*, which defined 70,000 words. For many years thereafter the name "Webster" was associated with the dictionaries that descended from this work. The name is now in the public domain and any publisher can use "Webster" as part of a dictionary title today. The original company now publishes under the name Merriam-Webster.

Another milestone in the history of the dictionary occurred in 1935, when Edward L. Thorndike published the *Thorndike-Century Junior Dictionary*, the first one ever directed to children. This dictionary was based on the words appearing most often in materials for children.

Today everyone uses dictionaries. These perennial best sellers are the most commonly used reference tool. Most families own some form of dictionary. The natural logic of dictionaries is such that even primary children soon learn that they are arranged in alphabetical order and are used to look up the meanings of unfamiliar words. Despite their basic ease of use, however, what students and most adults don't realize is the wide variety of dictionaries on the market, the different purposes they serve, and the various features available that make one dictionary more suitable than another to meet individual and personal needs.

There are different kinds of dictionaries: general dictionaries (including thesauruses), subject dictionaries (such as science or sports dictionaries), and foreign language dictionaries. General dictionaries break down into categories differing mainly in the number of words they include. The following categories are based on Kenneth F. Kister's *Dictionary Buying Guide* (Bowker 1977), which you may consult for further information:

- unabridged—generally contains over 250,000 words and is a huge volume.

- college—lists from 130,000 to 250,000 words, is a fairly scholarly work, and is much easier to hold.

- abridged—holds from 55,000 to 130,000 entries, is for the average adult, and is often based on a lengthier unabridged or college version.

- pocket—under 55,000 words, pocket-sized, often paperback.

- school—ranges from 1600 for the most elementary to as many as 95,000 words, depending on the grade level it is designed to serve.

Each publisher compiles more than one kind of dictionary, so if you already own a college dictionary and plan to purchase an abridged version, be sure to choose one that is from a different company so you will be getting a variety of definitions and supporting information.

Dictionaries also differ in other areas:

- format—one column or two with varying amounts of marginal white space
- method of presenting information—use of pictures, positioning of guide words, frequent repetition of pronunciation key, whether entries are letter-by-letter or word-by-word
- inclusion of sample sentences
- inclusion of synonyms and/or antonyms after the definitions
- inclusion of usage notes explaining differences in the way words are used
- inclusion of detailed etymology (word history)

A typical ENTRY consists of: the MAIN ENTRY (the word or words being defined) in boldface type; broken up into syllables for pronunciation; its part of speech; definition(s); the origin of the entry (its etymology); synonyms/antonyms; cross references; and usage notes. Some dictionaries also contain separate lists of foreign words and phrases, geographical and biographical names, and even handbooks of style.

Although all dictionaries give definitions, each dictionary is unique in some way. Take a look at the various dictionaries available in your school's media center so that you can familiarize yourself with the different areas that are included. If you don't have access to a media center, choose dictionaries from the public library. It is a good idea to have a variety of different dictionaries on hand, either in the media center or in the classroom, rather than buying multiple copies of one dictionary to serve the entire class. Paperbacks can supplement hardbound versions.

The simplest way to compare dictionaries is to choose one word (or main entry) and look it up in a number of different ones. Although you will probably not be using it for skills lessons, first look briefly at an unabridged dictionary. Using the same main entry, now turn to a college dictionary. Then check an abridged and, finally, a pocket dictionary. Besides looking at the way the main entry is defined, look through the front and back to see what other features each dictionary includes. Be sure to use dictionaries from different publishers for further contrast.

Now take a school dictionary to see how it is similar to and different from the ones you have already examined. Some dictionaries in this category have very long and basic instructions on how they should be used. The *Scott Foresman Intermediate Dictionary* (Scott, Foresman 1979) for example, tells the reader "How to Find (different types of) Words" as well as "How to Use Pronunciation," "How to Find a Meaning," and "How to Use the Dictionary for Spelling and for Writing." Each section has exercises on how to use it, which students can do so that they will clearly understand. Student dictionaries also have a lot of illustrations.

The Thesaurus

A different kind of dictionary is a thesaurus, a book designed to help you find just the right word you need when you are seeking a precise term, aren't sure which word will best express your thoughts, or don't want to overwork a particular adjective. It is sometimes called a dictionary of synonyms. These books are arranged in two different ways—either alphabetically or topically.

A thesaurus arranged by topic will allow you to select a finer shade of word, but it is generally much more difficult to use. Students below the high school level will feel more comfortable with an alphabetical dictionary of synonyms.

A thesaurus for elementary school students, *In Other Words: A Beginning Thesaurus* by Andrew Schiller (rev. ed., Lothrop 1977), offers a painless introduction to young readers. (Two levels are available.) This is alphabetically arranged and contains sentences and illustrations to simplify the task, as well as introductory sections explaining synonyms, antonyms, and how to use the book.

Webster's Collegiate Thesaurus (Merriam 1976) contains 20,000 main entries and is also alphabetical. Besides giving the parts of speech and synonyms, it offers related words, contrasted words, and antonyms.

Roget's International Thesaurus (4th ed., Harper and Row 1977) is an example of the topical thesaurus covering 250,000 words and phrases that must first be looked up in an alphabetical index in the back of the book (covering over 500 pages). Readers are given a choice of meanings and then referred to a numbered category next to the word they are seeking, and then to a paragraph within that category.

The thesaurus is an important learning tool for enriching vocabulary in ways that a dictionary is not. Children should become familiar with it at an early age and get into the habit of referring to it whenever they have a writing assignment to do.

The skills required to use a dictionary are the same as those for using an alphabetical thesaurus and the purpose served is similar. Teaching units and games designed for one tool reinforce the other, particularly if you point out the connection. When you find frequent opportunities to consult the dictionary or thesaurus as part of the regular classroom work, you guarantee that your students will develop the dictionary habit.

TEACHING UNIT 1: EVERYTHING'S COMING UP DAISIES

When spring is in full flower, the outdoors is so inviting that school can take on a dusty, dreary appearance. With everyong longing to be out in the open, it can be difficult to motivate students to work on library skills.

Don't fight the mood; capitalize on it. You can bring in the spring by "growing" daisies all over the classroom. Not only will the place look bright and cheerful, but you will artfully be sneaking in practice in basic library skills.

Skills Practiced:

1. Students in grade 1 use first letters of words to practice newly acquired dictionary skills.
2. Students in grades 2 through 4 practice alphabetical/dictionary skills by looking for entries beginning with the second letter of a word.

3. Students in grades 5 through 8 practice the bibliographic search techniques they normally ignore.

Materials:

several sheets of construction paper in dark green, light green, white, and yellow
stick-glue

masking tape
scissors
markers in orange and black

Cutting Up Daisies:

1. Cut approximately 20 daisy bottoms—a stem and two leaves—from light and dark green construction paper. (See Figure 3-1.) You will need at least 20 to start.

Figure 3-1.

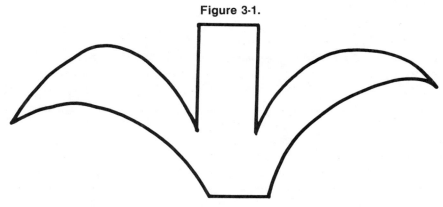

2. Cut 20 rectangles with jagged tops from light and dark green construction paper. (See Figure 3-2.) These should be at least 14″ wide and 2¼″ high to form the grass from which the daisies grow.

Figure 3-2.

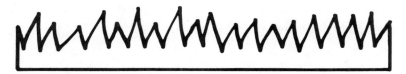

3. Cut 60 to 70 rectangles, 6½″ × 1¾″, from light and dark green construction paper. These will be stems.
4. Cut 30 5½″ squares from white and yellow construction paper.
5. Draw the daisy heads with an orange marker on the white and the yellow construction paper.

Getting Started:

1. Use the lists in Figure 3-3 as a guide. Print the name of the flower on the stem section of the daisy's base.

   NOTE: The lists include names that are long and short. You can distribute the words judiciously to meet the individual needs of students. Add or change the list according to your requirements. If you make additions to the two-letter list, be sure all two-letter combinations are possible beginnings of words.

2. Put up some signs inviting everyone to "grow daisies" and write simple directions.

3. Attach the grass at strategic places around the room.

Figure 3-3.

GRADE 1 (LIGHT GREEN)	GRADES 2-4 (DARK GREEN)	GRADES 5-8	
One Letter	*Two Letters*	*Cross-Reference List*	
orchid	violet	horticulture	grain
lily	hibiscus	agriculture	plant
forsythia	clover	flower	pollen and
phlox	thistle	botany	pollination
rose	columbine	tree	seed
daisy	crocus	weed	gardening
tulip	daisy		

Directions for Students in Grade 1:

1. Get a daisy base.
2. Look at the second letter in the name of your flower.
3. Go to the dictionary and find a word beginning with that letter.
4. Get a piece of stem from the desk—it can be the same green or a different shade.
5. Write your word on the stem.
6. Look at the third letter in the name of your flower.
7. Go to the dictionary and find a word beginning with that letter.
8. Put the word on another piece of stem.
9. When you find a word that begins with the last letter in the name of your flower, get a daisy head from the desk and write the last word at the top of the daisy.
10. Get help from the desk and "plant" your daisy base in the "grass" using stick-glue.
11. Using stick-glue, connect the pieces of the stem in the right order. Add the daisy head on top. Write your name on the bottom leaves.

Directions for Students in Grades 2-4:

1. Get a daisy base from the desk.
2. Go to the dictionary and find a word that begins with the same two letters as the name of your flower. For example, if your flower is "clover," find a word beginning with "cl."
3. Get a piece of stem from the desk and write the word on the stem.

4. Go to the dictionary and find a word that begins with the second and third letters of the name of your flower. For example, if your flower is "clover," find a word beginning with "lo."

5. Get another piece of stem and write the word.

6. When you find a word that begins with the last two letters, get a daisy head from the desk and write the word.

7. Borrow stick-glue from the desk and "plant" your daisy base in the "grass," connecting all your stem pieces in correct order. Add the daisy head on top.

8. Write your name on the bottom leaves.

Directions for Students in the Upper Grades:

1. Get a daisy base from the desk and write your name on the leaves.

2. With stick-glue, "plant" the base in the "grass."

3. Look up your subject in the encyclopedia. (*World Book* is excellent for this.)

4. Find the cross-references at the end of the article.

5. Choose two of those references and print them on two stem pieces available at the desk.

6. Paste your two stems so they branch off from the central stem.

7. Check for and follow up one of the cross-references at the end of the two new articles.

8. Try to narrow the topic and put the head on your daisy when you find no more cross-references. You should have *two* heads on your daisy.

NOTE: Avoid a circular type of reference. Some cross-references refer back to your original topic. Do not reuse a heading.

Once students take off on the project, you will need many more daisy parts. The original numbers are just to get you started.

You can expand the dictionary skill to include the upper grades and work on the cross-references at another time by altering the requirements slightly.

Students in grades five through eight can look for words, following the directions for grades two through four, but instead of selecting any word beginning with the correct two-letter combination, they must choose a descriptive word that might apply to their flower.

By the end of the month your room will be filled with daisies. You may be out of wall space, but the feeling of spring will be everywhere.

TEACHING UNIT 2: INTRODUCING THE THESAURUS

You can introduce the concept of the thesaurus to students as young as second grade in an informal and unstructured way. This can be done in a variety of situations.

Objectives:

At the end of this lesson students will:

1. Demonstrate their understanding of a thesaurus by using it to enrich the language choices they make when writing compositions.

2. Add to and use the class-made thesaurus, indicating their awareness that words have subtle shades of meaning and need to be chosen carefully.

Materials:

alphabetical thesaurus (as many as you can find)

overhead projector and supplies

oaktag and markers

Introductory Activities:

Begin with a common adjective that is relevant to the discussion.

1. If you have just read a fairy tale, there is sure to be a beautiful girl involved. Ask the children what other words they can think of to describe her besides "beautiful." If they are comfortable with language, you will immediately get contributions such as "lovely," "good looking," "attractive," "gorgeous," even "sexy." Where language experience is limited, the answers may be as simple as "pretty" or "nice."

   When all the words students can think of have been exhausted, try another. How about the villain in the story? How would you describe his or her actions? Again, words will come tumbling out: "mean," "wicked," "nasty," "cruel," "unkind," and "heartless" from students with an enriched environment. Others may be hard pressed to come up with much more than "bad" or "no good."

2. Another time, use the weather as the start of the lesson. A cold, clammy, nasty, inclement day can elicit a number of different descriptions. On a clear, sunny, day ask children how today's weather makes them feel.

3. Call attention to a new bulletin board display. Again, depending on the type of display, there are many descriptive words that can be used.

Explain Synonyms:

After the class has participated in one of the above introductory activities, tell them that what they have been doing is using synonyms, or words that are similar in meaning. Explain that when they have compositions to write they will want to use many different words in their writing. Being able to use a wide variety of words is similar to drawing a picture using a box of 64 crayons rather than a box of 8 crayons. Let the class discuss the implications of this simile.

Show students one or two copies of the thesauruses you have and explain how they can look up words. (Of course, you will only show them the simpler alphabetical thesauruses, not the topical ones.) Choose one of the words that you used as a springboard and look it up. Put the words from the thesaurus on an overhead projector and have the class discuss the "shades" of meaning. Encourage sentences using these words. Could the words be interchanged?

Make a visible and continuing thesaurus of your own to keep students attuned to shades of meaning and aware of the variety of the English language. Choose some common words used regularly in writing, such as "say" or "go." Hang a smiling mouth (see Figure 3-4) with the word "say" above it. Turn it into a mobile of alternate words from the thesaurus, dictionary, or student reading. When students write, they can consult the mouth so their characters can "an-

Figure 3-4.

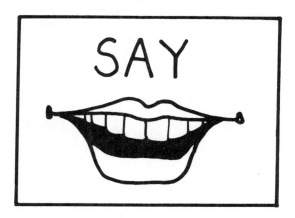

nounce," "state," "growl," or "snap" their replies instead of "saying" them. A footprint will do the same for "go." You can branch out. A smiling face can start a "happy" mobile. A contrasting frowning face serves for "sad."

For grades 2 to 4 prepare a chart to record the successes of your word detectives. Whenever students find a new synonym, give them a point. If you use different colors for each month you can reward the student who has added the most synonyms to the mobile. The mild competition and the hanging reminders will make writing easier and help your students begin paying attention to the language they are using.

TEACHING UNIT 3: DICTIONARY SKILLS

Students develop basic dictionary skills without much class time being devoted to actual teaching. It is important, however, to require some evidence that they have attained a level of proficiency. This unit not only lets you check students' skills, but also is an exploration of the way words are constructed. It is an excellent follow-up to a unit on prefixes.

Objectives:

By the conclusion of this unit students will be able to:

1. Locate a word in a dictionary.
2. Define some common prefixes and stems.

Materials:

felt marker

1 sheet of chart paper or oaktag

acetate sheet (transparency) and markers

35   4" × 6" cards

Preparation:

1. Make a chart of the 14 prefixes listed in Figure 3-5.
2. With a felt marker, write a different stem word (see Figure 3-6) on each of the 4" × 6" cards.

Figure 3-5.

PREFIXES				
AB	(7)		IN	(21)
AC	(5)		OB	(7)
COM	(7)		PER	(8)
CON	(21)		PRE	(11)
DE	(20)		PRO	(12)
DIS	(8)		RE	(28)
EX	(8)		TRANS	(10)

Figure 3-6.

STEMS				
BATE	(3)		PLETE	(3)
CEDE	(4)		PORT	(7)
CEPT	(7)		POSE	(7)
CESS	(6)		PRESS	(4)
CORD	(4)		QUIRE	(3)
DUCT	(6)		SCRIBE	(6)
FECT	(5)		SENT	(5)
FER	(6)		SOLVE	(3)
FINE	(3)		SPECT	(4)
FLECT	(3)		SPIRE	(5)
FORM	(7)		STRUCT	(4)
FUSE	(5)		TAIN	(5)
GRESS	(5)		TEND	(5)
JECT	(6)		TRACT	(7)
JURE	(4)		VENT	(3)
LATE	(5)		VERSE	(5)
MAND	(3)		VERT	(3)
MIT	(4)		VIOUS	(3)
PEL	(5)			

3. Put a transparency with the following words on the overhead projector:

> AUTOGRAPH
> BIOGRAPH (Y)
> GEOGRAPH (Y)
> PHONOGRAPH
> TELEGRAPH

Procedure:

1. Give students a minute or so to look at the transparency, then ask them what is the common element in all the words. They will have little difficulty in identifying "graph" as the part that reappears in each word.

2. If all the words contain the same stem, what meaning do they have in common? This is a much more difficult question. It is necessary to ask the definition of each word and then, by adroit questioning, help students realize that "graph" means "write." The prefixes extend the concept of writing into new meanings.

3. You can generate interest by encouraging students to list words that use the same prefixes with other stems or endings. They may come up with:

GEOLOGY

BIOLOGY

TELEPHONE or PHONETICS

TELESCOPE or TELEVISION

AUTOMOBILE or AUTOBIOGRAPHY

4. Now that the class sees how prefixes, suffixes, and stems join to make new words, explain that they will be finding some less obvious prefixes and stems.

5. Distribute the cards of stems to the class. (One stem per student is enough. You can use the remainder for extra credit.) Direct their attention to the chart. Students are to check each prefix in conjunction with the stem on their card to see if it forms a word.

6. When students find a word, they are to write it below the stem and give the definition.

7. After students have located all possible words, gather the group around the chart and ask how many have found words with the first prefix *ab*. There should be seven (*ab*scess, *ab*duct, *ab*ject, *ab*jure, *ab*late, *ab*sent, and *ab*solve).

8. Have students read their definitions and attempt to define the prefix. Write the prefix definition on the chart. Continue through the remaining prefixes. (See Figure 3-7 for the answer key.)

9. Display the stem cards with definitions around the room. (See Figure 3-8 for the answer key.)

Figure 3-7.

```
                                 ANSWER KEY
                             DICTIONARY PREFIXES

AB    abscess      DE    debate       IN    inception     PRO    probate
      abduct             deduct             induct               process
      abject             defer              infer                product
      abjure             define             inflect              profuse
      ablate             deflect            inform               progress
      absent             deform             infuse               project
      absolve            defuse             ingress              propel
                         deject             inject               propose
AC    accept             demand             injure               proscribe
      accede             deplete            inquire              prospect
      access             deport             inscribe             protract
      accord             depose             inspect              proportion
      acquire            depress            instruct
                         describe           intend        RE     rebate
COM   command            destruct           invent               recede
      commit             detain             inverse              recess
      compel             detract            invert               record
      complete           devious            incessant            reduction
      comport            deception          intractable          refer
      compose            defect             infect               refine
      compress                              inspire              reform
                   DIS   discord                                 reflect
CON   concede            dispel       OB    object               refuse
      concept            disport            oblate               regress
      concord            dispose            obstruct             reject
      conduct            dissent            obtain               relate
      confection         distend            obverse              remand
      confer             distract           obvert               remit
      confine            dissolve           obvious              repel
      conform                                                    replete
      confuse      EX    except       PER   perception           report
      congress           excess             perform              repose
      conjure            expel              perjure              repress
      conscript          expose             permit               require
      consent            express            pertain              resent
      construct          extract            perspective          respect
      contain            extend             perfect              respire
      contend            export             perspire             retain
      contract                                                   retract
      convent                        PRE    precede              reverse
      converse                              precept              resolve
      convert                               prefer
      conspire                              preform       TRAN/  transfer
                                            prelate       TRANS  transform
                                            prescribe            transgress
                                            present              translate
                                            pretend              transmit
                                            prevent              transport
                                            previous             transcribe
                                            prefect              transpire
                                                                 transpose
PLEASE NOTE: The underscores in some words                       transverse
indicate that in addition to having prefixes and
stems the words also have suffixes.
```

Figure 3-8.

```
                        ANSWER KEY
                     DICTIONARY STEMS

BATE    debate      FORM    conform     PORT    comport     STRUCT  construct
        probate             deform              deport              destruct
        rebate              inform              disport             instruct
                            perform             export              obstruct
CEDE    accede              preform             report
        concede             reform              transport   TAIN    contain
        precede             transform           proportion          detain
        recede                                                      obtain
                    FUSE    confuse     POSE    compose             pertain
CEPT    accept              defuse              depose              retain
        concept             infuse              dispose
        except              profuse             expose      TEND    contend
        inception           refuse              propose             distend
        precept                                 repose              extend
        perception  GRESS   congress            transpose           intend
        deception           ingress                                 pretend
                            progress    PRESS   compress
CESS    abscess             regress             depress     TRACT   contract
        access              transgress          express             detract
        excess                                  repress             distract
        process     JECT    abject                                  extract
        recess              deject      QUIRE   acquire             intractable
        incessant           inject              inquire             protract
                            object              require             retract
CORD    accord              project
        concord             reject      SCRIBE/ conscript   VENT    convent
        discord                         SCRIPT  describe            invent
        record      JURE    abjure              inscribe            prevent
                            conjure             prescribe
DUCT    abduct              injure              proscribe   VERSE   converse
        conduct             perjure             transcribe          inverse
        deduct                                                      obverse
        induct      LATE    ablate      SENT    absent              reverse
        product             oblate              consent             transverse
        reduction           prelate             dissent
                            relate              present     VERT    convert
FECT    defect              translate           resent              invert
        infect                                                      obvert
        perfect     MAND    command     SOLVE   absolve
        prefect             demand              dissolve    VIOUS   devious
        confection          remand              resolve             obvious
                                                                    previous
FER     confer      MIT     commit      SPECT   inspect
        defer               permit              prospect
        infer               remit               respect
        prefer              transmit            perspective
        refer
        transfer    PEL     compel      SPIRE   conspire
                            dispel              inspire
FINE    confine             expel               perspire
        define              propel              respire
        refine              repel               transpire

FLECT   deflect     PLETE   complete    PLEASE NOTE: The underscores in some words
        inflect             deplete     indicate that in addition to having prefixes and
        reflect             replete     stems, the words also have suffixes.
```

LEARNING CENTER:
LOOKING UP UNUSUAL WORDS IN THE DICTIONARY

This lesson relates to the "Inflate Your Vocabulary" bulletin board in Part Three. It can be used from second grade on and is particularly effective during the month of October to mark Noah Webster's birthday.

Tell your class that you are highlighting Noah Webster and the dictionary this month. Suggest that they participate in finding unusual words in the dictionary by writing them down and posting the cards for others to see. This may be done during a class period or when the children have free time.

Materials:

> several different dictionaries
>
> pack of 3″ × 5″ index cards
>
> pens
>
> tape

Procedure:

1. Give each student some 3″ × 5″ cards and a pen.

2. The students may check any dictionary to find words that interest them.

3. Each word is written on the center of the card and the pronunciation is written in parentheses next to it. At the bottom of the card the name of the dictionary in which the word was found is noted. The card is then turned upside down and the meaning of the word is written on the back.

4. The cards (and the pens) are returned to you to post around the room. If there is time it is a good idea to do this right away so that the students can see where you place their cards.

5. Stick a piece of tape to the top of each card and attach it to the bulletin board. Leave the bottom free so that the card can be turned over and the definition can be read easily. Place each card low enough so that the children can read it.

6. The cards can be posted near the bulletin board, near the area where the dictionaries are kept, or around your room, depending on the amount of space you have.

The children will enjoy looking for unusual words and will learn the meanings of several new ones.

Chapter 4

ENCYCLOPEDIAS

BACKGROUND INFORMATION

Encyclopedias began in the classical age as the product of a single author. It was not until the eighteenth century that they emerged as the combined effort of many writers who were concerned with simplifying an extensive range of complex subjects and keeping the material as up to date as possible. Because they perform these functions so well, encyclopedias—along with dictionaries—are the most widely used reference tools.

They are so frequently used it almost seems unnecessary to explain much about encyclopedias. Although you probably used them extensively in your own student days and still do now as an adult, you probably are familiar with only one particular set of encyclopedias. As a teacher, your concerns about students copying directly from the encyclopedia may create a situation in which this valuable resource is regularly ignored or misused.

In order to develop the broad background needed to instruct students in the proper use of encyclopedias, you should take a closer look at the various types, their differences in presentation, and their similarities of overall purpose. You need to appreciate that there are times when it is appropriate and important for students to consult an encyclopedia. An added bonus comes as you discover that encyclopedias can be used as a teaching tool for improving students' ability to organize material and read intelligently.

Various Types

Encyclopedias are classified by length, type, and audience. Some consist of only one or two volumes, yet still serve a useful purpose. They don't always have an index and their entries are much shorter and usually less comprehensive than those having twenty-plus volumes.

They are also divided into two types: general and subject. General encyclopedias include the whole body of knowledge, while subject encyclopedias focus on one area. In some instances their coverage may be defined extremely narrowly, such as *The Illustrated Encyclopedia of the Animal Kingdom.* Check your media center for specialized encyclopedias in science, geography, and history.

Subject encyclopedias may be single- or multi-volume works and should be included as part of the research skills that students must develop.

Editors of encyclopedias gear their work to a specific audience. *Encyclopedia Americana* and *The New Encyclopedia Britannica* are designed for adult use. *World Book Encyclopedia, Compton's Encyclopedia,* and *Merit Students Encyclopedia* are aimed at students in upper elementary through high school grades. *New Book of Knowledge* provides material for still younger readers. Because of curriculum requirements and the range of student capabilities, all but the adult encyclopedias are customarily found in elementary media centers while high schools include all those mentioned. If you want a detailed analysis of general encyclopedias look through Kenneth F. Kister's *Encyclopedia Buying Guide*, 3rd ed. (Bowker 1981).

Differences in Presentation

You should compare encyclopedias in the same way you compare dictionaries. Choose two subjects, one which you know a great deal about and one with which you are unfamiliar. Look both up in several sets and see how they are handled. If you were making a purchase you would be deciding which one of the many sets most suited your needs. As a teacher you should become familiar with the different ways subject matter is presented. Each of the acceptable encyclopedias tends to do something well, and no matter how comprehensively one set treats a subject, another set may add still more information.

As you turn from one encyclopedia to another you become aware that there are major differences as to scope, length of entries, illustrations (color versus black and white), and other special features. Adult encyclopedias generally have more entries than those for young adults. Some encyclopedias, particularly those intended for younger users, have fairly short articles. Color illustrations are expensive but they make the work more inviting. Special features vary widely and may include tables, diagrams, fact summaries, study aids, outlines, and extensive cross references. Other helps or hindrances to ease of use are variations in type face. Some encyclopedias can cause eyestrain with prolonged use.

Similarities of Purpose

General encyclopedias seek to present their users with the broadest possible range of human knowledge made comprehensible for their audiences' reading levels, limited by the total number of the volumes the publishers consider to be cost effective. To accomplish this purpose the major encyclopedias do an excellent job of simplifying information, making them the perfect first step when you want an introduction to a subject. Another specialty of encyclopedias is the short entry that gives brief explanations on a wide variety of topics. The encyclopedias vary as to the fields they cover well. Some include extensive biographies; others may give summaries of literary works.

To maintain accuracy in an everchanging world, it is of critical importance for encyclopedias to be up to date. They have a policy known as CONTINUOUS REVISION, which means they update a percentage of the entries each year. Optimally, ten percent of the set should be revised each year, but many publishers, feeling the economic pinch, have not met this figure. A recent copyright date is no guarantee that the article you are reading has been revised recently. As a means of checking how current some entries are, look up science areas such as astronomy, in which there have been recent discoveries, to see whether the latest theories on the origin of the universe, or information on the solar sytem have been included.

The continuous revision policy causes the strange page numbering in some encyclopedias. Pages become 125a, 125b, 125c, and so forth, when new material is added. When an article is lengthened as a result of revision, it is far too costly to change all subsequent page numbers, as it would entail changing every plate and correcting all affected page references in the index.

The quality of the index is of major importance in an encyclopedia. It must be easy to use and have a comprehensive range of entries to anticipate the many ways a user might look up a subject. The index should give extensive subdivisions of a subject and have adequate cross-references.

Students do not naturally consult an index unless they have been trained or encouraged to do so. They automatically turn to the letter and volume where they think the material should be located. They must be taught that the compiler of the encyclopedia doesn't necessarily think about placing information in the same area where the student wants to look for it; therefore, the index must be used. Some elementary students are confused by the reference to the volume letter or number that precedes the page number in the index, so this must be clearly explained also.

Another problem students encounter is that encyclopedias have different ways of alphabetizing. Some follow the word-by-word arrangement as in the card catalog (see Chapter 2). Others use a letter-by-letter entry. Also, there is no consistency in whether a singular or plural version of the entry is in use. It is easy for students to assume that the subject they are seeking is not listed unless they are aware of these distinctions.

TEACHING UNIT 1:
HOW TO USE AN ENCYCLOPEDIA
EVEN IF YOU CAN HARDLY READ

This simple unit is more than an introduction to encyclopedias; it is also an introduction to research methods. The skills that are taught to beginning readers are the same skills that are needed by students at higher reading levels who must sift through greater quantities of material. The teaching is done in one forty-five-minute period or two thirty-minute periods. The learning, however, occurs only as the students apply what was taught to writing a report.

If you want to expand the teaching time, you can adapt the overhead projector techniques described at the conclusion of Part Three. Students can use the techniques to make maps and report covers and to illustrate whatever is of interest or importance to them.

To obtain the best results, work from the curriculum. Consider areas that students would enjoy exploring. Countries such as Japan, Mexico, or Egypt with their interesting foods, dress, and housing are good subjects. Another subject that might be selected is food, with individual reports on different grains, fruits, and dairy products.

Objectives:

At the conclusion of this unit students should be able to:

1. Identify an encyclopedia as an alphabetically arranged set of books containing information on all subjects. (This is obviously a rudimentary explanation.)
2. Select one volume from a multi-volume encyclopedia set that contains information on the topic to be researched.
3. Locate an article within a volume.
4. Scan an encyclopedia article and extract the needed information.
5. Explain that a bibliography is a list of books that were used in research.
6. Make a simple bibliography.

Some students will also be able to use an index in an encyclopedia or other book to find additional information. Students in grades 4 and above should be taught how to use the index.

Materials:

ditto masters

enough paper to run off copies for every student in the class

3 sheets of acetate—2 sheets to make permanent transparencies and 1 sheet to be used during class (be sure that a thermal copier that makes permanent transparencies is available in your school)

at least one set of encyclopedias (additional sets are helpful)

overhead projector

transparency markers

Preparation:

1. Prepare worksheets on each country to be researched by students. You can approach this in two different ways. If you prefer this to be done during regular class time, try to have two different encyclopedia sets and assign no more than two students to each country. If the reports can be worked on during free time, you need select only three or four countries from the following list: Afghanistan, Bolivia, China, Denmark, Egypt, France, Hungary, Japan, Mexico, Netherlands, Peru, Switzerland, Turkey, U.S.S.R., Venezuela. Before you assign a country make sure that all the information asked for on the worksheet is covered in the encyclopedia article. The sample worksheet in Figure 4-1 is designed for students at the second-grade level.
2. Make a permanent transparency of the worksheet.
3. Make a permanent transparency of a page in an encyclopedia. Be sure to select a page that uses various type sizes to set off sections. You can make a transparency from a sample page sent by the publisher or from a photocopy of a page in an encyclopedia.

Procedure:

1. If you can, take students to the media center and have them sit in or near the reference section. Briefly discuss with them the kinds of books found

Figure 4-1.

WORKSHEET ON A COUNTRY

Do a report on _____.
Your report should have a cover, a table of contents, and a bibliography. In your report, you should have:

1. the name of two big cities, including the capital

2. the name of a big river or mountain

3. some foods eaten in that country

4. information about the language spoken there

5. the name of a national holiday and how it is celebrated

6. facts you found interesting about this country

The last page of your report will be your bibliography.

---

there. For second and third graders, it is sufficient to define reference books as dictionaries, encyclopedias, and atlases.

2. Inform students that they will need to use encyclopedias to do their reports.

3. Pick up one volume and flip through the pages so that the class can see the text.

4. Although students might observe that the encyclopedia looks difficult, reassure them that you are about to teach them some "tricks" to make it simple.

5. The first thing for them to realize is that they do not have to read an entire set of encyclopedias. They need only begin with one volume. Go through the following steps to help them realize this for themselves:

   a. Put the transparency of the worksheet on the overhead projector. (Assign yourself "Japan" as the country you will research.)

   b. Ask the students, "What is the subject of this report? What will it be about?"

   c. Once they have responded, ask for the first letter of the subject.

   d. Point to a set of encyclopedias and ask which volume will be needed.

   e. Have one student select the correct volume.

   f. Congratulate the student and point out the letter or letters on the spine. Also show the letters on the volumes before and after the one chosen.

6. Give an audible sigh of relief because the class has now isolated the one book that is needed. But even one book is far too much to read. Show the children the first and last articles in the volume. Ask what has to be done to locate the article on Japan. Ask questions that will help the students realize that they must go to the second letter. Turn to the *Ja* section. Be sure to show the class the guide words at the top of each page. Show them that you go to the third letter and fourth letter and so on until "Japan" is found.

7. Distribute the encyclopedia set (one volume per group of three or four is usually sufficient) to allow some practice. Tell each group to look for a different country in its volume.

8. When an article on Japan has been located, the first step of the research project is complete and the children know how to find an article on their own. Now slowly turn the pages in the article and express dismay at the number of pages.

9. Go back to the transparency of the work sheet. Note that the first topic is the name of two large cities. Pick up the *J* volume again. Ask the students if they know what special picture has names of cities, mountains, and rivers. If no answer is forthcoming, give them a clue by suggesting that their families might use one before going on an automobile trip. Once you have elicited the word *map*, flip through the pages until you come to a map of Japan.

    NOTE: If you have an unusually alert class you may introduce atlases (see Chapter 5) at this point.

10. Refer to the volumes that are being shared by several students and have the students find maps of various countries.

11. Explain to the students that the size of the type indicates the size of the city. Ask them to read or spell the name of a big city on the map at which they are looking. Select a student to repeat this procedure with the map of Japan. Question 1 is now answered.

12. Next, ask what color is used to show water. Tell the children that the squiggly blue lines indicate rivers. Let them find rivers on their maps. Ask how they can tell a big river from a small one. You are, of course, looking for "length of the line" as the response. Ask how they would find a mountain and have them locate one.

13. Point out to the students that they have answered two questions of the assignment and that almost no reading has been required. Now they need only copy the information.

14. Put the transparency of an encyclopedia page on the overhead projector. In order to answer the next questions the class will have to learn how encyclopedia articles are divided. Remind the students that the larger and darker typeface on maps shows the more important cities. The same idea is used within the article itself. The larger or bolder type is used to set off sections. Students need only look for key words and phrases such as **Way of Life, People,** or **Food** printed in bold type. Encourage them to check the volumes in front of them to locate similar key words. By now, you have isolated one paragraph on food that the students can read since it is only a few sentences long. If some students cannot read the paragraph, remind them that you would be more than willing to read a few lines to them, especially since they have done all of the work in locating the material.

15. The same techniques can be applied to the question about language.

16. Additional information—on housing, holidays, or whatever else is important about a particular country—can be found by using the methods just learned or by looking at pictures.

17. Point out to the students that the articles they have been looking at have many pictures. If they see one that shows something special about the

country they can try to read the caption aloud. You can use the word *caption*, but explain it immediately. Again, if the caption proves too difficult to read they can ask for help. The important thing is that they have found the information; they have done research.

18. Students in grades 4 or above should be shown the index volume of the encyclopedia and asked if they know what an index is. They have probably used an index in a book and the concept is easily expanded. They should be told that the first letter or number given in the encyclopedia index refers to the volume and the other number(s) to the page. Although students doing research on as large a topic as a country can go straight to the appropriate volume, they may locate more items of interest if they first consult the headings in the index. (NOTE: For more practice on an advanced level using subject encyclopedias, see Teaching Unit 2 further on in this chapter.)

19. One more item needs to be covered. The children should be told that whenever they do research and write down information they must also list where they found the information. This list is called a bibliography. Let them feel impressed with themselves for being responsible for such a grown-up requirement. Use the acetate sheet to make a very simple bibliographic citation. All you need to list are the underlined name of the encyclopedia and the volume number. The form of the bibliography is not important; at this time you are teaching it to set an example that all researchers must acknowledge the sources they used.

20. If students can go to the media center to do research, the more gifted students can be directed to the regular nonfiction shelves and taught to use an index to obtain further information. The titles of the books they used would also be included in their bibliographies. These would be more extensive than the one, two, or three volumes listed by the majority of the class.

TEACHING UNIT 2:
USING ENCYCLOPEDIAS ARRANGED BY SUBJECT

Many students find it difficult to apply skills learned in one area to another area—even when the skills are similar. For example, although students may be able to use a general encyclopedia and an index in a book, some of them seem unable to put the two skills together to use an encyclopedia that is arranged by subject. Students who have been taught to use the index volume of alphabetically organized encyclopedias may be able to deal with a subject arrangement, but don't count on it!

Because the students don't perceive the similarities between the skills they know and the ones they will have to use, they do not turn readily to subject encyclopedias. They seem to regard such sets as *Book of Popular Science* (Grolier) and the *Undersea World of Jacques Cousteau* (Grolier) as non-encyclopedias and non-helpful.

By teaching students about entries arranged by subject you can accomplish at least two things: (1) you will introduce students to additional reference tools, and (2) you will reinforce skills in using indexes, cross-references, entry words, and so forth.

Since most encyclopedias having this arrangement specialize in a subject area, your instructions will be given during a science or social studies class, therefore, the students will also discover that these skills apply to all subject areas, not just English or language arts.

When you begin a new science or social studies unit incorporate the use of subject encyclopedias into your teaching. The instruction takes only one class period and can be adapted to serve the needs of any grade level. When you are going through the encyclopedias in preparation for your lesson be alert to information that goes beyond what is given in the textbook that would further enrich your lesson.

Objectives:

At the conclusion of this unit students will be able to:

1. Name at least one subject encyclopedia.
2. Locate a topic in the index of the subject encyclopedia.
3. Find the volume and page where the information on that topic is located.
4. Identify the volume and page where illustrations on that topic can be found.
5. Employ a subject encyclopedia for research purposes.

Preparation:

Choose the most appropriate encyclopedia for the lesson. For example, a junior high school science class beginning a unit on oceanography will need the *Undersea World of Jacques Cousteau*. Use that as the base for the lesson.

Prepare three transparencies.

1. On the first (see Figure 4-2) list approximately fifteen to twenty entries as they appear in the index volume. Do not include subheadings or page numbers, but include at least one "see" reference. Point out the way the index

Figure 4-2.

Sea bass
Sea birds
Sea city
Sea cow
Sea cucumber
Sea elephant
Sea-floor spreading
Sea gull, *see* Gull, sea
Sea hags
Sea hawk
Seahorse
Seal
Sealab I
Sealab II
Sea level

(From: *Undersea World of Jacques Cousteau*, 20v, Grolier, 1973)

is alphabetized. The one illustrated in Figure 4-2 lists entries in letter-by-letter order. Some indexes use a word-by-word listing. In such an arrangement, "Sea level" would come right after "Sea hawk."

2. On the second transparency (see Figure 4-3) list entries from another section of the index. You need only three or four main entries. One can be expanded to include about four subheadings. Each of the main entries and subheadings should contain a volume and a page reference.

3. On the third transparency (see Figure 4-4) make a detailed list of another section of the index. Use pens of different colors or use boldface type to distinguish between typefaces used to indicate illustrations. For this transparency there should be about ten subheadings from the entry on which you will focus.

4. Prepare a fourth transparency (see Figure 4-5) that illustrates the index of another encyclopedia having a subject arrangement. You can use one or two of the entry words you had earlier pointed out to the class to show how the two indexes are alike and how they are different.

Figure 4-3.

```
Disease
        egg and, II 6
Disruptive coloration. See Coloration, disruptive
Divers and diving, XII 10
        adaptations for, X 60–61, 62–63
        archaeology and, XII 24–25
        breath-holding ability and, X 58–59
        coral, XVII 62–63
        sunken treasure, XVII 10–19
Diving bells, XII 37, 64, 65, 66, 68–69, 78; XVII 17
```

(From: *Undersea World of Jacques Cousteau*, 20v, Grolier, 1973)

Figure 4-4.

```
Shark, I 30, 33, 35, 36, 42, 75, 106; II 27; III 8, 9; IV 83; V 17, 78, 94; VI 29, 140–141;
        VII 86, 100, 101; IX 111; X 8; XI 74, 89, 95; XII 13; XV 92, 106; XVII 95

        aggression, VIII 56–57
        angel, VI 92
        birth, II 118–119
        curiosity, XVII 69
        diet, VII 86
        dolphin versus, VI 140–141
        eyes, IV 122
        foodgetting, III 10; VI 28, VII 86; VIII 10
        jaws, VI 31
        teeth, III 84
```

(From: Undersea World of Jacques Cousteau, 20v, Grolier, 1973)

Figure 4-5.

```
OCEAN 2-223-32, 260-68; illus 2-269
        bioluminescence, 3-432
        caves, formation from ocean waves 2-101
        currents 2-250
        deep-sea exploration 2-269
        earthquakes 2-31
SHARK (fish) 4-316-26
        fossils 4-481, 482

(From: New Book of Popular Science, 6v, Grolier, 1980)
```

Avoiding Yawns:

Teaching a skill lesson can be deadly dull, and even you are likely to yawn unless you use an approach that will grab the attention of the class. The transparencies are one aid because they will switch the focus from you to the screen and back. If you fall into the lecture trap, however, most of the class will tune out. The trick is to ask questions that will force the students to see analogies between the information they already have and that which they are learning.

Do not tell the students that the entry to the encyclopedia is through an index volume. Instead, ask them what they would do to find information on seahorses. Their first response might be to "look under 's.'" Allow some more students to make guesses. If no one gives the correct answer, ask the class how they would use a one-volume book about ocean life to find out about seahorses. At least one student will now remember the index. Use this answer to guide the class to the realization that the last volume in an encyclopedia arranged by subject contains an index. Remind them that there are always exceptions; indexes can also be at the beginning or at the end of each volume.

Procedure:

Each of the transparencies mentioned earlier helps students to understand how the index volume functions. The following instructions will give you a better idea of how to use them.

1. The alphabetical arrangement of the index is highlighted in the first transparency. For the oceanography unit, a selection of entries beginning with the word "sea" serves to illustrate how detailed the index can be. You will need to point out the difference between a letter-by-letter alphabetical sequence, as used in the *Undersea World of Jacques Costeau*, and a word-by-word arrangement, as used in the card catalog and other encyclopedias and dictionaries. Choose two or three of the entries and say which position they would occupy if a word-by-word arrangement were followed. Ask the class to explain the "see" reference to make sure the concept is understood.

NOTE: Experience has shown that at some time during the lesson, it is necessary to make it clear to students that the index volume refers only to the books in that particular encyclopedia set.

2. After talking about alphabetical sequence draw the group's attention to the second transparency's key-word alphabetical arrangement of subheadings and discuss how they relate to the entry word. If the entry words are "Divers and diving," then the subheading "treasure" refers to diving for treasure. (The connection between entry and subheading is now always obvious to students.) As you review the transparency ask the students where they would find information on diving for treasure. Students need to understand that an index to a multi-volume set must first give the volume number and then the page number. Careful questioning can bring them to that understanding. If the set uses Roman numerals to indicate the volume number, as does the *Undersea World of Jacques Cousteau*, be sure the students know how to decipher them. Many students have never learned about Roman numerals and others may have forgotten.

3. The complete concept is brought together in the third transparency. Explain that you have used two colors of ink or used boldface type, if possible. Ask why the different typefaces are used. For classes unable to figure out the reason, ask them what they expect to find when they look up something in the index. Have them check subheadings, one from each ink color, to see if they can determine the reason for using different typefaces. Help the students to realize that there are many subdivisions under an entry that may be applicable to a topic being researched. For instance, if "Shark" were being used as an entry and if someone were researching the eating habits of sharks, he or she should be able to recognize that the words "feeding," "eyes," "mouth," and "jaws" are possibly relevant subdivisions.

General Hints and Follow-Up:

Throughout the lesson, ask students to tell you which entry they would use to find something. Then have one of them locate the information and bring it to you when found. The interruptions caused by this procedure actually keep the lesson moving.

If there is an extra set of the encyclopedias you used during the demonstration, or if the set in the media center is not in heavy demand, you may ask to keep it in your classroom during the teaching of this unit.

As you continue to teach research techniques students begin to truly learn. Soon you will notice a change in behavior. It will not happen immediately but after a while you will see students seeking needed information in a logical, efficient manner.

TEACHING UNIT 3:
ENCYCLOPEDIAS—TOOLS WITH A TWOFOLD PURPOSE

Students from elementary grades onward, when faced with any reference question, invariably turn to encyclopedias. This reaction is so common that teachers often try to limit the practice. The unspoken question then becomes: if encyclopedias are not to be used are they a poor tool? If so, why do media centers own so many sets? The answer is that they *are* valuable and serve an important function in preparation for research. Even better, they can be used to teach students a basic writing skill—how to outline. Unfortunately, misuse has created a situation in which an invaluable tool is disdained.

By now, teachers as well as students must be reintroduced to the purpose and value of encyclopedias. For someone unfamiliar with a topic, encyclopedias are an excellent introduction. Users need to appreciate how admirably they present a new and difficult subject, so the reader can then organize a research project and learn what aspects are of interest to him or her and what direction the paper might take.

Because of the general coverage and the need to communicate essential information rapidly, long encyclopedia articles are tightly constructed and follow a careful outline. This structure can be used to train students to read selectively, to become aware of how a topic is divided, and then to go on to learn how to construct their own outlines. The latter skill can be used in a variety of ways from writing a research paper, to studying for an exam, to organizing personal activities.

Preparation:

Before students begin a research assignment or are taught outlining, instruct (or perhaps reinstruct) students in using encyclopedias intelligently.

1. Look carefully at multi-volume encyclopedias. The media center undoubtedly owns at least three or four different sets, one of which is probably *World Book*. (NOTE: If you don't have access to a media center borrow additional classroom sets from other teachers.) At the end of every long article *World Book* includes the basic outline that was followed, giving the Roman numeral and capital letter headings. Further subdivisions that may be used within the articles are not given in the outline. Although the information is there to help, it is rarely used.

2. Choose a large topic—perhaps in science—that is being studied by the class. Possibilities include "oceans," "sound," "electricity," or "weather." Prepare a transparency of the outline at the end of the *World Book* article. Leave space under the capital letter headings so you can make added entries as necessary.

3. During the course of the lessons students will be comparing articles on the same subject in different encyclopedias. If there are twenty-eight students in your class and you have four different encyclopedias, you will need to choose seven different subjects in addition to the one for which you prepared the transparency. Be sure you select topics that are sufficiently long to have outlines given in *World Book*.

4. Before class set up seven tables. If one of the topics is "Texas," that table will have the proper volume from *World Book* as well as volumes from *New Book of Knowledge, Compton's,* and *Merit Students Encyclopedia* (if those are the ones available in your school's media center).

Procedure:

1. After explaining the objective of the session, tell students at each table their topic and have them look it up. If at all possible, there should be one volume per student. Have them page through the article. Ask if they would really like to read the entire article. The response will be obvious and emphatic. What can they do instead? Let them come up with suggestions. You want them to discover the numerous ways encyclopedias capsulize and present information in the form of charts, graphs, tables, and captioned photographs.

2. Have students using *World Book* turn to the outline at the end of their article. Using the transparency you made, explain that by looking at the outline students can choose the sections of interest in the article. They need not read the whole thing.

3. Now that they know what part of the article applies, the problem is how to locate it. The holders of *World Book* should soon see how the different typeface and spacing tells whether the section is a Roman numeral (which indicates a major heading) or a capital letter (which indicates a major subdivision of that Roman numeral). They may also find further subdivisions of the heading not given in the outline but shown by the typeface. You can add the Arabic number headings to your transparency if your chosen article is so organized.

4. It is quite surprising to hear quiet exclamations as the light dawns on the class. It seems so obvious to you that you may be startled to realize that students have been using encyclopedias without being aware of the purpose of the different typeface. Their new-found knowledge can now be applied when the outline is not given at the end of the article. Students with other encyclopedias should look through their articles and see how type is used to show the organizational plan. The *New Book of Knowledge*, for example, employs a triangular arrow before a boldface type to indicate a major heading. Subdivisions are in boldface above the paragraph, with further subdivisions in boldface at the left margin beginning a paragraph.

Follow-Up:

Students can now extract the outline of an article. This serves to give them practice in both using encyclopedias and making outlines. The list given in Figure 4-6 for articles in the *New Book of Knowledge* allows you to assign subjects based on students' abilities.

One small problem may arise from the fact that these articles do not always adhere to the rule for outlining that requires a "B" whenever there is an "A," and a "2" whenever there is a "1." When the editors have failed to follow the conventional form, students can try to come up with their own headings.

Since outlining is a method of organizing plans and materials, two other activities are possible. The first, slightly frivolous but fun, is to have students outline the planning of a party. The individual results can be combined to show how well prepared the students can be with a little organization.

The second activity will continue to benefit students throughout their school years. Have them outline a unit in their science and social studies (history in high school) texts using the typeface in the same way they did with the encyclopedias. Vocabulary words or names given in boldface within the body of the text should be listed as subdivisions of the headings under which they fall.

Students will now learn another valuable lesson—outlining the text as a method of preparation for tests. Once the outline is complete, they can star any section they don't fully understand, then go back to the text and review only that section. In this way, outlining becomes a valuable study skill. Where once they reread an entire unit, wasting time needed for working on problem areas, they now have confidence that they have covered all the material and can concentrate on their weak points.

Figure 4-6.

Subjects to Outline from *New Book of Knowledge*

VOL.	EASY	MODERATE	DIFFICULT
1.	Airplane Models		Anthropology
2.	Balloons and Ballooning	Bats	Basketball
3.	Cartoons	Chess	Computers
4.	Darts	Dolphins and Porpoises	Dogs
5.		Eisenhower, Dwight D.	Energy Supply
6.	Flying Saucers	Football	Fire Fighting and Prevention**
7.	Genealogy	Gymnastics	Gardens and Gardening
8.	Halloween	Hurricanes and Tornadoes	Hawaii
9.	Ink		Indians of North America
10.		Kites	Jewelry
11.		Lighthouses	Libraries
12.	Magic	Money	Missiles
13.	Noise	Names and Nicknames	New Jersey
14.	Outlines	Observatories	Olympic Games
15.	Pens and Pencils	Plants, Poisonous	Psychology
16.		Racket Sports	Rockets
17.	Study, How to*	Sharks, Skates and Rays	Snakes
18.	Teachers	Telegraphs and Cables	Tennis**
19.	Vikings	Volcanoes	Vermont
20.		Whales	World War II**
	*very easy		**very complex

Once students become familiar with outlining you can prepare a unit on writing research papers. But even if you don't follow up with another unit, the students will have learned a skill they can use for the rest of their lives.

LEARNING CENTER: ENCYCLOPEDIAS

Encyclopedia skills need to be practiced and you can't include student research as part of every unit. An effective alternative is to set up a learning center on encyclopedias. Depending on your class needs and how you select the questions, it can be used for remediation, extra credit, or as a required part of the unit.

Begin small. The center can be started with three question cards and a single answer card. (See Figures 4-7 through 4-10.) As you move into a new unit, make more cards, selecting questions that will add to students' understanding or pique their interest in the subject while also reinforcing their library skills. Be sure to number the cards and key the numbers to the answer card, which may be kept separately.

As the learning center grows, you may withdraw cards on a topic covered earlier. To keep your management of the center simple make one answer card for each topic and consider color coding. For example, you may have four question cards on "heat." The four cards and the answer card can be on yellow posterboard. When you move on to "sound" and add new cards, put them on white

Figure 4-7.

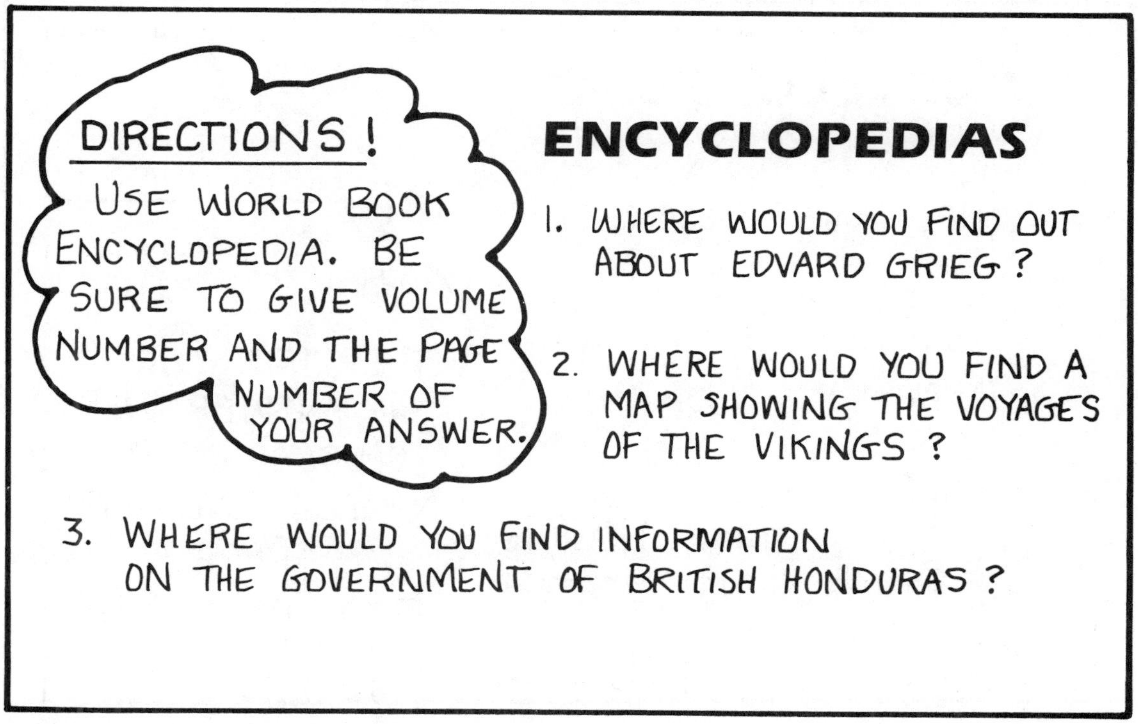

Figure 4-8.

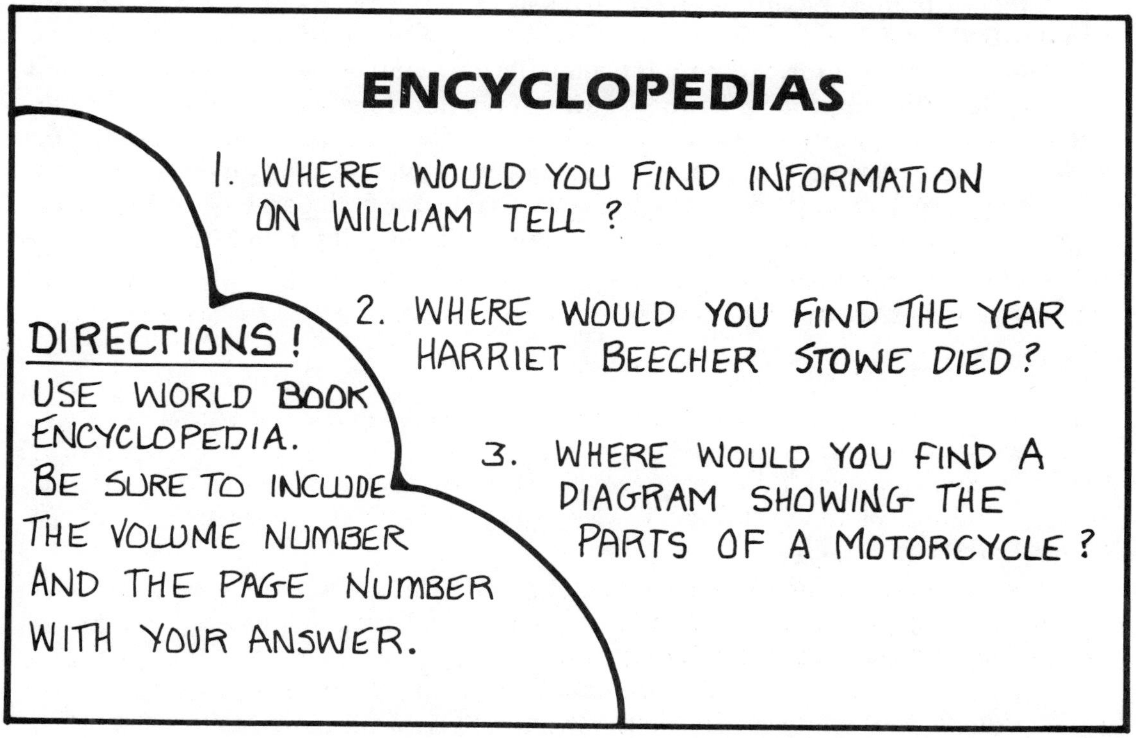

Figure 4-9.

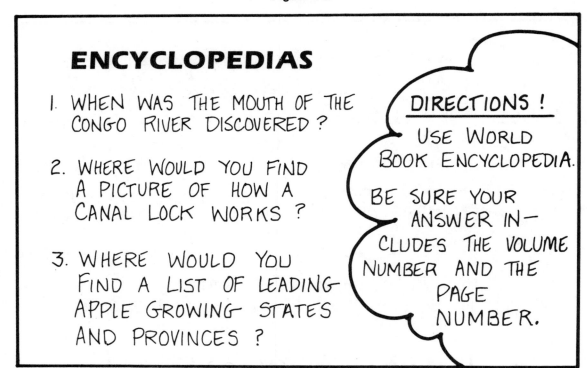

posterboard. By the time the class is working on an earth science unit you can remove the yellow cards until the following year.

The cards may be any size you choose. A size that has proven to be convenient is 6″ × 9″.

The learning center, if set up for remediation, can be a way to use a modified mastery learning approach. Students who have not done well on a unit test can get the same basic information from encyclopedias and then be retested. You will have exposed them to the subject in another way, and thus given them a second chance to learn. If you schedule class time for independent study, your slower students can work with encyclopedias and not fall further behind. Meanwhile, they will develop proficiency in a vital research skill.

Figure 4-10.

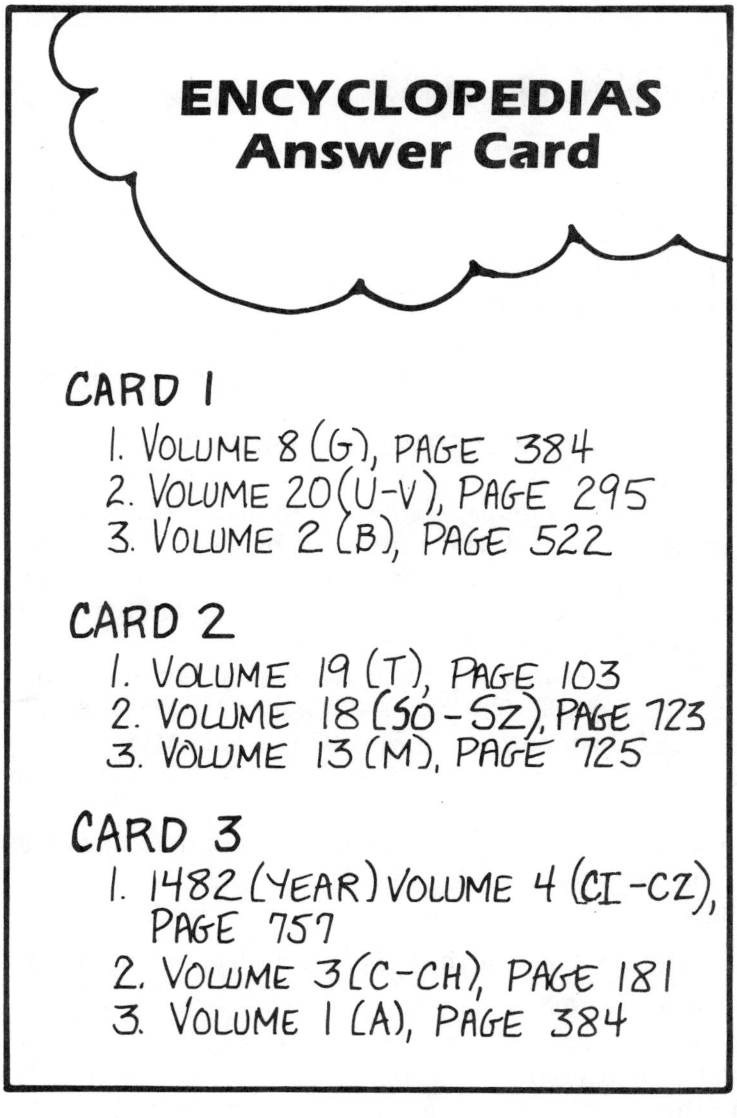

ENCYCLOPEDIAS
Answer Card

CARD 1
1. Volume 8 (G), page 384
2. Volume 20 (U-V), page 295
3. Volume 2 (B), page 522

CARD 2
1. Volume 19 (T), page 103
2. Volume 18 (SO-SZ), page 723
3. Volume 13 (M), page 725

CARD 3
1. 1482 (year) Volume 4 (CI-CZ), page 757
2. Volume 3 (C-CH), page 181
3. Volume 1 (A), page 384

Chapter 5

ATLASES

BACKGROUND INFORMATION

An atlas is a book of maps, a simple definition which does not seem to require much explanation. Yet the simplicity of its design sometimes obscures your awareness that students must employ a combination of skills to use it effectively, that there are many variations distinguishing one atlas from another, and that there are two very different types of atlases.

Most third graders can grasp the general idea that maps are small representations of the larger world. They usually learn this through assignments that have them map the classroom (example: "Unmarked Map of the Media Center," from Chapter 1), map a room in their house, map their route to school or the school itself.

Large wall maps can be used to help students understand some of the cartographers' conventions:

- blue lines represent rivers
- the size and boldness of the typeface indicate comparative sizes of cities
- stars show capitals

You may have introduced them to these facts if you used the encyclopedia teaching unit in Chapter 4.

Knowing the meaning of these symbols is a start, but people use atlases for a different purpose. The function of an atlas is to pinpoint where a geographic feature can be found and where it is relative to other locations. To do this, students must be able to search an extensive index requiring good alphabetical skills and find not only the page reference but the location key as well. They must then be able to examine the box formed by the letter and number of the key and find the name they looked up in the index. On a more advanced level, they may have to interpret a key and scale of distances to determine where the place lies in relation to a given point. The quality of printing varies from map company to map company and from atlas to atlas. Sometimes the more obscure place names are printed in such small letters as to be virtually unreadable, particularly for young (and old) users. Maps use color to differentiate among countries or feet above sea level, but these can be too dark and make reading place names difficult. Before you assign atlas reference work check the volumes students will be using so you can anticipate whether there will be any problems.

Atlases come in several sizes. Although you might be envisioning those heavy oversized editions that libraries tend to store in special cases, there are some that are just about the size of a standard page. The *Rand McNally World Atlas, Goodes Edition* is designed for school use. It measures 8¾" × 11¼" and has fifty pages of special maps in the introductory pages, including global maps of manufacturing regions, agricultural production and natural resources, as well as the more usual weather and population maps. Twenty more pages of maps of the world cities follow before the regular atlas begins. Enrich social studies teaching from grade five and up by using maps and allowing students to have further practice with atlases.

Other subject areas can use the introductory information found in other atlases. The *Hammond Medallion World Atlas* devotes fifteen pages to "Environment and Life" including pages on the Geological Record, the Structure of the Earth, the Biosphere, and Life Support Cycles.

Rand McNally publishes two versions of *Cosmopolitan World Atlas*. One is the "Planet Earth Edition" and has fifty pages on such subjects as the Moon, the Ocean World, and Planet Earth. The second version has thirty pages on the characteristics of United States geographic regions and twenty pages of travel maps. The company also publishes a *Concise Atlas* with fifty pages, having another approach to explaining the Earth. The first twenty-five pages explore such topics as the Life and Death of Earth, Earth Under the Sea, and the Active Earth. This is followed by a section showing the influence of Man on Earth, the Water Energy and Food Resources, Religion, Language, Population, and Pollution.

The National Geographic Society has taken another approach. Its atlases are square, measuring 10¾" × 10¾". *Our Fifty States*, for example, divides the United States into geographic regions, explaining the features, major cities and characteristics of the area. Each state in that region is given a two-page spread with one page being an easy-to-read monochromatic map. Scattered throughout the volume are discussions using maps or graphics on Weather, America at Work, and Energy and Its Uses. The text is difficult for children below the fourth grade, but the maps are simple enough for a second grader to use.

No one atlas is better than the others. They are all accurate but each has a distinctive quality. Map tones and printing density vary. You need to examine several atlases to decide what you consider to be the positive and negative qualities of each.

The historical atlas is a specialized type. Probably the best known one is *Shepherd's Historical Atlas* (Shepherd, William B., 9th edition, revised, Barnes and Noble, 1967), which, although difficult for younger students to use, is the most comprehensive with a chronological sequence of maps from 3000 B.C. to 1967 A.D.

Historical maps are included as part of the *Hammond Medallion Atlas* discussed earlier. Three sections contain biblical maps, world history maps, and U.S. history maps.

One of the best historical atlases, suitable for browsing, is the *American Heritage Pictorial Atlas of U.S. History* (American Heritage 1966). Virtually every double page has at least one map. For major events in U.S. history, such as the Revolutionary War and the Civil War, large sections are organized to give maps of battles—famous ones as well as little-known ones. Major battles often have labeled pictorial spreads that show the terrain clearly so students can easily visualize the progress and difficulties of the engagement. These maps can make a dry account in the textbook come alive.

Maps are compelling for many people, perhaps because they make remote places seem real. With a little planning you can incorporate them into your teaching and open the world for your students.

TEACHING UNIT 1: ATLASES AS VACATION PLANNERS

As a break or when a holiday season approaches, you can hold the attention of your students and give them practical experience in using atlases and maps by having them plan vacations. The unit works well for grades five to eight and can be adapted to tie into any cities or countries that are included in the social studies curriculum.

The use of a combination of tools is an approach that shows the interrelation among reference sources to answer real-life questions. Many students have seen their parents do similar planning. This motivates them to develop what they can appreciate as adult skills.

Resources Needed:

You need a standard collection of atlases, encyclopedias, and books on each state. Road atlases are most useful and, since these are available in paperback, you might purchase two or three. An optional extra that can make the teaching unit more realistic is a supply of directories from national hotel/motel chains. To randomly choose vacation destinations, students might draw their selections from one of two coffee cans or small boxes that you have prepared.

Preparation:

1. First, write the names of major U.S. and Canadian cities not in your immediate area on slips of paper. You might include:

Los Angeles	Boston
Chicago	Toronto
New York City	Oklahoma City
Montreal	Tampa
Washington, D.C.	Portland
New Orleans	San Francisco

2. Next, write the names of scenic, historical, and recreational attractions not in your immediate area on other slips of paper. You might include:

Independence Hall	Prince Edward Island National Park
Statue of Liberty	Golden Gate Park
Knott's Berry Farm	Mount Rushmore
West Point	The Freedom Trail
Pearl Harbor	Jasper National Park
Walt Disney World	Annapolis

3. If you are using the coffee cans or boxes, decorate them with pictures from travel folders. Most travel agencies are cooperative about giving you all the old brochures you need. Label one can (or box) CITIES and the other AT-TRACTIONS.

4. While at the travel agency see if you can get old posters of different cities and use them to create an exciting atmosphere in the room. Finally, make copies of the worksheet in Figure 5-1.

The Assignment:

Divide the class into groups of about four students each. Although the project could be done by students working individually, it is more efficient to use a group approach because of the time factor, and students will enjoy it more.

Each group selects one member as recorder to: (1) keep track of materials used in completing the assignment, (2) know who is responsible for which part, and (3) unify the final project.

Each group decides whether to go to a city or an attraction. If coffee cans or boxes are used, the groups can make their own selections; otherwise, assign the destinations.

After distributing a copy of the worksheet to each group, review the tools to be used in completing the assignment. Suggest that each group divide the questions and illustrations among its members and then share the information with each other so that all group members will understand what was done to complete the group project.

As an aid in organizing their research, the groups should write the name of the research tool they expect to use next to each question on the worksheet. You might also walk among the groups and check their initial approach while they are deciding who will be doing what question.

A Colorful Presentation:

When the groups hand in their work, display it along with travel sections from the Sunday newspapers. Invite other classes to your room and have your junior travel agents discuss great places to visit.

Figure 5-1.

WORKSHEET

Destination _____

Group Members _____

_____

1. How far is the city or attraction from your point of origin? (Do not give miles "as the crow flies," but calculate distance using major highways.) Which highways would you use?

2. How many days will it take you to get there? Base your answer on a maximum drive of 400 miles a day for one driver and 600 miles per day if two or more drive. Where would you plan to stop each night? (Choose the nearest town or use the motel directories for a specific location.)

3. What weather (average temperature, precipitation) would you expect for a July vacation?

4. For CITY groups only: What five sights would you be sure not to miss? Describe them. Why are these attractions special?

5. For ATTRACTION groups only: In what state is this attraction located? What is the nearest major city?

6. For ATTRACTION groups only: What activities would you plan while visiting this attraction? Why do people visit this attraction?

7. For all groups: Present your project.
   - Make a travel poster promoting your destination.
   - Prepare a travel brochure that includes the answers to the above questions.
   - Hand in your completed worksheet and a bibliography of all sources you used.

TEACHING UNIT 2: MAKE YOUR OWN MAPS

An unusual way to teach map and atlas skills is to have students create maps for others to read, not maps of areas they know, but rather imaginary worlds they design. They will develop their creativity as they brainstorm a theme and then the locations of their fictitious kingdoms. At the same time they are forced to incorporate map skills into their planning. This unit is an extension of one taught by Beverly Zinze to fifth and sixth graders at Harry S. Truman School in Sayreville, New Jersey. It should be taught after students know the basics, but you can explain the terms as you go along.

Objectives:

At the conclusion of this unit students will be able to:

• use a legend to decode map symbols

• use coordinates from an index to find a location on a map

• understand colors as a source of physical information given

Introduce the unit by reading a simple story, such as *Authorized Autumn Charts of the Upper Red Canoe River Country* by Peter Zachary Cohen or a chapter from *The Phantom Tollbooth* by Norton Juster. In either of these books the map devised by the author helps readers visualize where the characters are, just as maps of real places do. Encourage students to tell how they feel about maps in books and the use of maps in general. Then say that they will create their own maps of places that have never been.

The guidelines are simple. The country they create must have a name that indicates what the land is about and determines the places that will be found within. Work through one idea with the whole class. Suggest "School Dazia" as an example of your invented country. Places might include Mathville, Social Studies Town, and Science City. Geographical features could be Homework Mountains, Pencil Forest, and the Chalk River.

As you begin, the class will groan a bit about the puns but soon they will join in and add their own. After you have listed enough places, draw a sketch of your new country and ask for suggestions as to where these places should be located on the map. Next, the class must decide on other information to be given in the map. Which town is to be largest and how is that represented? Is the map to be physical as well as political? If so, which is the highest section and which is the lowest? What colors illustrate the difference? How do you show the distance in miles/kilometers between cities? How do you decide what route to use between cities? As the questions are answered, the key or legend is developed.

Complete the illusion of a real map by requiring boundaries. Other countries or bodies of water need to be included. Some obvious frontiers for your creation a. e: Vacationland to the south, Adulthood in the north, United Universities in the west, and the Sea of Information in the east. Draw light vertical and horizontal lines evenly spaced over your map. Label the vertical lines 1, 2, 3, etc. and the horizontal lines A, B, C, etc.

Distribute the worksheet (see Figure 5-2) and divide the class into assigned or self-organized groups with not more than four students in them. Each group should be given a number. Review the requirements and directions on the worksheet. Suggest that each group begin with a brainstorming session similar to the one they had as a class to first choose the name of their country and then the locations. Of course, they can add places as they go along, at least until they prepare the final map.

It should not take too long to complete the project. Preliminary sketches are helpful, and you can check group progress this way. Remind the class to follow all directions on the worksheet. Each group is responsible for preparing its section of what will be the index. All the locations included on their maps (cities, rivers, mountains, whatever they invent) must be listed on separate 3" × 5" cards with the letter/number identification *and* their group number. Cards should be put in alphabetical order and turned in along with the map.

Try to have several atlases available for the groups to consult for ideas. As the projects develop, students will be looking at them more closely to see relative size of print, the way color is used, and how legends are added. Instead of your requiring them to look at the atlases, the assignment gives them the direction and the motivation to pay close attention to the details.

The most difficult part of the assignment, however, is for the groups to devise the questions that other groups are to answer. In general, they should follow a basic format such as: "How far is it from X to Y? What is the best route? Name the bodies of water that can be found in Z land."

At the close of the unit each group turns in an oaktag sheet with their fully colored map. The group number should be in the upper right-hand corner of the oaktag when it is held with the shorter width across the top and bottom and the name of the country should be centered as a title. Their map question sheet with separate answer key is required at this time along with the cards.

You can punch holes in the oaktag sheets and put rings through them to turn the individual maps into an atlas. Have some students interfile all the cards to serve as an index. Keep the question-and-answer sheets in a separate file. Make copies of the question sheet so students can answer those written by other groups.

As you teach this unit over a period of several years, your student-made atlas and index will continue to grow and become even more useful. You might use it as a springboard for creative writing assignments. Students can choose one of the maps and write an adventure about someone who lives in the imaginary place.

Figure 5-2.

WORKSHEET

First Steps:

1. Choose name of country.
2. Create place names and geographical locations.

   • you must have at least 15
   • extra credit is given for more than 20 places
   NOTE: You can have special locations (parks, streets, etc.) within a large city.

3. Plan boundaries.
4. Decide whether your map will be physical or political.

Planning It Out:

1. Draw sketch of country.
2. Fill in places you created.
3. Sketch in highways to be included. Be sure to give them numbers.
4. Lightly draw vertical and horizontal lines on sketch and label with letters and numbers.

Completing the Project:

1. Take oaktag sheet.
2. Draw your country neatly.
3. Put in all locations neatly.

   • suggestion: Use self-stick labels

4. Color map. This may be done before Step 3 if you use labels.
5. Rule vertical and horizontal lines. Be sure they are evenly spaced.
6. Add legend to map.
7. Prepare 3″ × 5″ cards.

   • make one card for each place with letter and number and group number.

example:

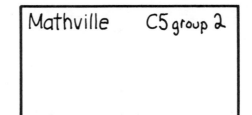

8. Write worksheet and separate answer key. Be sure group number is on both.
9. Before handing in work, check the following:

   • Group number in corner
   • name of country on top
   • group member names on back
   • all boundaries drawn in

TEACHING UNIT 3: ALONG THE SAME LINES

Students commonly assume that latitude determines climate, something that is true to a limited extent. Although altitude, prevailing winds, and proximity to ocean currents ultimately have greater effects, few students would believe that New York City and Madrid share a common latitude. Since their map study is generally regional, students rarely realize which countries are north or south of each other on a global scale. As they complete this assignment, they will increase their skills in reading latitude lines and learn to use the specialized maps that are found in the front of many atlases.

Objectives:

At the end of this unit students will be able to:
- locate cities around the world when given the latitude
- use climate and rainfall maps
- use product maps

Preparation:

1. On a ditto master make an alphabetical list of all the cities you want students to find. (See Figure 5-3 for suggestions.) Include either your state cap-

Figure 5-3.

Cities to Locate

Ankara	Florence	Omaha
Antwerp		Ottawa
Atlanta	Hartford	
		Paris
Barcelona	Kiev	Peking
Berlin		Philadelphia
Boise	Las Vegas	Phoenix
Boston	London	
	Los Angeles	Richmond, VA
Calgary		Rome
Casablanca	Madrid	
Cedar Rapids	Málaga	San Francisco
Chicago	Manchester, NH	
Copenhagen	Marseille	Tangiers
	Milan	Teheran
Denver	Milwaukee	Tokyo
Detroit	Minneapolis	Toronto
Dublin	Moscow	
		Vancouver
Edinburgh	Naples	Volgograd
Edmonton	New York City	
		Wichita

ital or the largest city in your state. You may have to add additional cities to match that latitude line.

2. Divide the class into groups, one group for each assigned line of latitude. (See Figure 5-4 for suggested latitude lines.) Students never see this master list.

3. Make a ditto master of the worksheet shown in Figure 5-5.

Figure 5-4.

ANSWER KEY
CITIES BY LATITUDE

33°N–34°N
Atlanta
Casablanca
Los Angeles
Phoenix

35°45'N–36°45'N
Las Vegas
Tangiers
Teheran
Tokyo

37°N–38°N
Málaga
Richmond, VA
San Francisco
Wichita

39°45'–40°45'N
Ankara
Denver
Madrid
New York City
Peking
Philadelphia

41°N–41°45'N
Barcelona
Hartford
Naples
Omaha

42°N–42°30'N
Boston
Cedar Rapids
Chicago
Detroit
Rome

43°N–43°45'N
Boise
Florence
Manchester, NH
Marseille
Milwaukee
Toronto

45°N–45°30'N
Milan
Minneapolis
Ottawa

49°N
Paris
Vancouver
Volgograd

51°N–51°45'N
Antwerp
Calgary
Kiev
London

53°N–53°30'N
Berlin
Dublin
Edmonton

56°N
Copenhagen
Edinburgh
Moscow

GROUP MEMBERS _____

Figure 5-5.

LATITUDE RANGE _____

CITY	COUNTRY and CONTINENT	TEMPERATURE		ANNUAL PRECIPITATION	MAJOR PRODUCTS
		WINTER	SUMMER		

Procedure:

1. Explain the assignment to the class. Distribute the alphabetical list of cities. Reassure them that they need not find all the cities on the list, just the ones along their assigned latitude lines.

2. Distribute the worksheets. Be sure all students know the latitude range their group has been assigned.

3. Review with the class how to read latitude lines. Special attention must be paid to the way maps vary even within one atlas. When the area is large (for example, Texas or U.S.S.R.), there may be 5° to 10° between each latitude line. For smaller areas there may be only 1° between each line. Occasionally the map will divide within the degree. Be sure students know that one-half a degree of latitude is equal to 30'.

4. Direct students to look for the product and climate maps. Most of these can be found in the early pages of the atlas, although product maps may also be placed alongside regular political maps. *Goode's World Atlas* (Rand McNally) is particularly suited to this part of the assignment.

Optional Display Idea:

Have students transfer their worksheets onto large sheets of oaktag. They can include additional information such as:

- outline maps of the country or state where their cities are located

- flags of the countries

- additional facts of interest (language, money, food, national dress)

Hang the results along with a world map. Use colored pushpins to mark the cities. All cities along the same line should have the same color pushpins.

TEACHING UNIT 4: PLOTTING THE CONTINENTS
(for grades 5–8)

If you really want to challenge your students and test their comprehension of latitude and longitude, offer them these six dot-to-dots that have them plotting the coordinates of the continents. The puzzles are a variant on a unit developed by Beverly Zinze for her sixth grade class at the Harry S. Truman School in Sayreville, New Jersey.

The exercise is a difficult one, and few students in the fifth and sixth grades will be able to do more than the first three maps. Not only do students need to locate and connect the dots, but once they have successfully completed drawing the outline, they will most likely have to check an atlas to verify the continent they have drawn.

Plotting the points is tedious work, and if you assign too many maps students can become resistant and careless. Instead of spending too much time on the project divide the class into groups. The number of students per group is determined by how many of the six maps you plan to assign. Each *student* then prepares only one map. Thus, if you have a group of six, a complete set will be made.

Maps are of different levels of difficulty. The higher the number, the more difficult the map, as follows:

Map 1	Australia	(Figure 5-7)
Map 2	Africa	(Figure 5-8)
Map 3	South America	(Figure 5-9)
Map 4	Europe	(Figure 5-10)
Map 5	North America	(Figure 5-11)
Map 6	Asia	(Figure 5-12)

Note particularly that the latitude and longitude on the maps of North America and Asia have 10° separations rather than the 5° separations of the other four maps. Some additional difficulties students face include observing carefully:

- the East/West notation as some maps cross the 180° longitude line
- the North/South notation when plotting coordinates near the equator

To simplify the activity somewhat, give students wide-ruled graph paper (see Figure 5-6) with the latitude and longitude degrees indicated along the top and side of the paper. Use the answer sheets to guide you in preparing the correct degree range for each map. For fifth and sixth graders, you might even place the first point on the map to get them started. If you feel this assignment is very difficult, walk your class through the map of Australia to plot the course together. Make a transparency of the grid so that everyone can see what is being done.

To make the activity even more challenging for a bright seventh or eighth grade class, just tell students the range of latitude and longitude degrees they will need. Check their work, at least on the first map, to be sure they have the right idea before they begin plotting the coordinates.

Objectives:

As a result of this activity students will:

- demonstrate an understanding of the meaning of latitude and longitude
- identify continents from their shape and by checking the latitude and longitude of these continents in an atlas

Directions for Students:

1. Plot the coordinates one at a time.

2. As soon as you have two points plotted, *connect the dots.*

3. When you have completed the map, see if you can identify the continent you have drawn.

4. Check your answer by looking up the continent in an atlas. Be sure the latitude and longitude points match.

Figure 5-6.

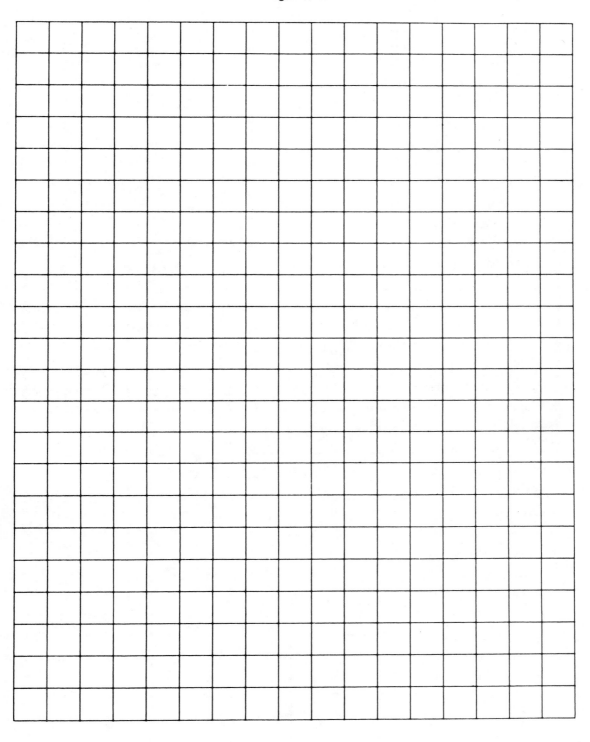

Figure 5-7.   Map 1 — Australia

Latitude	Longitude	Latitude	Longitude
35°S	116°E	15°S	145°E
30°S	115°E	20°S	148°E
25°S	114°E	23°S	150°E
22°S	114°E	25°S	152°E
22°S	115°E	30°S	153°E
20°S	120°E	35°S	151°E
15°S	125°E	37°S	150°E
14°S	127°E	38°S	146°E
15°S	130°E	38°S	143°E
13°S	130°E	37°S	140°E
12°S	132°E	35°S	136°E
11°S	133°E	32°S	131°E
12°S	135°E	33°S	125°E
12°S	137°E	34°S	123°E
15°S	136°E	34°S	120°E
18°S	140°E	35°S	118°E
11°S	143°E	35°S	116°E

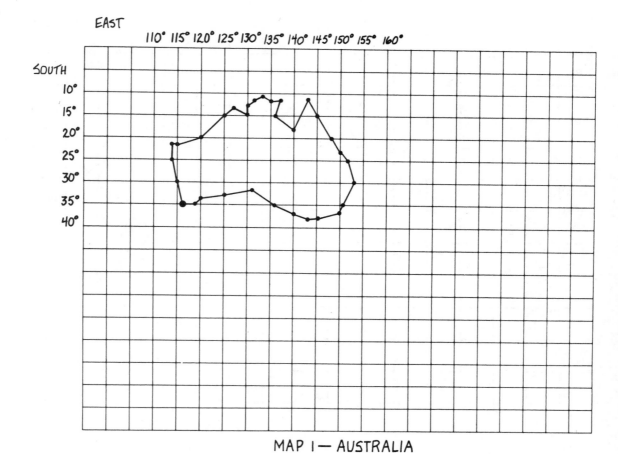

MAP 1 — AUSTRALIA

Figure 5-8.   Map 2 — Africa

Latitude	Longitude			Latitude	Longitude
6°N	8°W			33°N	30°E
8°N	12°W			32°N	32°E
12°N	18°W			14°N	40°E
16°N	18°W			12°N	42°E
19°N	17°W			10°N	44°E
25°N	15°W			12°N	61°E
30°N	10°W			5°S	39°E
34°N	8°W			11°S	41°E
36°N	7°W			15°S	41°E
35°N	6°W			20°S	33°E
35°N	3°W			25°S	35°E
36°N	0°			30°S	31°E
38°N	10°E			34°S	26°E
34°N	10°E			35°S	20°E
33°N	15°E			18°S	12°E
31°N	20°E			12°S	13°E
33°N	21°E			10°S	14°E
34°N	22°E			3°S	9°E
32°N	29°E			5°N	9°E
				6°N	8°W

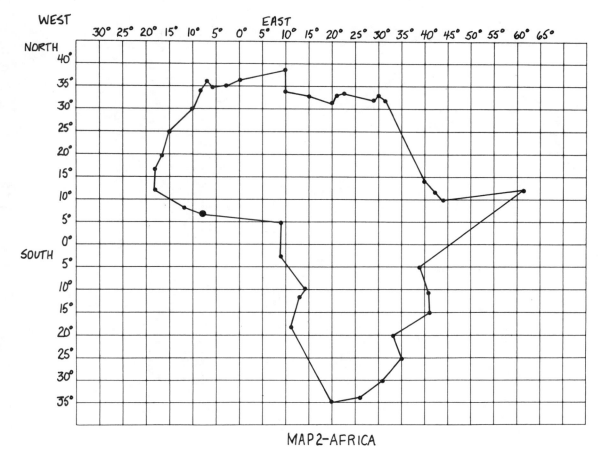

MAP2-AFRICA

Figure 5-9.   Map 3 — South America

Latitude	Longitude		Latitude	Longitude
0°	80°W		25°S	49°W
3°N	77°W		28°S	49°W
7°N	77°W		35°S	55°W
8°N	78°W		38°S	58°W
9°N	77°W		39°S	63°W
8°N	76°W		42°S	63°W
11°N	75°W		41°S	65°W
12°N	72°W		45°S	67°W
12°N	70°W		47°S	65°W
10°N	63°W		50°S	69°W
9°N	60°W		54°S	70°W
7°N	58°W		55°S	65°W
7°N	54°W		55°S	70°W
4°N	52°W		50°S	74°W
3°N	51°W		40°S	74°W
2°N	50°W		20°S	70°W
1°N	50°W		18°S	71°W
2°S	45°W		15°S	76°W
3°S	40°W		10°S	78°W
5°S	35°W		5°S	82°W
10°S	34°W		3°S	82°W
13°S	41°W		1°S	81°W
20°S	40°W		0°	80°W

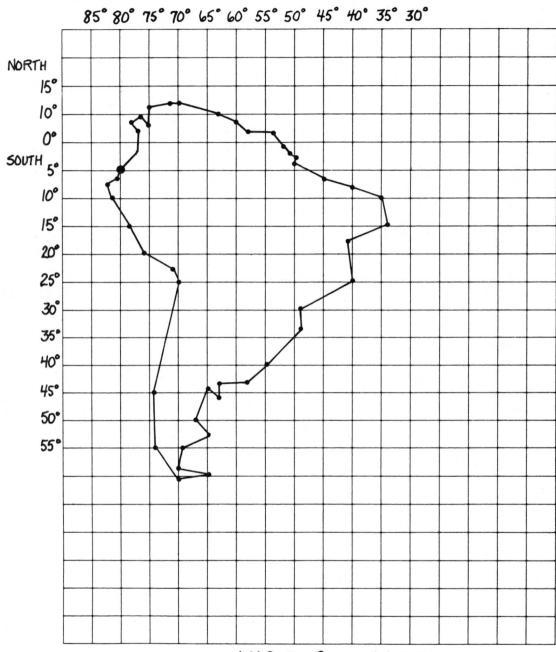

WEST
85° 80° 75° 70° 65° 60° 55° 50° 45° 40° 35° 30°

NORTH
15°
10°
0°
SOUTH 5°
10°
15°
20°
25°
30°
35°
40°
45°
50°
55°

MAP 3—SOUTH AMERICA

Figure 5-10.   **Map 4 — Europe**

Latitude	Longitude	Latitude	Longitude	Latitude	Longitude
44°N	9°W	66°N	22°E	41°N	31°E
43°N	2°W	63°N	18°E	41°N	23°E
46°N	1°W	60°N	19°E	38°N	25°E
48°N	4°W	56°N	16°E	36°N	23°E
48°N	3°W	56°N	14°E	40°N	20°E
50°N	2°W	55°N	14°E	46°N	14°E
50°N	1°W	55°N	13°E	45°N	13°E
50°N	1°E	60°N	10°E	41°N	19°E
53°N	5°E	58°N	8°E	40°N	18°E
54°N	9°E	58°N	6°E	42°N	17°E
57°N	8°E	62°N	5°E	39°N	17°E
58°N	11°E	65°N	12°E	38°N	15°E
57°N	10°E	72°N	25°E	39°N	16°E
55°N	9°E	72°N	30°E	40°N	16°E
54°N	11°E	67°N	41°E	42°N	12°E
54°N	14°E	66°N	38°E	44°N	9°E
55°N	21°E	67°N	32°E	43°N	3°E
59°N	24°E	64°N	38°E	42°N	3°E
59°N	28°E	70°N	65°E	40°N	0°
60°N	30°E	68°N	65°E	38°N	1°W
61°N	28°E	60°N	60°E	37°N	2°W
60°N	24°E	51°N	60°E	37°N	4°W
61°N	22°E	52°N	52°E	36°N	6°W
63°N	22°E	48°N	52°E	37°N	7°W
65°N	25°E	42°N	50°E	37°N	9°W
66°N	25°E	45°N	40°E	44°N	9°W
		42°N	42°E		

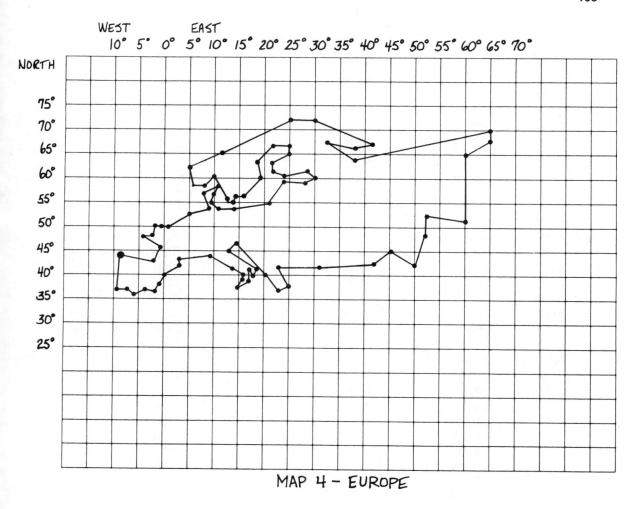

MAP 4 — EUROPE

Figure 5-11.   Map 5 — North America

Latitude	Longitude	Latitude	Longitude	Latitude	Longitude
40°N	124°W	72°N	90°W	46°N	60°W
45°N	124°W	74°N	87°W	43°N	65°W
50°N	127°W	74°N	80°W	45°N	67°W
55°N	133°W	73°N	75°W	44°N	70°W
60°N	140°W	71°N	70°W	41°N	74°W
60°N	150°W	67°N	65°W	35°N	76°W
60°N	153°W	66°N	62°W	33°N	80°W
58°N	155°W	65°N	64°W	31°N	82°W
56°N	160°W	66°N	67°W	27°N	80°W
54°N	165°W	64°N	65°W	25°N	79°W
53°N	170°W	63°N	65°W	30°N	85°W
52°N	180°	63°N	70°W	30°N	90°W
53°N	173°E	64°N	75°W	29°N	89°W
55°N	165°W	64°N	78°W	30°N	94°W
58°N	157°W	66°N	73°W	25°N	98°W
58°N	162°W	68°N	73°W	20°N	98°W
60°N	162°W	70°N	77°W	18°N	95°W
61°N	165°W	70°N	80°W	19°N	91°W
62°N	167°W	65°N	82°W	21°N	91°W
68°N	167°W	64°N	80°W	21°N	87°W
71°N	160°W	64°N	90°W	18°N	86°W
71°N	155°W	60°N	95°W	15°N	92°W
70°N	145°W	59°N	85°W	17°N	95°W
69°N	136°W	50°N	83°W	18°N	100°W
70°N	130°W	52°N	80°W	20°N	105°W
70°N	125°W	54°N	79°W	27°N	110°W
68°N	115°W	60°N	77°W	31°N	115°W
68°N	105°W	63°N	77°W	30°N	114°W
68°N	95°W	63°N	73°W	25°N	111°W
70°N	96°W	60°N	70°W	23°N	109°W
74°N	96°W	57°N	68°W	23°N	110°W
74°N	90°W	60°N	65°W	30°N	117°W
73°N	94°W	55°N	60°W	34°N	118°W
69°N	90°W	50°N	55°W	34°N	121°W
67°N	87°W	47°N	53°W	37°N	122°W
70°N	85°W	47°N	57°W	40°N	124°W

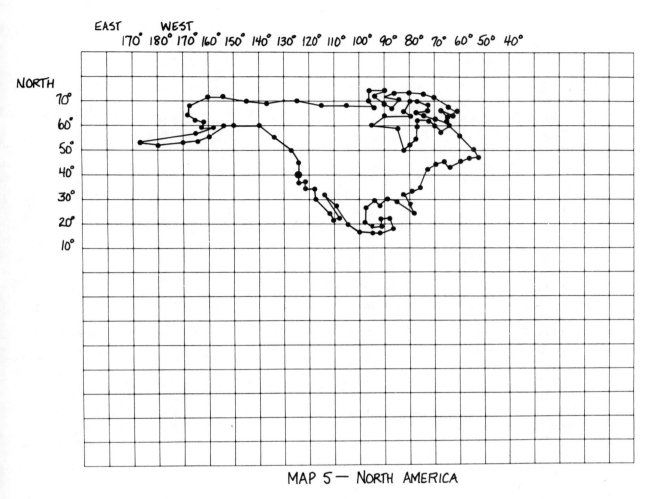

EAST   WEST
170° 180° 170° 160° 150° 140° 130° 120° 110° 100° 90° 80° 70° 60° 50° 40°

NORTH
70°
60°
50°
40°
30°
20°
10°

MAP 5 — NORTH AMERICA

Figure 5-12.   Map 6 — Asia

Latitude	Longitude	Latitude	Longitude	Latitude	Longitude
30°N	31°E	60°N	165°E	7°N	100°E
35°N	30°E	54°N	163°E	5°N	104°E
40°N	35°E	52°N	156°E	2°N	105°E
41°N	31°E	55°N	156°E	5°N	100°E
41°N	40°E	60°N	162°E	8°N	98°E
42°N	42°E	62°N	162°E	17°N	97°E
45°N	40°E	60°N	150°E	15°N	95°E
42°N	50°E	60°N	143°E	20°N	93°E
48°N	52°E	58°N	140°E	22°N	90°E
52°N	52°E	55°N	135°E	16°N	80°E
51°N	60°E	54°N	140°E	10°N	79°E
60°N	60°E	49°N	140°E	9°N	77°E
68°N	65°E	43°N	132°E	20°N	73°E
70°N	65°E	42°N	130°E	21°N	70°E
73°N	70°E	40°N	127°E	25°N	68°E
76°N	90°E	35°N	129°E	25°N	60°E
78°N	105°E	35°N	125°E	28°N	58°E
75°N	112°E	40°N	125°E	30°N	48°E
72°N	120°E	41°N	123°E	28°N	50°E
72°N	140°E	39°N	117°E	24°N	52°E
71°N	150°E	38°N	122°E	27°N	58°E
70°N	160°E	35°N	120°E	22°N	60°E
69°N	162°E	30°N	121°E	20°N	58°E
70°N	171°E	21°N	118°E	18°N	58°E
70°N	175°E	21°N	110°E	13°N	45°E
69°N	180°	20°N	105°E	20°N	40°E
68°N	177°W	15°N	109°E	30°N	35°E
67°N	180°	11°N	109°E	30°N	31°E
64°N	180°	8°N	105°E		
60°N	170°E	12°N	100°E		

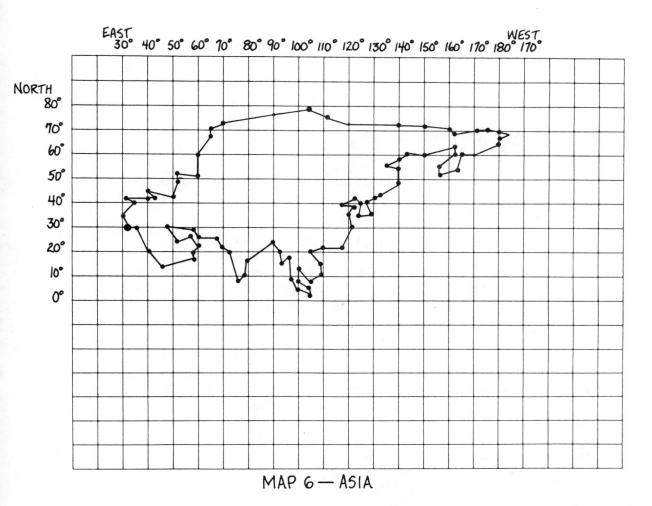

EAST
30° 40° 50° 60° 70° 80° 90° 100° 110° 120° 130° 140° 150° 160° 170° 180° WEST 170°

NORTH
80°
70°
60°
50°
40°
30°
20°
10°
0°

MAP 6 — ASIA

Chapter 6

ALMANACS

BACKGROUND INFORMATION

If you need to check when the last amendment to the Constitution was actually adopted, what number it was, and what it said; or how many member nations make up the United Nations and who they are; or what the current tuition rate is for a specific college, go to an almanac. If your students want to know where they can write to their favorite sports stars, or when their birthdays fall in the year 1999, or how fast a cheetah can run, send them to an almanac.

As you can see from the numerous and varied examples above, almanacs are sources for lots of different information and cover a broad range of subjects of interest to the public. They are published annually, with updated statistics and current news, are relatively inexpensive, and are a good reference tool for the home shelf as well as the school classroom and media center. Browse through an almanac for even fifteen minutes and you are bound to find at least one or two interesting tidbits of information that you never knew before.

Because the information in an almanac is placed randomly, a good index is essential to help the reader find the facts quickly and painlessly. Most almanacs have more than one index—a comprehensive one that runs many pages with three columns per page, as well as either a quick reference index or an alphabetical contents list. Any time you need to look up something specific you must turn to the index to gain an entry to the information. It is almost impossible to find what you are looking for by leafing through the pages. Choosing the specific word that is most likely to be listed in the index comes with time and practice.

Its annual publication schedule makes the almanac a good tool for finding the answers to statistical questions. The government statistics, census reports, voting results, and so forth, included are as current as can be found in a bound volume (as opposed to a magazine or newspaper). Information on almost any subject—financial, political, social, educational, and historical—is listed. Many segments, such as natural disasters or prize winners, are unchanged from year to year except for necessary updating.

Almanacs have a journalistic style. The information is presented in a compact and compressed manner. They include both current and retrospective events.

The World Almanac, the oldest one around, was founded in 1868 by Joseph Pulitzer of the *New York World Telegram*. It was followed by the *Information*

Please Almanac in 1947 and a number of others. Although *The World Almanac* is considered by standard reviewing sources to be the most useful and comprehensive of the almanacs, each one includes the same basic information but tries to cover certain things that the others don't. Look through whatever almanacs are available in your media center or public library to see how material is presented. You may find that you like one type more than another; however, there is not a great deal of difference.

To get some idea of what is covered in an almanac, *The World Almanac and Book of Facts*, 1983 edition, published by the Newspaper Enterprise Association, Inc. of New York, consists of 976 pages including some maps. The general index is in the front of the volume. It begins with a third-of-a-page listing of 1983 highlights which include:

- America's 25 most influential women
- A "Consumer Survival Kit"
- Heroes of Young America: the third annual poll
- Off-beat news stories of 1982
- World Almanac high school records
- World's refugees in 1982

You may consider some of these listings trivial but they will probably capture your students' interest. The index itself is 34 pages long with three columns per page. The final page has a "Quick Reference Index" listing information under such headings as: education, holidays, the population of the United States, postal information, and world history.

Generally, instruction on the almanac is begun around fifth grade. The small typeface and very thin pages (reminiscent of its newspaper style and background) make the almanac difficult for younger children to use. Of course, there are exceptions and if a subject comes up at a lower grade level for which the almanac will be helpful (such as third or fourth graders wanting the addresses of major league teams), you can always introduce it then.

The Guinness Book of World Records, edited and compiled by Norris McWhirter, while not actually an almanac, also belongs in this section. It was first published in 1955 by the Guinness Brewing Company "to provide a means of settling peacefully arguments about record performances" and has been revised annually ever since. Its popularity is attested to by the fact that it is published in 23 languages, can be purchased in 141 countries, and had sold over 42 million copies worldwide by late 1981. The paperback edition, published by Bantam, makes this book available at a price range that everyone can afford.

The *Guinness Book* lists all kinds of records—the tallest, shortest, fastest, slowest, longest, most, first, and so on. It is arranged by broad topics and the 1982 edition has twelve chapters headed:

The Human Being	The World's Structures
The Animal and Plant Kingdom	The Mechanical World
The Natural World	The Business World
The Universe and Space	The Human World
The Scientific World	Human Achievements
The Arts and Entertainment	Sports, Games, and Pastimes

There is a comprehensive index at the back of the book. Browsing through it, students will find superlatives like the tallest man, the highest I.Q., the rarest animal, the biggest apple, the most powerful drugs, the rarest language, the tallest chimney, the largest chocolate factory, the shortest war, the most parking tickets, the record number of cotton threaded in the eye of a needle, the longest throw in baseball, and the youngest Wimbledon champion. It is no wonder that students are fascinated by this book at an early age and retain their interest as they grow older.

Once they are introduced to the *Guinness Book* and learn a little about how it is arranged and how they can look things up, students will not need any urging or reinforcement to keep on using it. They will eagerly thumb through copies whenever they have free time, looking for the oddities that appeal to them.

This wide appeal of the *Guinness Book* has been used by other writers and publishers in different ways. SVE has a series of sound filmstrips (Reading Comprehension Using Guinness World Records and Reading Quizzes from Guinness World Records) based on *The Guinness Book of World Records.* Occasionally, the book will feature prominently in fiction stories for children. (One title is *The Highest Hit* by Nancy Willard, Harcourt, 1978.)

Students who learn to be comfortable using an almanac will have gained an important skill that will help them throughout their lives. At the same time, they will gain a lot of pleasure from using this special tool, not only for browsing, but for purposes of gaining information.

TEACHING UNIT 1: THE TRIVIA TROVE

Students in the fifth to eighth grades who are able to accomplish simple research (using the card catalog, general and subject encyclopedias, and perhaps a periodical index) should be encouraged to broaden their knowledge of reference books. This teaching unit takes the form of a classroom learning center and introduces students to the use of an almanac.

Include enough books to allow several children to work at the same time. Several back issues of almanacs can be used but students must record what year they used because answers may change over the years. Although only *The World Almanac* (Newspaper Enterprise Association, Inc.) is used in this unit, you could expand the learning center by also including other almanacs.

No introductory lesson is necessary for this unit. The students learn as they search, asking questions when they have a problem. The answer key directs them to the proper heading for searching. You may want to separate the search information from the answers. In that case, make a separate card, calling it "Clues for the Puzzled." Students who have no idea how to locate an answer can check the "clues" card, try again, then check their results against the answer card.

Objectives:

At the conclusion of this unit students will be able to:
- determine the key word needed to search an almanac index
- locate facts from tables in the almanac

Materials:

> 11 pieces of 6″ × 9″ posterboard
>
> 1 manila envelope large enough to hold the cards
>
> a piece of oaktag about 18″ × 24″
>
> felt markers
>
> masking tape

Preparation:

1. Use the posterboard to prepare five task cards with questions (see Figure 6-1), one task card as an answer key (see Figure 6-2), and, if you choose, five clue cards (see Figure 6-3). The clue cards and answer card can go on a second and third posterboard color for ease in separating them from the questions. You should keep the answer card.

2. Print "WORLD ALMANAC" on the outside of the manila envelope. Place the cards inside.

3. Print "THE TRIVIA TROVE" on the piece of oaktag. Attach the manila envelope, with the task and clue cards inside, to the oaktag.

4. Mount the oaktag on a bulletin board or wall.

Figure 6-1.

Task Card 1

Use *The World Almanac* to answer these questions:

1. What is the address of the American Motorcyclist Association? The National Basketball Association?
2. In what year was there a tie for the Cy Young Award? Who were the winners?
3. Where were the 1980 Winter Olympics held?
4. Which team won the Stanley Cup in 1980?
5. Which teams played in the Super Bowl in 1982? What was the score?

Task Card 2

Use *The World Almanac* to answer these questions:

1. What was the date of the first manned orbital flight? Who was the astronaut?
2. Who was the first American in orbit? What was the date?
3. Who were the crew members on the first manned lunar landing? What were the dates of the mission?
4. Who were the American astronauts and Russian cosmonauts involved in the first international manned rendezvous and docking? How many hours was the American flight? How many hours was the Russian flight?

Task Card 3

Use *The World Almanac* to answer these questions:

1. What is the world's longest river? How many miles is it?
2. How large is the Gobi Desert?
3. What is the world's highest mountain? How high is it?
4. Where is the second deepest lake in the world? How deep is it?
5. How deep is the deepest ocean in the world?

Task Card 4

Use *The World Almanac* to answer these questions:

1. What was the date of the San Francisco Earthquake? On March 27, 1964 an earth-quake hit Alaska. What did it measure on the Richter Scale?
2. What is the earliest date given for a major flood in the U.S.? Where was it?
3. When did the *Titanic* sink? How many lives were lost?
4. When did the zeppelin *Hindenberg* explode? How many lives were lost?

Task Card 5

Use *The World Almanac* to answer these questions:

1. Who invented the helicopter?
2. Who is credited with inventing the first gasoline automobile?
3. Who invented the first electronic television? When?
4. Who invented the first automatic toaster?
5. Who invented the first submarine?

Figure 6-2.

Answers to Task Cards

Card 1

1. American Motorcyclist Association, 33 Collegeview, Westerville, Ohio 43061. National Basketball Association, 645 Fifth Avenue, New York, New York 10022.
2. Dennis McLain (Tigers) and Mike Cuellar (Orioles) tied for the American League award in 1969.
3. Lake Placid, New York
4. New York Islanders
5. San Francisco 49ers, 26 points; Cincinnati Bengals, 21 points

Card 2

1. April 12, 1961; Yuri A. Gagarin
2. John H. Glenn, Jr.; February 20, 1962
3. Neil A. Armstrong, Edwin E. Aldrin, Jr., and Michael Collins; July 16–24, 1969
4. Americans: Vance Brand, Thomas P. Stafford, and Donald K. Slayton; Russians: Alexi Leonov and Valeri Kubason; 217 hours, 30 minutes for the American flight; 143 hours, 31 minutes for the Russian flight

Card 3

1. Nile River in Egypt; 4,145 miles
2. 500,000 square miles
3. Mount Everest in the Himalayas; 29,028 feet
4. Lake Tanganyika in Africa; 4,823 feet
5. Mariana Trench in the Pacific Ocean; 38,635 feet

Card 4

1. April 18, 1906; 8.5
2. May 31, 1889; Johnstown, Pennsylvania
3. April 14–15, 1912; 1,503 lives lost
4. May 6, 1937; 36 lives lost

Card 5

1. Sikorsky
2. Daimler
3. Farnsworth; 1927
4. Strite
5. Holland

Figure 6-3.

Clues for the Task Cards

Card 1

1. Look under "Addresses, to find," subheading "Associations and Societies." When you find the proper page, note that addresses are arranged according to key words in the titles.
2. Look under "Young, Cy, award winners (baseball)" or under "Awards, prizes," subheading "Baseball."
3. Look under "Winter Olympics" or "Olympic games."
4. Look under "Stanley Cup (hockey)."
5. Look under "Super Bowl" or "Football, professional," subheading "Super Bowl."

Card 2

Look under "Space developments," subheading "Astronauts."

Card 3

1. Look under "Rivers," subheading "World." Check carefully to determine the correct answer.
2. Look under "Deserts, world."
3. Look under "Mountains." When you find the page read the information carefully.
4. Look under "Lakes." When you find the page, check carefully to determine the correct answer.
5. Look under "Oceans and seas."

Card 4

1. Look under "Disasters," subheading "Earthquakes."
2. Look under "Disasters," subheading "Floods."
3. Look under "Disasters," subheading "*Titanic* disaster (1912)"; or look under "Ships," subheading "Disasters."
4. Look under "Disasters," subheading "*Hindenburg* (dirigible)"; or look under "Aircraft," subheading "Disasters."

Card 5

Look under "Inventions."

TEACHING UNIT 2: GETTING GOOD AT *GUINNESS*

You may think that teaching *The Guinness Book of World Records* is unnecessary because so many of your students seem to read it avidly. If you observe them, however, you will find they are browsing through it rather than looking up facts in the index. Their fascination with it makes *The Guinness Book* the perfect choice for teaching them how to select key words to search an index. Once you set up the learning station students will vie for the opportunity to work at it. It is helpful to have several paperback copies of the same edition. Since records can change with each edition, either update your answer key when necessary, or keep the old editions at the center and have students use them exclusively.

Objectives:

At the conclusion of this unit, students will be able to:
- select the key word in a question and look it up in an index
- locate required information within a body of text

Materials:

6 pieces of 6″ × 9″ posterboard (if you have made Teaching Unit 1, use a different color posterboard)

1 manila envelope large enough to hold the cards

1 piece of oaktag about 18″ wide

felt markers

masking tape

Preparation:

1. Use the posterboard to prepare the five task cards (see Figure 6-4) containing the questions. Prepare the answer key (see Figure 6-5) on the remaining card.
2. Print "GUINNESS BOOK OF WORLD RECORDS" on the outside of the manila envelope. Put the five task cards inside.
3. Print "GETTING GOOD AT GUINNESS" on the piece of oaktag. Attach the manila envelope, with the task cards inside, to the oaktag. Keep the answer card at your desk.
4. Mount the oaktag on a bulletin board or wall.

Figure 6-4.

Task Card 1

1. What is the longest recorded attack of hiccuping?
2. Who holds the record for sneezing?
3. Who voluntarily remained motionless for the longest recorded time? How long?
4. How long did the longest recorded dream last?

Task Card 2

1. What is the largest number of dominoes set up by one person and then toppled?
2. How wide was the biggest bubble gum bubble?
3. What was the greatest number of stories constructed in a free standing house of cards?
4. What is the longest record for nonstop talking?

Task Card 3

1. How big was the largest pizza?
2. Describe the largest single dish or recipe designed to feed the most people. (Look under "Foods, consumption.")
3. Where is the largest chocolate factory?
4. What is the ravioli-eating record?

Task Card 4

1. What is the most venomous snake?
2. What was the wingspan of the largest flying prehistoric animal?
3. What was the weight of the heaviest lobster caught?
4. What was the weight of the largest carnivorous fish ever caught? What type of fish was it?

Task Card 5

1. What is the most expensive private house ever built?
2. Where is the tallest lighthouse located? How tall is it?
3. Where is the world's crookedest street?
4. How tall is the tallest totem pole and where was it raised?
5. How high are the largest tires that have ever been made?

Figure 6-5.

Answers to Task Cards (based on the 1982 edition of *The Guinness Book of World Records*)

Card 1

1. Charles Osborn started hiccuping in 1922. He still is.
2. Tricia Reay began on October 15, 1979 and ended April 25, 1980, a total of 194 days of sneezing.
3. Wolfgang Kreuzer; 7 hours, 2 minutes
4. Two hours, 23 minutes

Card 2

1. 169,713 dominoes (stretched 4.3 miles and took 13 days to set up)
2. 19¼ inches wide
3. 61 stories (using 3,650 cards)
4. 150 hours

Card 3

1. 80 feet, 1 inch in diameter or 18,664 pounds (cut into 60,318 slices)
2. roasted camel (cooked eggs are stuffed in fish; the fish are stuffed in cooked chickens; the chickens are stuffed into a roasted sheep carcass; and the carcass stuffed into a camel
3. Hershey, Pennsylvania
4. 250 pieces in 66 minutes (by John Keogh of Manchester, England)

Card 4

1. the sea snake
2. the pterosaur's wingspan was 36 to 39 feet
3. 44 pounds 6 ounces
4. more than 10,000 pounds; a great white shark

Card 5

1. the Hearst Ranch at San Simeon, California (cost more than $30 million to build)
2. Yokohama, Japan; 348 feet tall
3. Lombard Street in San Francisco, California
4. 173 feet; Alert Bay, British Columbia, Canada
5. 11 feet 6 inches

Chapter 7

PERIODICAL INDEXES

BACKGROUND INFORMATION

Magazines and newspapers are more than brief material to be read for immediate recreation and information interests and then tossed out. When indexed so that the information can be retrieved, they serve as sources of current knowledge and opinion. The most widely available reference for finding needed magazine articles is the *Readers' Guide to Periodical Literature* (covering approximately 175 periodicals) or the less extensive *Abridged Readers' Guide to Periodical Literature* (covering approximately 60 periodicals), both published by the H. W. Wilson Company. *Readers' Guide* or the *Abridged Readers' Guide*, as they are commonly called, can be found in the reference section of virtually every academic, public, and senior high school library. Junior high schools and some elementary schools may also subscribe.

Readers' Guide to Periodical Literature

The *Readers' Guide* has long been the basic tool for researching magazines. The term PERIODICAL, which means a publication issued at regular and recurring intervals, is generally regarded as a synonym for magazine.

Although *Readers' Guide* is an important reference tool, it is not simple to use. Some of the difficulties encountered are caused by the demands placed on the tool itself. Issues appear on a semimonthly and monthly schedule, including cumulative booklets and an annual, bound, cumulative volume.

Nonetheless, it is somewhat intimidating to face the row of annual volumes lined up in their green bindings (red in the case of *Abridged Readers' Guide*) with the flimsier paper-covered current issues standing alongside the latest bound volume. Where to begin? You must hone in on a time frame to avoid being totally overwhelmed.

Finding the subject you want is often difficult. Anyone familiar with the card catalog realizes that the subject headings in use are often quite different from those an occasional user might look under. *Readers' Guide* has the same problem and only frequent use will make you comfortable with some of the constructions. A librarian can help you through the early stages.

Once the entry is found, deciphering the information can be another stumbling block. Abbreviations specific to the two readers' guides are confusing, although each issue does have a "Key to Abbreviations."

Children's Magazine Guide

Since *Readers' Guide* primarily indexes adult magazines, elementary schools may prefer to subscribe to *Children's Magazine Guide* (7 North Pinckney Street, Madison, WI 53703), published ten times a year including two semi-annual cumulations. Its approximately 45 periodicals include those commonly found in elementary media centers, such as *Cricket, Ranger Rick*, and *Penny Power* as well as professional magazines including *Horn Book, Learning*, and *School Library Journal*. The list of magazines indexed is revised periodically to reflect new publications of interest and to eliminate those that are no longer popular.

The general structure is similar to *Readers' Guide*, though not as complicated, so that students who use *Children's Magazine Guide* can transfer the skills they learn to the adult indexes when it becomes necessary. As with *Readers' Guide*, the explanation of the abbreviations used is printed on the inside front cover of each issue. A sample entry is explained on the inside back cover.

The New York Times Index

Searching for magazine articles is difficult. Finding information in newspapers is even more complicated. Although public and secondary school libraries usually subscribe to several newspapers only the *New York Times* has a printed index that allows a search to be made. Unfortunately, in contrast to *The New York Times Index, Readers' Guide* is childishly simple to use.

As with *Readers' Guide*, there are annual cumulations of *The New York Times Index* although earlier editions combine several years. Volume I covers 1851–1862. Biweekly issues and quarterly cumulations are intended to keep the index current; however, they are invariably published around three months after the dates covered.

The arrangement is by subject in word-by-word ("New York" before "Newark") alphabetical order. A brief description of the article is given to aid the user. Subdivisions are used when there is a substantial amount of material entered under one heading. Entries under the main heading and those under the subdivisions are listed *not* in alphabetical order (as there is no title that could be logically used), but in chronological sequence.

After finding the article you want, including the section, page, and column, you normally search the microfilm print and read the information. Many libraries have a printer so that an article can be copied for a minimum charge.

Some Newer Indexes

Many public libraries today have two additional tools to help users—the *Magazine Index* and the *National Newspaper Index*. These are generally too expensive to be in the schools and not all public libraries have them, but you should be aware of their existence.

The *Magazine Index* (Information Access Company, Belmont, CA 94002) covers 400 magazines and each reel spans a five-year period. It begins with January 1977. For anything earlier you must still use the *Readers' Guide*. The user sits in front of a microfilm viewer with a 12" × 14" screen and, by pushing buttons either forward or backward, quickly gains access to the entries. A knob is provided for browsing or looking through one section slowly.

Listings are alphabetical and you can look up subjects, brand names of products, book, record, and movie reviews (graded to show the reviewer's opinion) as well as restaurant reviews. The *Magazine Index* is very simple to use (magazine titles are spelled out) and fun to browse through.

The *National Newspaper Index* (also issued by Information Access Company) includes, all in one alphabetical listing updated monthly, the *New York Times*, the *Wall Street Journal*, and the *Christian Science Monitor* (with coverage dating back to 1979), with the addition of the *Washington Post* and the *Los Angeles Times* since the fall of 1982. The information appears on a viewer similar to that of the *Magazine Index* and also includes book, theatre, and restaurant reviews along with listings for all the items you would normally expect to find in a newspaper index. After your students have mastered the *Readers' Guide* and *The New York Times Index* tell them about these new tools designed for use in the computer age.

Organization of the Teaching Units

The following three teaching units are arranged in ascending order of difficulty. The first introduces elementary students to a simple periodical index as they begin research. The second unit, on *Readers' Guide*, explains this standard research tool. The third and most difficult prepares students for the complexities of searching for newspaper articles.

TEACHING UNIT 1: USING *CHILDREN'S MAGAZINE GUIDE*

Designed for students in grades 4–6, this teaching unit is a learning center activity that introduces them to the *Children's Magazine Guide*.

Objectives:

At the conclusion of this unit students will be able to:

- interpret an entry in *Children's Magazine Guide*
- find magazine articles on a given subject using *Children's Magazine Guide*

Material:

for sample entry display:

- sheet of 11″ × 14″ oaktag
- black felt marker
- small sheets of light-colored construction paper
- string (optional)
- rubber cement

several 9″ × 12″ sheets of posterboard

10 strips of 6″ × 2″ posterboard

clear self-stick vinyl

6 sheets of 6″ × 9″ posterboard

2 large manila envelopes to hold large posterboard

1 small manila envelope for the strips

6″ × 9″ sheet of light-colored construction paper

Preparation:

1. Make a large sample entry copied from an issue of the *Children's Magazine Guide* or use Figure 7-1. Label all parts as shown.
   - Print the entry on 11″ × 14″ oaktag.
   - Use the light-colored construction paper to prepare labels to explain the different parts (magazine title, subject heading, etc.) of the entries.
   - Paste labels as shown on Figure 7-1.
   - Draw lines or use string to connect the labels to the appropriate section of the entry as shown on Figure 7-1.
2. Make several copies of a page in *Children's Magazine Guide* (see Figure 7-2) and one or two copies of the abbreviation page (see Figure 7-3). Cover these with clear self-stick vinyl.
3. Paste each copy on a sheet of 9″ × 12″ posterboard.
4. Select ten subject headings from *Children's Magazine Guide* that are of interest to your class or are represented in most issues, or use the ones listed below. Print the headings on the posterboard strips and cover with the clear vinyl. NOTE: If you use the posterboard strips in the card catalog teaching unit (see Chapter 2), be sure the strips for this unit are of a different size and color to prevent materials from getting mixed up.
   Sample subject headings:

ASTRONOMY	MOVIES
COMPUTERS	OCEAN LIFE
EXERCISE	ROCK GROUPS
GAMES	SPACE SHUTTLES
HAIR CARE	TREES

5. Prepare the five task cards (see Figure 7-4) on the 6″ × 9″ posterboard. Use the remaining card for the answer key (see Figure 7-5) to be kept at your desk. Note that the first four task cards apply to the sample page. This gives students practice with entries for which you have the answer key. The fifth card requires them to use the *Children's Magazine Guide* itself. Have one of your better students check the answers on the fifth card for further practice.
6. Display the unit that includes the sample entry, the manila envelope containing the sample and abbreviation pages, another manila envelope containing the five task cards, and a small envelope holding the strips on a bulletin board or wall.

Figure 7-1.

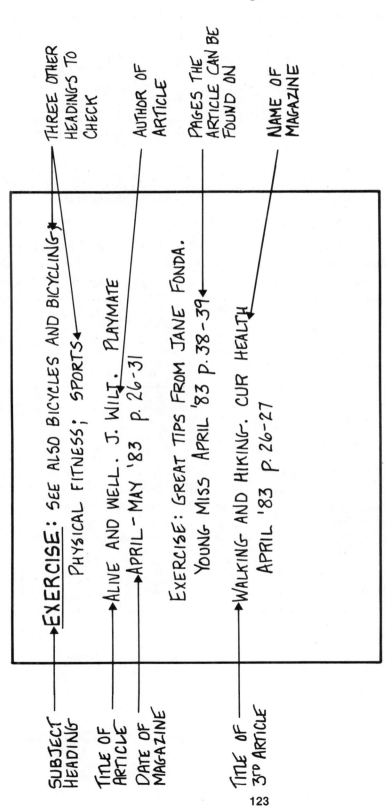

THREE OTHER
HEADINGS TO
CHECK

AUTHOR OF
ARTICLE

PAGES THE
ARTICLE CAN BE
FOUND ON

NAME OF
MAGAZINE

EXERCISE: SEE ALSO BICYCLES AND BICYCLING;
PHYSICAL FITNESS; SPORTS

ALIVE AND WELL. J. WILT. PLAYMATE
APRIL - MAY '83 P. 26-31

EXERCISE: GREAT TIPS FROM JANE FONDA.
YOUNG MISS APRIL '83 P. 38-39

WALKING AND HIKING. CUR HEALTH
APRIL '83 P. 26-27

SUBJECT
HEADING

TITLE OF
ARTICLE

DATE OF
MAGAZINE

TITLE OF
3RD ARTICLE

CAN YOU...

NAME 3 MAGAZINES WITH ARTICLES ON EXERCISE ?

FIND THE LONGEST ARTICLE ?

LIST THE 3 OTHER PLACES TO CHECK ?

IF NOT...ASK FOR HELP

Figure 7-2.

SRI LANKA - WILDLIFE
   CONSERVATION: see Wildlife
   Conservation - Sri Lanka
STAMP COLLECTING
   Americans on Stamps: Rachel
   Carson. Boys' Life Mar '83 p50
   Stamps & Coins. J.C.Halter.
   See issues of Boys' Life
   Starting in Stamps. Odyssey Jun '83
   p10
STAR WARS: see Movies
STARGAZING: see also Astronomy
STARS: see also Astronomy;
   Constellations; Galaxies; Nebulae
STARS - CLUSTERS: see also Nebulae
   Backyard Universe. G.F.Chaple.
   Odyssey Apr '83 p16D-16E
STARS - POETRY
   Night Skies. H.B.Julian. Ebony Jr
   Aug-Sep '83 p36
   Summer Stars. C.Sandburg. Cricket
   Jul '83 p4
STATUE OF LIBERTY
   New Life for Lady Liberty? Jr Schol
   Feb 18 '83 p8

STORIES: see Fiction
STRIKES - TRUCKERS
   Truckers' Strike Fueled by Anger.
   Cur Ev Feb 14 '83 p1
STRINGED INSTRUMENTS: see also
   Musical Instruments
   Two String Players Talk About Their
   Instruments. B.L.English. Cricket
   May '83 p12-14
STUDENT EMPLOYMENT: see also
   Babysitting; Summer Jobs
   Jobs for Students. Career World
   Mar '83 p15; Apr '83 p12-13
   Relax Rules on Hiring Teenagers?
   (Interviews) Career World May '83
   p28-29
   A Stop-Out—Sometimes It May Be the
   Only Way to Go. A.White.
   Career World May '83 p16-18
STUDY HABITS
   Study Hard: It's Easy. H.B.Julian.
   Ebony Jr Aug-Sep '83 p30-31
SUCCESS
   If You Think You Can... R.W.Stump.
   Career World Apr '83 p24-25
   10 Ways to Be a Winner (and How to
   Cope When You Aren't One).
   L.Graeber. Young Miss Mar '83
   p46-48+

SUICIDE
   Youth Suicide on Rise. Cur Ev
   Apr 11 '83 p4
SUMMER
   Dynamite Sings the Summertime
   Blues. Dyn Jul '83 p10-11
SUMMER ACTIVITIES: see also Arts and
   Crafts; Rainy Day Activities
   Grab Bag of Summer Fun!
   C.A.Batzer. Young Miss May '83
   p76-77
   Six Ways to Make Summer Sizzle!
   L.Graeber. Young Miss
   Jun-Jul '83 p19
   Things To Do This Summer. Ebony Jr
   Jun-Jul '83 p17
   25 Things To Do in the Summer When
   You Don't Have Anything To Do.
   M.Stine. Dyn Aug '83 p18-19
SUMMER CAMPS: see Camps
SUMMER JOBS
   Green Grow the Gardening Jobs.
   Pen Pow Jun-Jul '83 p2-5
SUMMER - POETRY
   Quiet Time. S.Luther & others.
   Ranger Rick Jul '83 p8-9
   A Slide. R.Woodard. Ebony Jr
   Jun-Jul '83 p46
   Summer. L.Leurgans. Ebony Jr
   Jun-Jul '83 p46
SUMMER SCHOOLS - CANADA
   Summer at Ukkivik. M.Sanderson.
   Beaver Spring '83 p30-35
SUN: see also Solar System
   Daylights Poster. Odyssey Jul '83
   p14-16+
   Far-Out Facts. World Jun '83 p30-31
   Sun Power. G.Laycock. Boys' Life
   Jun '83 p10-11
SUNGLASSES
   Sunglasses. S.R.Schlanger. Sci World
   Mar 4 '83 p7
SUNKEN TREASURE: see Underwater
   Archeology
SWANS
   High Season for Swans. L.Hales.
   Nat Wildlife Jun-Jul '83 p50-55
   Snowed Under. World Mar '83 p28-30
SWAZILAND
   Sibusiso of Swaziland. J.A.Jones.
   Highlights Mar '83 p12-13
SWEAT: see Perspiration
SWIMMERS
   Mary T. Meagher. F.Dortmand.
   Insports Apr '83 p18-21
SWIMMING
   Improve Your Swimming. D.Pryce.
   Boys' Life Aug '83 p48-49

Permission has been granted by *Children's Magazine Guide*, Madison, WI, to use this material.

Figure 7-3.

ABBREVIATIONS OF MAGAZINES INDEXED

Check the magazines your library subscribes to
as a quick reference for users.

Ahoy – AHOY
Backyard – YOUR BIG BACKYARD
Beaver – THE BEAVER
Book Rep – THE BOOK REPORT
Boys' Life – BOYS' LIFE
Career World – CAREER WORLD
Chickadee – CHICKADEE
Child D – CHILDREN'S DIGEST
Child Life – CHILD LIFE
Class Comp L – CLASSROOM
    COMPUTER LEARNING
Cobble – COBBLESTONE
Contact – 3-2-1 CONTACT
Cricket – CRICKET
Cur Ev – CURRENT EVENTS
Cur Health – CURRENT HEALTH 1
Cur Sci – CURRENT SCIENCE
Digit – DIGIT
Dyn – DYNAMITE
Early Yrs – EARLY YEARS
Ebony Jr – EBONY JR!
Electric Comp – THE ELECTRIC
    COMPANY MAGAZINE
Enter – ENTER
Good Apple – THE GOOD APPLE
    NEWSPAPER
Highlights – HIGHLIGHTS FOR
    CHILDREN
Horn Bk – THE HORN BOOK
    MAGAZINE

Humpty D – HUMPTY DUMPTY'S
    MAGAZINE
Insports – INSPORTS
Instr – INSTRUCTOR
Int Wildlife – INTERNATIONAL
    WILDLIFE
Jack & Jill – JACK & JILL
Jr Schol – JUNIOR SCHOLASTIC
K-Power – K-POWER
Learn – LEARNING
Muppet – MUPPET MAGAZINE
Nat Geog – NATIONAL GEOGRAPHIC
    MAGAZINE
Nat Wildlife – NATIONAL WILDLIFE
Odyssey – ODYSSEY
Owl – OWL MAGAZINE
Pen Pow – PENNY POWER
Playmate – CHILDREN'S PLAYMATE
    MAGAZINE
Plays – PLAYS
Ranger Rick – RANGER RICK
Sci World – SCHOLASTIC SCIENCE
    WORLD
Sciland – SCIENCELAND
SLJ – SCHOOL LIBRARY JOURNAL
Teach & Comp – TEACHING AND
    COMPUTERS
Wee Wisdom – WEE WISDOM
World – NATIONAL GEOGRAPHIC
    WORLD
Young Miss – YOUNG MISS

ABBREVIATIONS

bc – back cover
concl. – conclusion
cont. – continued
ed. – editor

fc – front cover
no. – number
p – page(s)
pt – part

supp – supplement
trans. – translator
+ – cont. on later pages
... – words omitted

Jan – January
Feb – February
Mar – March

Apr – April
May – May
Jun – June

Jul – July
Aug – August
Sep – September

Oct – October
Nov – November
Dec – December

Permission has been granted by *Children's Magazine Guide*, Madison, WI, to use this material.

Figure 7-4.

Task Card 1

Use the sample page from *Children's Magazine Guide* to answer these questions:

1. What is the title of the article listed under SUMMER JOBS?
2. In what magazine did the article appear?
3. In what month and year did the article appear?
4. On what page did the article appear?

Task Card 2

Use the sample page from *Children's Magazine Guide* to answer these questions:

1. What is the title of the article listed under SUNGLASSES?
2. Who wrote the article?
3. In what magazine did the article appear?
4. In what month and year did the article appear?
5. On what page did the article appear?

Task Card 3

Use the sample page from *Children's Magazine Guide* to answer these questions:

1. How many articles are listed under SUMMER ACTIVITIES?
2. What other headings should you check for more articles on SUMMER ACTIVITIES?
3. Who wrote the article on SUMMER ACTIVITIES for *Dynamite* magazine?
4. Where should you look to find information on SUMMER CAMPS?

Task Card 4

Use the sample page from *Children's Magazine Guide* to answer these questions:

1. How many subjects are listed on this page?
2. Which article on SWANS appeared in *National Geographic World*?
3. What magazine had an article on STUDY HABITS? Who wrote it?
4. Which two headings on this page give ideas for jobs and what other subject headings would you check?
5. If you are looking for something unusual to add to a report on the SUN, which one article should you check?
6. Which is probably the longest article on the SUN? How do you know?

Task Card 5

Use the ten strips in the small manila envelope and follow these directions:

Take one strip and look it up in *Children's Magazine Guide*. Answer the questions:

1. Which issue did you use?
2. How many entries are listed under the subject heading you checked?
3. Give the names of the magazines that have information on this subject.
4. Put a star next to the name of any magazines we have in our media center.

Repeat the same questions for each strip.

Figure 7-5.

Answers to Task Cards

Card 1

1. "Green Grow the Gardening Jobs"
2. *Penny Power*
3. June/July, 1983
4. Page 2 through page 5

Card 2

1. "Sunglasses"
2. S. R. Schlanger
3. *Science World*
4. March 4, 1983
5. Page 7

Card 3

1. Four
2. There are two headings — Arts and Crafts; Rainy Day Activities
3. M. Stine
4. Look under CAMPS

Card 4

1. 30 subjects
2. "Snowed Under"
3. *Ebony Jr!* written by H. B. Julian
4. SUMMER JOBS, STUDENT EMPLOYMENT, also check BABYSITTING
5. "Far Out Facts" in *National Geographic World*, June 1983, pages 30–31
6. "Daylights Poster"; the other articles are two pages long; this one goes from page 14 to 16 and then continues on another page — that's what the + means

TEACHING UNIT 2: GUIDE TO *READERS' GUIDE*

Whether or not they have in-school access to the *Readers' Guide* or the *Abridged Readers' Guide*, by the seventh grade, students *must* be introduced to this reference tool. If *Children's Magazine Guide* is not available in the elementary school, then this unit should be started in sixth grade or even the second half of fifth grade.

Readers' Guide is not a simple tool and this classroom learning center gives students an opportunity to develop familiarity with its structure before they try to use it on their own. If you want a number of students to work at the center at the same time make one copy per student of the sample card, abbreviation cards, and task cards. You may introduce the center if you like, but most students can follow the directions with little difficulty.

Objectives:

At the conclusion of this unit students will be able to:

- decipher the various parts of a *Readers' Guide* entry
- understand what is meant by "see" and "see also" references in the *Readers' Guide*
- evaluate articles to determine which are likely to meet their information needs
- derive general information from the article titles

Materials:

4 pieces of 9″ × 12″ posterboard

1 copy of sample page from *Readers' Guide* (Figure 7-6)

1 copy of "Abbreviations" page (Figure 7-7)

1 copy of "Abbreviations of Publications Indexed" (Figure 7-8)

6 pieces of 6″ × 9″ posterboard

18″ × 24″ piece of oaktag

felt marker

rubber cement

clear self-stick vinyl

10″ × 14″ manila envelope

small manila envelope

Preparation:

1. Paste the copy of the sample page (see Figure 7-6) and both abbreviation pages (see Figures 7-7 and 7-8) onto the 9″ × 12″ posterboard. Cover with clear self-stick vinyl.

2. Copy the sample entry (see Figure 7-9) onto the remaining pieces of 9″ × 12″ posterboard. Cover with clear self-stick vinyl.

3. Prepare the five task cards (see Figure 7-10) that refer to the sample page onto the 6″ × 9″ posterboard. Make an answer card (see Figure 7-11) on the remaining piece of posterboard to keep at your desk.

4. Print "*Readers' Guide to Periodical Literature*—Samples" on the 10″ × 14″ manila envelope and place the sample and abbreviation pages inside.

5. Print "*Readers' Guide to Periodical Literature*—Questions" on the smaller manila envelope and put the task cards inside.

6. Print "Guide to *Readers' Guide*" on the 18″ piece of oaktag and mount on a bulletin board or wall.

7. Attach the manila envelopes to the oaktag.

8. Post the sample entry alongside the oaktag. (See Figure 7-12.)

Figure 7-6.

Solar heating—*cont.*

Energy answers. T. Dean. il *Workbench* 39:55-6+ Jl/Ag '83

Passive solar design. T. Dean. il *Workbench* 38:39+ Jl/Ag '82

Passive solar design. T. Dean. il *Workbench* 38:120-3 S/O '82

Passive solar design. T. Dean. il *Workbench* 38:40+ My/Je '82

Solar additions that heat your home. D. Haupert. il *Better Homes Gard* 61:110-13 S '83

Solar heating industry *See* Solar energy industry

Solar houses

Building the Sun Cottage: cost control. A. W. Macdonald. il *Mother Earth News* 82:176-7 Jl/Ag '83

Energy answers. T. Dean. il *Workbench* 39:78-81 Mr/Ap '83

Energy answers. T. Dean. il *Workbench* 39:17-19 Ja/F '83

For passive solar, it's so long, slanted glass. R. Stepler. il *Pop Sci* 223:70-3 Ag '83

Passive solar plus [design by Charles G. Woods] il *Mother Earth News* 82:124-5 Jl/Ag '83

Progress makes perfect [modified thermal envelope house] T. Smith. il *Mother Earth News* 82:158-60 Jl/Ag '83

State-of-the-art solar home. T. Dean. il *Workbench* 39:8-12+ My/Je '83

Solar magnetic field *See* Sun—Magnetic properties

Solar Optical Telescope *See* Space vehicles—Telescopes

Solar oscillations *See* Oscillations

Solar power *See* Solar energy

Solar power plants *See* Solar energy

Solar power satellites *See* Artificial satellites—Solar energy use

Solar radiation

See also

Solar wind
Sunspots
Ultraviolet rays

Physiological effects

See also

Suntan

Solar reflectors

Keeping the sun out and savings in [sun-reflecting plastic films for windows; study by Steve Treado] *Sci News* 124:126 Ag 20 '83

Solar research *See* Sun

Solar system

See also

Moon
Planets
Sun

Another solar system? [Vega system; Infrared Astronomy Satellite discovery] J. Eberhart. *Sci News* 124:100 Ag 13 '83

Another world? [IRAS detects possibility of a new solar system] il *Time* 122:71 Ag 22 '83

NASA verifies solid objects orbit Vega [Kuiper Airborne Observatory confirmation of infrared astronomical satellite discovery] B. A. Smith. *Aviat Week Space Technol* 119:78 Ag 29 '83

New clue to solar system's origin [carbonaceous chondrites; work of Robert Pepin and Urs Frick] *USA Today* 111:7 Je '83

A new world forming out there? [IRAS discovery of new solar system] il *U S News World Rep* 95:9 Ag 22 '83

New worlds in the making [possible discovery of new solar system by IRAS] S. Begley. il *Newsweek* 102:76 Ag 22 '83

Planet-size stars or star-size planets? [extrasolar planet infrared survey] il *Sky Telesc* 66:114-15 Ag '83

Signal from a new world [Infrared Astronomy Satellite detects new solar system around Vega] E. Hillen. *Macleans* 96:46 Ag 22 '83

A solar system at Vega? [Infrared Astronomy Satellite discovery] M. M. Waldrop. *Science* 221:846 Ag 26 '83

Vega & Co.: what's being born out there? [Infrared Astronomy Satellite and Kuiper Airborne Observatory findings] J. Eberhart. *Sci News* 124:116 Ag 20 '83

Exploration

See Space flight

Solar water heaters

Batch solar water heaters. D. Reif. il *Mech Illus* 79:48+ Ag '83

Solar-assist heat pump follow-up report: a year of savings. D. A. Warren. il *Pop Mech* 160:112-13 S '83

Solar wind

Celestial winds, polar lights. F. Reddy. il *Astronomy* 11:6-15 Ag '83

Cosmic rays meet the solar wind [study of heliosphere by Pioneer 10] S. P. Maran. *Nat Hist* 92:22-3 Ag '83

Solarex Corp.

Oil industry buys a place in the sun [proposed take over of Solarex by Amoco] C. Norman. *Science* 221:839 Ag 26 '83

Sun sets at RCA, rises at Solarex. C. Norman. *Science* 221:532-3 Ag 5 '83

Solariums *See* Sun rooms

Soliciting donations *See* Fund raising

Solid state devices *See* Semiconductors

Solidarity (Trade union) *See* Trade unions—Poland

Solitude

See also

Loneliness

Solnick, Steven L.

The politics of apathy. il *Technol Rev* 86:9-11 Jl '83

Solomon, Anthony M.

about

Solomon's choice. B. Weberman. il por *Forbes* 131:32-3 Je 20 '83

Solomon, Norman

Watching the death train roll. il *Progressive* 47:14 Jl '83

Solomon, Stephen

Hot computer news: the portables are here. il *Sci Dig* 91:14-15+ Je '83

The Idaho chip. il *Sci Dig* 91:16+ Jl '83

Solomon, Susan

Your words. il por *Seventeen* 42:66-7 Je '83

Solondz, Gary

about

Suing the guru. R. L. Stern. il por *Forbes* 132:158+ S 12 '83

Solter, Davor

(jt. auth) *See* McGrath, James, and Solter, Davor

Solution (Chemistry)

See also

Buffer solutions
Diffusion
Precipitation (Chemistry)

Solzhenitsyn, Aleksandr, 1918-

Men have forgotten God [adaptation of Templeton Prize acceptance address, May 10, 1983]; tr. by A. Klimoff. il *Natl Rev* 35:872-6 Jl 22 '83

Soman, Florence Jane

Tender moments [story] il *Good Housekeep* 197:148-9+ S '83

Something wicked this way comes [film] *See* Motion picture reviews—Single works

Sommer, Harold

about

Wander Bird. J. Kortum. il por *Oceans* 16:14-18 Jl/Ag '83

Sommer, Mark

Forging a preservative defense. il *Bull At Sci* 39:5-7 Ag/S '83

Song titles *See* Titles of musical compositions

Songs

See also

Phonograph records—Songs
Popular music
Rock music

Songs of birds *See* Birds—Song

Sonnenberg Gardens (Canandaigua, N.Y.) *See* Gardens and gardening—New York (State)

Sontag, Susan, 1933-

The unseen alphabet: Kafka's inner world. il pors *Vogue* 173:202-3+ Jl '83

Sony Corp.

Sony: not the one and only. J. Brecher. il *Newsweek* 102:54 S 5 '83

Tone-deaf in the marketplace. il *Fortune* 108:6 Jl 25 '83

Soo Canal *See* Sault Sainte Marie Canals

Soot

Soot carbon and excess fine potassium: long-range transport of combustion-derived aerosols [biomass and fossil-fuel burning] M. O. Andreae. bibl f il map *Science* 220:1148-51 Je 10 '83

Sopher, Crea, and Penrose, Nancy

Burying radioactive waste in the deep-sea floor. il map *Sea Front* 29:210-17 Jl/Ag '83

Sorabji, Kaikhosru Shapurji

about

Geoffrey Madge, piano: Sorabji Opus clavicembalisticum. D. Garvelmann. *High Fidel* 33:MA24 Ag '83

Sorcery *See* Witchcraft

Sore throats [drama] *See* Brenton, Howard, 1942-

Figure 7-7.

ABBREVIATIONS

*	following name entry, a printer's device	Jr	Junior
+	continued on later pages of same issue	jt auth	joint author
Abp	Archbishop	Ltd	Limited
abr	abridged		
Ag	August		
Ap	April	m	monthly
arch	architect	Mr	March
Assn	Association	My	May
Aut	Autumn		
Ave	Avenue	N	November
		no	number
Bart	Baronet		
bibl	bibliography	O	October
bibl f	bibliographical foot-notes		
bi-m	bimonthly	por	portrait
bi-w	biweekly	pseud	pseudonym
bldg	building	pt	part
Bp	Bishop	pub	published, publisher, publishing
Co	Company		
comp	compiled, compiler	q	quarterly
cond	condensed		
cont	continued	rev	revised
Corp	Corporation		
		S	September
D	December	sec	section
Dept	Department	semi-m	semimonthly
		Soc	Society
		Sp	Special
		Spr	Spring
ed	edited, edition, editor	Sq	Square
		Sr	Senior
		St	Street
F	February	Summ	Summer
		supp	supplement
Hon	Honorable	supt	superintendent
		tr	translated, transla-tion, translator
il	illustrated, illustra-tion, illustrator		
Inc	Incorporated	v	volume
int	interviewer		
introd	introduction, intro-ductory	w	weekly
		Wint	Winter
Ja	January		
Je	June	yr	year
Jl	July		

Figure 7-8.

ABBREVIATIONS OF PERIODICALS INDEXED

For full information consult the list of Periodicals Indexed

*50 Plus — 50 Plus

A

Aging — Aging
Am Artist — American Artist
Am Craft — American Craft
Am Educ — American Education
*Am Herit — American Heritage
Am Hist Illus — American History Illustrated
Am Sch — The American Scholar
*America — America
Americana — Americana
Américas — Américas
Antiques — Antiques
Archit Rec — Architectural Record
Art Am — Art in America
Art News — Art News
Astronomy — Astronomy
*Atlantic — The Atlantic
Audubon — Audubon
Aviat Week Space Technol — Aviation Week & Space Technology

B

*Better Homes Gard — Better Homes and Gardens
BioScience — BioScience
Black Enterp — Black Enterprise
Blair Ketchums Ctry J — Blair & Ketchum's Country Journal
Bull At Sci — The Bulletin of the Atomic Scientists
Bus Week — Business Week

C

Car Driv — Car and Driver
Cent Mag — The Center Magazine
Change — Change
*Changing Times — Changing Times
Child Today — Children Today
Christ Century — The Christian Century
Christ Today — Christianity Today
Commentary — Commentary
Commonweal — Commonweal
Comput Electron — Computers & Electronics
Congr Dig — Congressional Digest
Conservationist — The Conservationist
*Consum Rep — Consumer Reports
*Consum Res Mag — Consumers' Research Magazine
Creat Crafts Miniat — Creative Crafts & Miniatures
Curr Health 2 — Current Health 2
Curr Hist — Current History
Current — Current (Washington, D.C.)
Cycle — Cycle

D

Dance Mag — Dance Magazine
Dep State Bull — Department of State Bulletin
Des Arts Educ — Design for Arts in Education
Down Beat — Down Beat

E

Earth Sci — Earth Science
*Ebony — Ebony
Educ Dig — The Education Digest
Encore Am Worldw News — Encore American & World-wide News
Environment — Environment
Esquire — Esquire
Essence — Essence

F

Fam Handyman — The Family Handyman
FDA Consum — FDA Consumer
*Field Stream — Field & Stream
Film Comment — Film Comment

First World — First World
Flower Gard — Flower and Garden
Flying — Flying
Focus — Focus (New York, N.Y.: 1950)
*Forbes — Forbes
*Foreign Aff — Foreign Affairs
Foreign Policy — Foreign Policy
*Fortune — Fortune
Futurist — The Futurist

G

Glamour — Glamour
*Good Housekeep — Good Housekeeping
*Gourmet — Gourmet

H

*Harpers — Harper's
Harpers Bazaar — Harper's Bazaar
*Health — Health (New York, N.Y.)
High Fidel — High Fidelity (Musical America edition)
Hist Today — History Today
Hobbies — Hobbies
*Horizon — Horizon (Tuscaloosa, Ala.)
House Gard — House & Garden
Humanist — The Humanist

I

Int Wildl — International Wildlife

L

*Ladies Home J — Ladies' Home Journal
Living Wilderness — The Living Wilderness

M

Macleans — Maclean's
Mademoiselle — Mademoiselle
Mankind (U S) — Mankind (Los Angeles, Calif.)
McCalls — McCall's
Mech Illus — Mechanix Illustrated
Mon Labor Rev — Monthly Labor Review
*Money — Money
Mot Boat Sail — Motor Boating & Sailing
Mot Trend — Motor Trend
Mother Earth News — The Mother Earth News
*Ms — Ms.

N

N Y — New York
N Y Rev Books — The New York Review of Books
N Y Times Book Rev — The New York Times Book Review
N Y Times Mag — The New York Times Magazine
*Nat Hist — Natural History
Nation — The Nation
Nations Bus — Nation's Business
*Natl Geogr — National Geographic
*Natl Geogr World — National Geographic World
Natl Parks — National Parks
*Natl Rev — National Review
Natl Wildl — National Wildlife
Negro Hist Bull — Negro History Bulletin
New Leader — The New Leader
New Repub — The New Republic
New Yorker — The New Yorker
*Newsweek — Newsweek

O

Oceans — Oceans
Opera News — Opera News
Org Gard — Organic Gardening
*Outdoor Life — Outdoor Life (Northeast edition)

Figure 7-8, continued

ABBREVIATIONS OF PERIODICALS INDEXED

P

*Parents — Parents
People Wkly — People Weekly
Petersens Photogr Mag — Petersen's Photographic Magazine
Phi Delta Kappan — Phi Delta Kappan
Phys Today — Physics Today
*Pop Mech — Popular Mechanics
Pop Photogr — Popular Photography
Pop Sci — Popular Science
Progressive — The Progressive
*Psychol Today — Psychology Today
Publ Wkly — Publishers Weekly

R

Radio-Electron — Radio-Electronics
*Read Dig — Reader's Digest
*Redbook — Redbook
Road Track — Road & Track
Roll Stone — Rolling Stone

S

Saturday Evening Post — The Saturday Evening Post
*Saturday Rev — Saturday Review
Sch Update — Scholastic Update (Teachers' edition)
*Sci Am — Scientific American
Sci Dig — Science Digest
*Sci News — Science News
Science — Science
Sea Front — Sea Frontiers
*Seventeen — Seventeen
Sierra — Sierra
Skiing — Skiing
Sky Telesc — Sky and Telescope
*Smithsonian — Smithsonian
Society — Society
*South Living — Southern Living

Space World — Space World
Sport Mag — Sport Magazine
*Sports Illus — Sports Illustrated
Sr Sch — Senior Scholastic (Teachers' edition)
*Stereo Rev — Stereo Review
Success Farm — Successful Farming
Sunset — Sunset (Central edition)

T

Technol Rev — Technology Review
Teen — 'Teen
Theatre Crafts — Theatre Crafts
Time — Time
Todays Educ — Today's Education
*Travel Holiday — Travel Holiday

U

U S Cathol — U.S. Catholic
*U S News World Rep — U.S. News & World Report
UN Mon Chron — UN Monthly Chronicle
UNESCO Cour — The UNESCO Courier
USA Today — USA Today

V

Vital Speeches Day — Vital Speeches of the Day
Vogue — Vogue

W

Wash Mon — The Washington Monthly
Weatherwise — Weatherwise
Wilderness — Wilderness
Work Woman — Working Woman
Workbench — Workbench
World Health — World Health
World Press Rev — World Press Review
World Tennis — World Tennis
*Writer — The Writer

Figure 7-9.

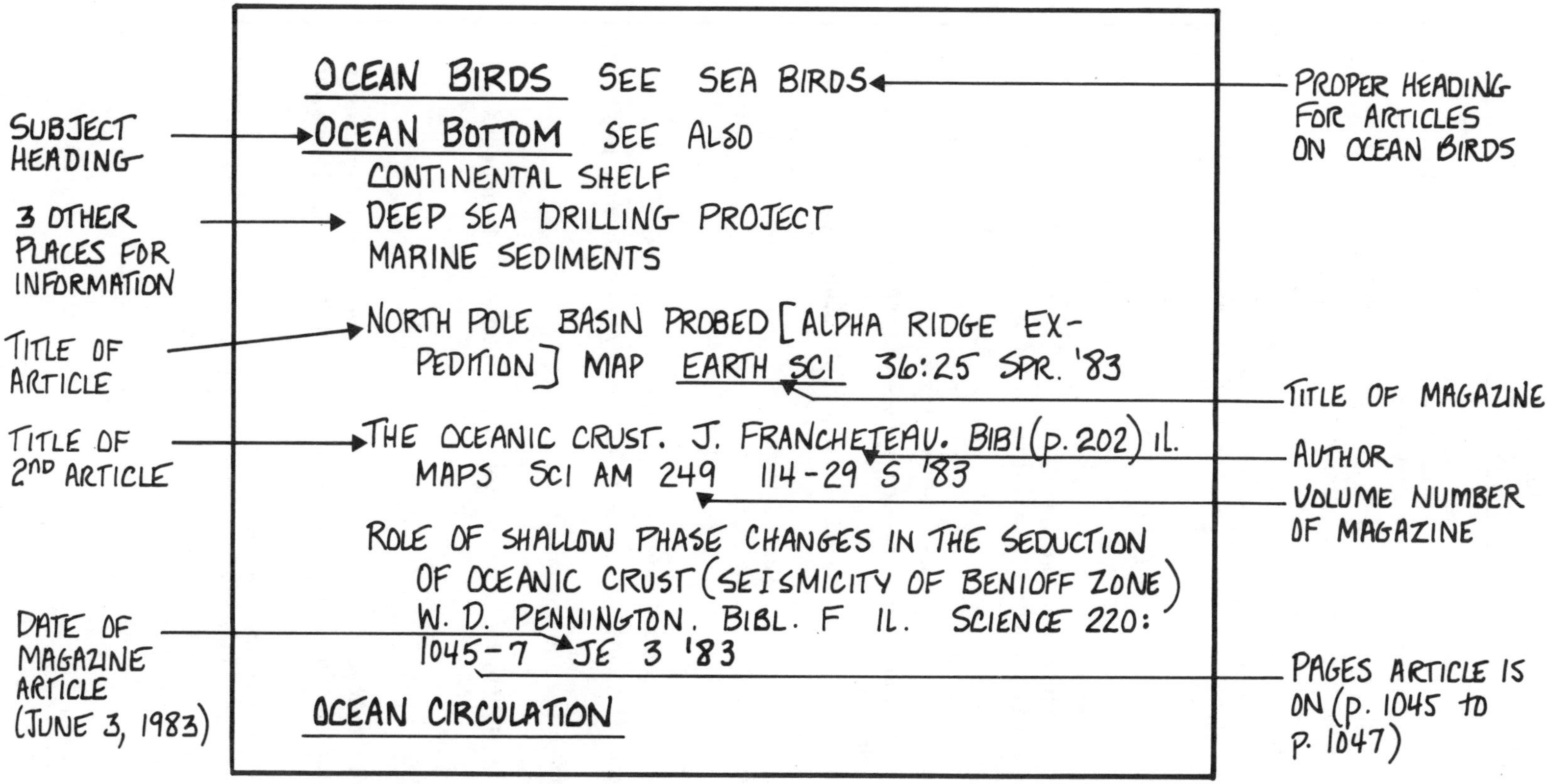

PROPER HEADING FOR ARTICLES ON OCEAN BIRDS

TITLE OF MAGAZINE

AUTHOR

VOLUME NUMBER OF MAGAZINE

PAGES ARTICLE IS ON (P. 1045 TO P. 1047)

OCEAN BIRDS   SEE   SEA BIRDS

OCEAN BOTTOM   SEE ALSO
  CONTINENTAL SHELF
  DEEP SEA DRILLING PROJECT
  MARINE SEDIMENTS

NORTH POLE BASIN PROBED [ALPHA RIDGE EXPEDITION] MAP EARTH SCI 36:25 SPR. '83

THE OCEANIC CRUST. J. FRANCHETEAU. BIBL (p.202) IL. MAPS SCI AM 249 114-29 S '83

ROLE OF SHALLOW PHASE CHANGES IN THE SEDUCTION OF OCEANIC CRUST (SEISMICITY OF BENIOFF ZONE) W. D. PENNINGTON. BIBL. F IL. SCIENCE 220: 1045-7 JE 3 '83

OCEAN CIRCULATION

SUBJECT HEADING

3 OTHER PLACES FOR INFORMATION

TITLE OF ARTICLE

TITLE OF 2ND ARTICLE

DATE OF MAGAZINE ARTICLE (JUNE 3, 1983)

CAN YOU...

NAME THE SUBJECT HEADING AFTER "OCEAN BOTTOM"?

NAME 2 ARTICLES WITH AUTHORS?

NAME THE 3 MAGAZINES THAT HAVE ARTICLES ON "OCEAN BOTTOM"?

IF NOT...ASK FOR HELP

Figure 7-10.

Task Card 1

Use the sample page of the *Readers' Guide* to answer these questions:

1. What is the proper heading for "Soo Canal"?
2. Where should you look for information about "Solidarity"?
3. If you want articles on "Sorcery," what heading should you check?
4. What other headings will give you information about the solar system?
5. How many other references are suggested for "Songs"?

Task Card 2

Use the sample page of the *Readers' Guide* to answer these questions:

1. How many articles are there about the "Sony Corp."?
2. Who seems to be the expert on the "Solarex Corp."?
3. For what magazine does Stephen Solomon write?
4. What two magazines have published several articles on "Solar Houses"?

Task Card 3

Use the sample page of the *Readers' Guide* to answer these questions:

1. Which article seems to suggest a connection between "Solar wind" and the polar lights? In what magazine can it be found?
2. Which article discusses the money saved by using "Solar water heaters"? In what magazine is it?
3. Which magazine has an article by Susan Sontag?
4. Which magazine has an article by Mark Sommer?

Task Card 4

Use the sample page of the *Readers' Guide* to answer these questions:

1. How many pages does the article by Aleksandr Solzhenitsyn run? On what page does it end?
2. What issue of *Science* magazine has an article on "Soot"?
3. How many articles on the "Solar system" have pictures?
4. What tells you that the story by Florence Jan Soman is continued on later pages of the magazine?

Task Card 5

Use the sample page of the *Readers' Guide* to answer these questions. All articles on "Solar system" are about the same discovery. Use the titles of the articles to answer the questions:

1. What do scientists think they have found?
2. Where is this phenomenon occurring?
3. What is the name of the observatory that confirmed the discovery?
4. What does the acronym IRAS stand for?

Figure 7-11.

Answers to Task Cards

Card 1

1. Sault Sainte Marie Canals
2. Trade Unions — Poland
3. Witchcraft
4. Moon, Planets, Sun
5. Three: Phonograph Records — Songs; Popular Music; Rock Music

Card 2

1. 2
2. C. Norman (He wrote both articles)
3. *Science Digest*
4. *Mother Earth News; Workbench*

Card 3

1. "Celestial Winds, Polar Lights"; *Astronomy*
2. "Solar-Assist Heat Pump Follow-up Report: A Year of Savings"; *Popular Mechanics*
3. *Vogue*
4. *The Bulletin of the Atomic Scientists*

Card 4

1. Five pages, p. 76
2. June 10, 1983
3. Four: "Another World," "A New World Forming Out There?" "New Worlds in the Making," "Planet-Size Stars or Star-Size Planets?"
4. The + after "148–9?"

Card 5

1. A new solar system seems to be forming
2. Around Vega
3. Kuiper Airborne Observatory
4. Infrared Astronomical Satellite

Figure 7-12.

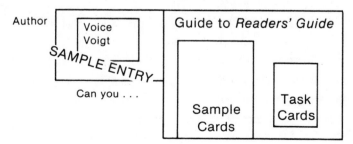

TEACHING UNIT 3: SEARCHING THE *TIMES INDEX*

Many students and adults avoid using *The New York Times Index* after their first frustrating confrontation with the complexities of its arrangement and the structure of its entries. If you eliminate newspaper articles from research, however, the report will lack the immediacy that many topics require.

This teaching unit will guide junior high school students past their initial confusion and familiarize them with the format of the *Times Index*. Since they can't be expected to complete the task cards just by reading the sample entry (as they can do with magazine indexes), you will have to introduce *The New York Times Index*.

Objectives:

At the conclusion of this unit students will be able to:

- cite the location of an article in the *Times* from the abbreviations used in the *Index*
- search the *Index* for articles relevant to a topic

Materials:

4 copies of the abbreviations key (Figure 7-13)

4 copies of the sample page (Figure 7-14)

8 pieces of 10″ × 14″ posterboard

1 piece of 9″ × 12″ posterboard (may be larger)

1 permanent transparency of the sample entry (Figure 7-15)

5 pieces of 6″ × 9″ posterboard

2 manila envelopes (1 extra large, 1 small)

18″ × 24″ piece of oaktag

rubber cement

clear self-stick vinyl

felt markers

Preparation:

1. Paste the copies of "Key to Abbreviations" and the sample page onto the 10″ × 14″ posterboard.
2. Cover with clear self-stick vinyl.
3. Copy the sample entry onto the 9″ × 12″ posterboard. (You can make the sample larger if you have adequate room for display.)
4. Also make a permanent transparency of the sample entry.
5. Copy the four task cards (see Figure 7-16) onto the 6″ × 9″ posterboard and use the last piece for an answer key (see Figure 7-17).
6. Keep the answer key at your desk and put the four task cards into the small manila envelope and the abbreviation and sample pages into the large manila envelope.
7. Print "Searching the *Times*" on the 18″ × 24″ piece of oaktag and attach both manila envelopes. Place the sample entry alongside. Display the center on the bulletin board or a wall.

Figure 7-13.

KEY TO ABBREVIATIONS

ABBREVIATION AND ACRONYM LIST

ACLU	AMER CIVIL LIBERTIES UNION
ad	ADVERTISEMENT
adm	ADMINISTRATION
AFT	AMER FED OF TEACHERS
agr	AGRICULTURE
ALA	AMER LIBRARY ASSN
ALPA	AIR LINE PILOTS ASSN
AMA	AMER MED ASSN
Amb	AMBASSADOR
anniv	ANNIVERSARY
ANPA	AMER NEWSPAPER PUBLISHERS ASSN
API	AMER PETROLEUM INST
Apr	APRIL
ASCAP	AMER SOC OF COMPOSERS, AUTHORS & PUBLISHERS
ASE	AMER STOCK EXCH
ASNE	AMER SOC OF NEWSPAPER EDS
ASPCA	AMER SOC FOR THE PREVENTION OF CRUELTY TO ANIMALS
assn	ASSOCIATION
Aug	AUGUST
auth	AUTHORITY
biog	BIOGRAPHY; BIOGRAPHICAL
bldg	BUILDING
BLS	BUR OF LABOR STATISTICS
Brit	BRITISH
bur	BUREAU
CAB	CIVIL AERONAUTICS BD
CARE	CO-OP FOR AMER RELIEF EVERYWHERE
Cath	CATHOLIC
champ	CHAMPION (SHIP)
chap	CHAPTER
chem	CHEMICAL
chmn	CHAIRMAN; CHAIRMEN
CIA	CENTRAL INTELLIGENCE AGENCY
coll	COLLEGE
com	COMMITTEE
comdr	COMMANDER
comm	COMMISSION
comr	COMMISSIONER
COMSAT	COMMUNICATIONS SATELLITE CORP
conf(s)	CONFERENCE (S)
cong	CONGRESS(IONAL)
const	CONSTITUTION
conv	CONVENTION
CORE	CONG OF RACIAL EQUALITY
Czech	CZECHOSLOVAK(IA, IAN)
Dec	DECEMBER
dem	DEMOCRAT(IC)
dir	DIRECTOR
divd	DIVIDEND
econ	ECONOMIC(AL); ECONOMY
educ	EDUCATION
EEC	EUR ECON COMMUNITY
Eur	EUROPE
FAA	FEDERAL AVIATION ADM
FAO	UN FOOD AND AGR ORGN
FBI	FED BUR OF INVESTIGATION
FCC	FED COMMUNICATIONS COMM
FDA	FOOD AND DRUG ADM
FDIC	FED DEPOSIT INS CORP
Feb	FEBRUARY
Fed	FEDERAL
FHA	FED HOUSING ADM
FPC	FED POWER COMM
FTC	FED TRADE COMM
GATT	GEN AGREEMENT ON TARIFF & TRADE
GB	GREAT BRITAIN
GNP	GROSS NATL PRODUCT
govt	GOVERNMENT
GSA	GEN SERVICES ADM
hosp	HOSPITAL
HUD	HOUSING AND URBAN DEVELOPMENT DEPT (US)
IATA	INTERNATL AIR TRANSPORT ASSN
IBRD	INTERNATL BANK FOR RECONSTRUCTION & DEVELOPMENT
ICBM	INTERCONTINENTAL BALLISTIC MISSILE
ICC	INTERSTATE COMMERCE COMM
ILA	INTERNATL LONGSHOREMEN'S ASSN
ILGWU	INTERNATL LADIES GARMENT WORKERS UNION
illus	ILLUSTRATION
ILO	INTERNATL LABOR ORGN
ILWU	INTERNATL LONGSHOREMEN'S & WAREHOUSEMEN'S UNION
IMF	INTERNATL MONETARY FUND
indus	INDUSTRY
ins	INSURANCE
inst(s)	INSTITUTE(S)
IRS	INTERNAL REVENUE SERVICE
Ital	ITALIAN
ITU	INTERNATL TYPOGRAPHICAL UNION
Jan	JANUARY

KKK	KU KLUX KLAN
Luth	LUTHERAN
Mar	MARCH
math	MATHEMATICS(AL)
med	MEDICINE
met	METROPOLITAN
Meth	METHODIST
mil	MILITARY
min	MINISTER
misc	MISCELLANEOUS
MTA	MET TRANSPORTATION AUTH
NAACP	NATL ASSN FOR THE ADVANCEMENT OF COLORED PEOPLE
NAM	NATL ASSN OF MFRS
NASA	NATL AERONAUTICS AND SPACE ADM
NASD	NATL ASSN OF SECURITIES DEALERS
natl	NATIONAL
NATO	NORTH ATLANTIC TREATY ORGN
NCO	NON-COMMISSIONED OFFICER
NEA	NATL EDUC ASSN
NLRB	NATL LABOR RELATIONS BD
NMB	NATL MEDIATION BD
NMU	NATL MARITIME UNION
NORAD	NORTH AMER AIR DEFENSE COMMAND
Nov	NOVEMBER
NRC	NUCLEAR REGULATORY COMMISSION
NYSE	NY STOCK EXCH
NZ	NEW ZEALAND
Oct	OCTOBER
OCS	Officer Candidate School
OECD	ORGN FOR ECON COOPERATION AND DEVELOPMENT
orch	ORCHESTRA
orgn	ORGANIZATION
PATCO	PROFESSIONAL AIR TRAFFIC CONTROLLERS ORGANIZATION
PHS	PUBLIC HEALTH SERVICE
PO(s)	POST OFFICE(S)
pol	POLITICS
POW	PRISONER OF WAR
pres	PRESIDENT
Presb	PRESBYTERIAN
Prot	PROTESTANT
prov	PROVINCE
PSC	PUB SERVICE COMM
ptl	PATROLMAN(MEN)
PUC	PUB UTILITIES COMM
qr(ly)	QUARTER(LY)
RAF	ROYAL AIR FORCE
RCAF	ROYAL Canadian Air Force
REA	RURAL ELECTRIFICATION ADM
recd	RECEIVED
ref	REFERENCE(S)
regis	REGISTRATION
rep	REPRESENTATIVE
rept(s)	REPORT(S)
repub	REPUBLIC(AN)
rev(d,g)	REVIEW(ED, ING)
SAC	STRATEGIC AIR COMMAND
SAG	SCREEN ACTORS GUILD
SALT	STRATEGIC ARMS LIMITATION TALKS
SAS	SCANDINAVIAN AIRLINES SYSTEM
SBA	SMALL BUSINESS ADM
SEC	SECURITIES & EXCH COMM
sec	SECRETARY
Sen	SENATE; SENATOR
Sept	SEPTEMBER
SLA	STATE LIQUOR AUTH
SUNY	STATE UNIV OF NY
treas	TREASURY
TUC	TRADES UNION CONG
TVA	TENN VALLEY AUTH
TWU	TRANSPORT WORKERS UNION OF AMER
UAW	UNITED AUTO, AEROSPACE & AGR IMPLEMENT WORKERS OF AMER
UFA	UNIFORMED FIREFIGHTERS ASSN
UFT	UNITED FED OF TEACHERS
UMW	UNITED MINE WORKERS OF AMER
UNESCO	UN EDUC, SCIENTIFIC & CULTURAL ORGN
UNICEF	UN CHILDREN'S FUND
univ	UNIVERSITY
US	UNITED STATES
USAF	US AIR FORCE
USCG	US COAST GUARD
USMC	US MARINE CORPS
USN	US NAVY
USO	UNITED SERVICE ORGNS
VA	VETERANS ADM
VI	VIRGIN ISLANDS
VISTA	VOLUNTEERS IN SERVICE TO AMER
vp(s)	VICE PRESIDENT(S)
WHO	WORLD HEALTH ORGN

Figure 7-14.

SMITH, Tim. See also Corporations, Mr 14
SMITH, Walter M (Col). See also Roads – NYC, Mr 18,22
SMITH, Wayne S. See also Latin America, F 3,8
SMITH, William B. See also International Telephone & Telegraph Corp (ITT), Ja 17
SMITH, William French (Atty Gen). See also Crime – NJ, Ja 16. Crime – US, Ja 25,28, Mr 4,6. Drug Traffic, Mr 18. Educ – US, Mr 1. Environmental Protection Agency (EPA), Mr 16. Nazi Era, Mr 8,15,16,17. Tennis, Ja 7. US – Pol, Mr 8,9. Waste etc, F 16,23. Weather, Mr 6
SMITH, William R (Co Exec). See also Waste etc, F 7
SMITH Barney, Harris Upham & Co. See also Elec Light, Mr 28
SMITH College. See also Colls – US, F 28. UN, F 25. US – Pol, Mr 8

Smith College, reversing customary policy, announces it will give honorary degree in absentia to US Amb to UN Jeane J Kirkpatrick before college's commencement exercises in May; Kirkpatrick withdrew as Smith commencement speaker after she was informed that college could not assure her security during possible demonstrations against her visit (S), Mr 1,I,4:3

Letter from 5 Smith College faculty members who drafted and circulated petition protesting award of honorary degree to Jeane Kirkpatrick, US delegate to UN; insists that they never questioned Kirkpatrick's right to speak at campus, Mr 11,I,30:5

SMITH Haven Mall (Lake Grove, NY). See also Retail Stores, Mr 20
SMITH International Inc

Smith International appoints Fred J Barnes president, succeeding Jerry W Neeley, who continues as chairman and chief executive officer (S), Mr 29,IV,2:6

SMITH Richardson Foundation. See also Radio, Ja 13
SMITHERS, R Brinkley. See also US – Armament etc, Mr 27
SMITHERS, Robert Brinkley. See also Alcoholism, Ja 23
SMITHERS Alcoholism Treatment and Training Center (NYC). See also Alcoholism, Ja 23
SMITHKLINE Beckman Corp

SmithKline Beckman repts fourth quarter net income rose to $117.5 million, while sales were up to $771.3 million; repts earnings for '82 rose to $455.2 million, while sales were up to $2.97 billion (S), Ja 26,IV,6:6

SMITHSONIAN Institution (Washington, DC). See also Astronautics – US, Ja 30. Blacks, F 24. Culture, F 8. Evolution, Ja 13. Festivals, Ja 28. Kites, Mr 11. Mennonite Churches, Mr 25. Space, Ja 2

Regents reaffirm their custom of barring public and press from meetings; group instructs sr staff members to compile rept on precedents and on relevancy of such measures as Freedom of Information Act to closed sessions; regents meet 3 times annually to set Smithsonian policy (S), Ja 25, I,23:5

Article on controversy over Smithsonian Institution's proposed reorganization of its performing arts program, which musicians say will split its functions among several Smithsonian bodies and spell the end its highly regarded music projects or at least their major curtailment; Smithsonian insists that reorganization represents attempt to introduce proper management; drawing (M), F 11,I,16:3

Smithsonian Institution and WETA-TV public-TV station, Washington, DC, announce author David McCullough will host TV series that will portray Smithsonian's holdings (S), F 26,I,20:2

Article on changes now taking place at Smithsonian Institution: talk of search for eventual replacement for S Dillon Ripley as chief executive officer, $75 million Quadrangle project for Sackler Gallery or Oriental Art and National Museum of African Art, unusual high turnover among museum directors, spending cutbacks and layoffs and television series on Smithsonian; Ripley portrait (M), Mr 16,I,24:5

SMITHTOWN (NY). See also Asphyxiation, F 16. RRs – US, F 27. Waste etc, F 13
SMOKE. See Air Pollution. Fires

SMOKE Detectors. See also Fires and Firemen, Ja 16. Fires and Firemen – NJ, Ja 29. Fires and Firemen – NYC, Ja 25
SMOKING. See also Airlines, Ja 11,29. Taxation, Mr 28

Washington, DC, tobacconists are unfazed by customers' New Year resolution to stop smoking, saying most will be back in shop by Jan 15; cartoon (S), Ja 1,I,6:2

Lorillard Inc to go national with new female-oriented cigarette brand called Satin (S), Ja 6,IV,17:1

Follow-up item on Oct '82 Federal Appeals Court ruling upholding right of Fed worker Irene C Parodi, of Fremont, Calif, to work in smoke-free job; court ruled that Govt must give Parodi job in 'safe environment' or grant her disability pension; case remains unresolved and Parodi atty John R Browne 3d has asked ct to approve disability benefits (S), Ja 9,I,33:1

Article on growth of generic cigarettes; ad campaign by Liggett & Myers discussed; graph (L), Ja 16,III,4:3

Philip Morris Inc is closing in on R J Reynolds Tobacco Co as number 1 company in cigarette sales is US; graphs; chart (L), Ja 17,IV,1:3

Study conducted at Cleveland Metropolitan General Hospital/Case Western Reserve Univ, published in Amer Journal of Obstetrics and Gynecology, shows that when nonsmoking pregnant woman is exposed to cigarette smoke of other people, fetal blood contains significant amounts of tobacco smoke byproducts (S), Ja 18,III,2:1

R J Reynolds Industries asks more than 10% of cigarette workers to resign or retire early and cuts production schedule in anticipation of sales drop to follow Federal tax increase (S), Ja 22,I,36:6

Israeli Govt approves plan to impose tight restrictions on cigarette advertising effective in July (M), Ja 23,I,10:1

Arkansas House of Reps approves resolution urging members not to smoke in chamber (S), Ja 23,I,21:1

New York Assemblyman Alexander B Grannis letter urges support for bill he and others have introduced to permit sale of cigarettes in state only if they are designed to stop burning within fixed time or meet other performance standards to limit their potential to cause fires, F 15,I,22:4

Article on Brazilian cigar-making operations of Benjamin F, Alonso and Felix Menendez, who find conditions in Bahia state to be very like those of their native Cuba, which they were forced to leave 22 years ago when Cuban Government took over Menendez Garcia company; Menendez Amerino SA hopes to underprice competition in US, chief target, to achieve short-range goal of 2.5% of market there for imported handmade cigars; map; photo (M), F 21,IV,1:1

Yearlong study of hospitalized heart attack patients by Boston University Medical School and Harvard School of Public Health researchers shows that risk of suffering heart attack is just as great among smokers who use low-nicotine cigarettes as it is among those who use high-nicotine brands (S), F 24,I,16:5

Comment on 'ceremonial picketing' of Metropolitan Museum of Art to protest sponsorship of current Vatican art show by Philip Morris Inc; pickets were organized by DOC (Doctors Ought to Care), national coalition of health professionals, and NYC and NJ chapters of GASP (Group Against Smoking Pollution); Msgr Eugene V Clark says sponsor is not Philip Morris as cigarette company, but Philip Morris Inc (S), F 28,II,4:2

Letter from William D Toohey Jr of Tobacco Institute replies to Feb 15 letter from New York State Assemblyman Alexander B Grannis urging mandating of self-extinguishing cigarettes as means of reducing fires, Mr 1,I,22:5

US Office on Smoking and Health, in pamphlet Why People Smoke Cigarettes, reports cigarette smoking is 'most widespread example of drug dependence' in US; pamphlet is released as Reagan Administration was preparing to give Congress its views on legislative proposals to strengthen warnings on cigarette packages; Dr Edward N Brandt Jr, head of Public Health Service, is scheduled to testify on March 9 before House Committee on Energy and Commerce (S), Mr 7,II,9:5

Polish Government announces price increases for gasoline, coffee and cigarettes (S), Mr 15,I,3:3

Victor Lusinchi article describes shopping for pipes in St Claude, France, town that introduced briar pipes to smokers; illustrations; map (S), Mr 20,X,p6

Article on experiment being conducted in London in which snuff containing small amount of nicotine was used to satisfy nicotine addiction in people trying to stop smoking; project director Dr M A H Russell says he hopes smokers will eventually be able to wean themselves of snuff habit, which is less harmful than smoking (M), Mr 23,III,15:1

Federal Trade Commission reports low-tar cigarettes continue to dominate tobacco market, although there are only six brands, compared with 10 in Dec 1981, with 0.5 milligrams or less of tar; says that 157 of 208 brands tested have 15 milligrams or less of tar, level that Government defines as low-tar; other findings detailed (S), Mr 29,I,14:1

SMUGGLING. See also Drug Traffic, Ja 17,18,21,28, F 8, 19,24, Mr 19,26,30. Firearms, Ja 15,28. Iran, F 18. Ireland, Northern, F 15, Mr 25,29,31. Libya, Ja 6, Ja 22,25,29, F 3, 6,19. Nicaragua, Mr 30
SMUIN, John. See also Dancing, Ja 26
SMULLEN, Ivor. See also Gambling, Mr 12
SMYLIE, Ed. See also Astronautics – US, Mr 19
SMYRNA (Tenn). See also Autos – US, F 22. Trucks, F 24, Mr 30
SNAIL Darters. See also Fish, F 23
SNECMA (Co). See also Airplanes, F 10

SNELLING, Richard A (Gov). See also Vermont, Ja 7, 24, Mr 13
SNEPP, Frank (Ex-CIA Analyst). See also Intelligence Agency, Mr 24
SNEZHNEVSKY, Andrei (Dr). See also Mental Health, Ja 30
SNINSKY, John J. See also Proteins, F 26
SNIPERS and Sniping. Use Shootings
SNOW, Henry (Ptl). See also Blacks, Mr 27
SNOW, Robert. See also Reagan, Mr 25
SNOW and Snowstorms. See also Airlines, Ja 10,13. Autos US, Ja 16. Avalanches. Elec Light, Ja 23. Food, F 14. Murders – NYC, F 14. Retail Stores, F 14. Roads – US, Ja 27. Ships, F 13. Skiing, Ja 23, F 14. Weather, Ja 1,16,17, 19, Ja 22,27, F 1,2,3,7,8,11,12,13,14,15,16,17,18,19,20,21,22, 23,25, Mr 7,13,22,25,27,28,29
SNOW King Frozen Foods Inc. See also Campbell Soup Co, Mr 20
SNOW Removal. See Snow and Snowstorms
SNOWBIRD (Utah). See also Med, Ja 11
SNOWBIRD Sports Medical Clinic (Snowbird, Utah). See also Med – US, Ja 11
SNOWDON Mountains (Wales). See also Mountain Climbing, F 20
SNOWMOBILES. See also Shootings, Mr 2
SNUFF

Article on experiment being conducted in London in which snuff containing small amount of nicotine was used to satisfy nicotine addiction in people trying to stop smoking; project director Dr M A H Russell says he hopes smokers will eventually be able to wean themselves of snuff habit, which is less harmful than smoking (M), Mr 23,III,15:1

SNYDER, Adam. See also Athletics, Mr 20
SNYDER, Edward V. See also Plastics, Mr 30
SNYDER, Jed C. See also Arms Control, Mr 15
SNYDER, Joseph R. See also News – US, Mr 27

SNYDER, Leslie Crocker (Asst Dist Atty). See also Courts, Mr 9,23
SOAP. Use Cleansers
SOARES, Mario. See also Portugal, F 24
SOBOLEVSKY, Rafail. See also Music – Concerts, Ja 19
SOBOLEWSKI, Chester. See also Autos – US, Mr 6
SOBREIRO, Joaquim. See also Liquor, F 7
SOCCER

At least 9 persons are injured when 2 homemade bombs explode during soccer game, Amsterdam, Netherlands (S), Ja 10,III,11:1

Seattle Sounders franchise sold to Bruce Anderson and Jerry Horn; coach Alan Hinton dismissed (S), Ja 13,II,15:1

US Soccer Federation says recently-formed Team America will join North American Soccer League (NASL) for full 30-game schedule in '83 (M), Ja 21,I,19:4

39 players invited to attend first training camp of Team America (M), Ja 26,II,8:5

Julio Mazzei to be retained as New York Cosmos coach for '83 season (S), F 1,II,7:1; F 2,II,8:5

Don Popovic to resign as coach of New York Arrows of Major Indoor Soccer League at end of current season (S), F 22,II,11:4

New York Arrows dismiss coach Don Popovic, 4 days after he angered club officials by disclosing plans to retire (S), F 25,I,24:1

John Machnick named coach of New York Arrows of Major Indoor Soccer League, succeeding Don Popovic who was dismissed and is named coach of Golden Bay Earthquakes (M), Mr 1,II,7:1

Brazil formally withdraws as site for 1986 World Cup soccer tournament, apparently clearing way for US to be selected as site; US Soccer Federation lists 12 stadiums as possible sites as part of 92-page presentation bidding for tournament; Mexico and Canada are only two other countries vying for tournament (S), Mr 11,I,27:5

Robert K Lifton, NY businessman, provides financial backing and management for Team America, soccer team based in Washington that will start playing this spring as one of NASL's regular teams; Team America will use only American players in league that has been dominated by foreign players; will also be US national team training for '86 World Cup; Lifton comments; his photo (M), Mr 15,IV, 2:5

George Vecsey article on Federation Internationale de Football Assn (FIFA) entertaining bids from US, Mexico and Canada to host '86 World Cup soccer matches; predicts US will be named host country; illustration (M), Mr 20,V,5:1

Pres Reagan supports US bid to host 1986 World Cup soccer tournament, letter to United States Soccer Federation president Gene Edwards (S), Mr 24,II,16:5

SOCCER Federation, US. See also Soccer, Ja 21,26, Mr 11, 24

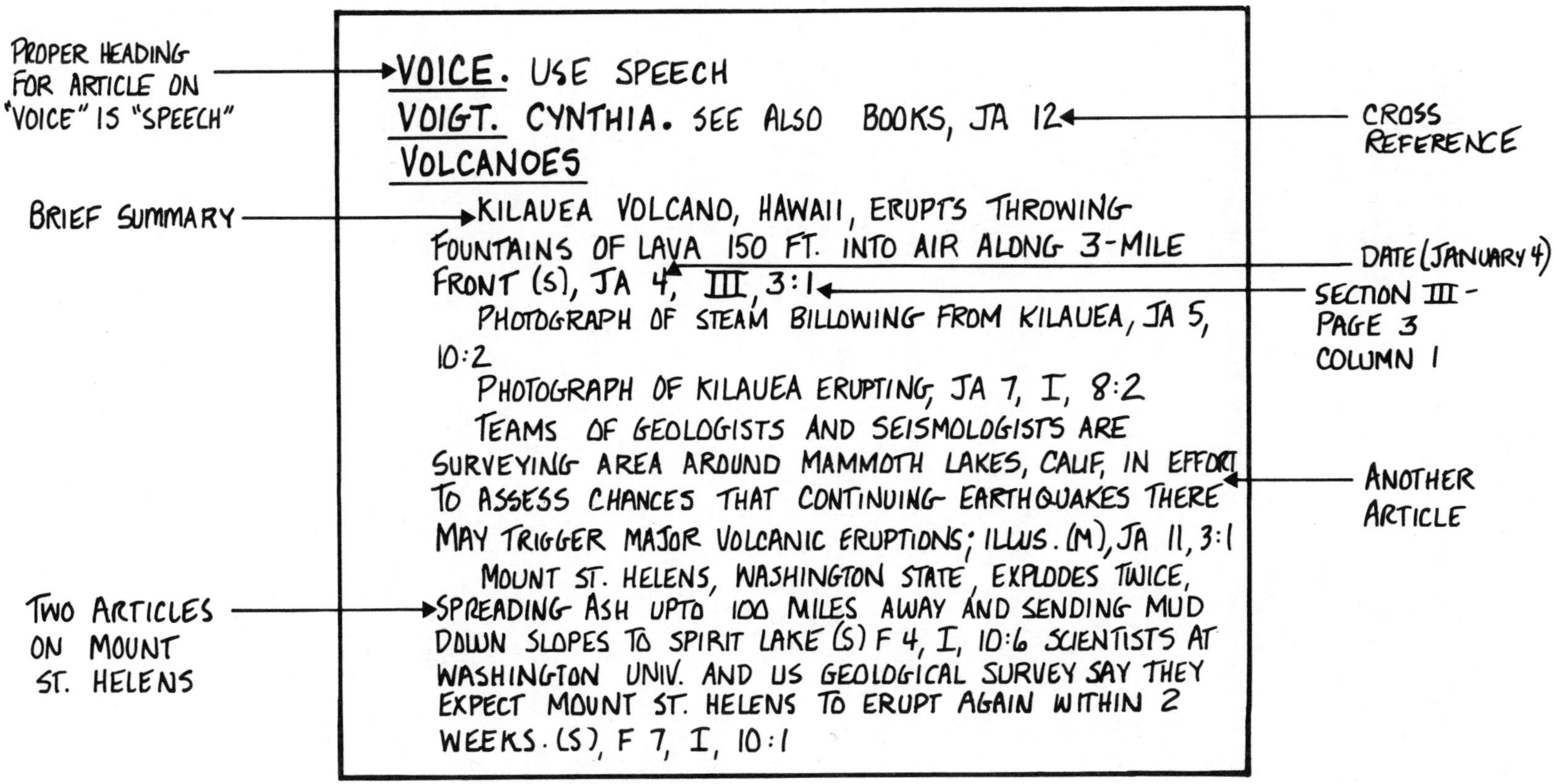

Figure 7-15.

Labels pointing to the card:
- CROSS REFERENCE
- DATE (JANUARY 4)
- SECTION III – PAGE 3 COLUMN 1
- ANOTHER ARTICLE
- PROPER HEADING FOR ARTICLE ON "VOICE" IS "SPEECH"
- BRIEF SUMMARY
- TWO ARTICLES ON MOUNT ST. HELENS

Card contents:

VOICE. USE SPEECH
VOIGT, CYNTHIA. SEE ALSO BOOKS, JA 12
VOLCANOES
KILAUEA VOLCANO, HAWAII, ERUPTS THROWING FOUNTAINS OF LAVA 150 FT. INTO AIR ALONG 3-MILE FRONT (S), JA 4, III, 3:1
PHOTOGRAPH OF STEAM BILLOWING FROM KILAUEA, JA 5, 10:2
PHOTOGRAPH OF KILAUEA ERUPTING, JA 7, I, 8:2
TEAMS OF GEOLOGISTS AND SEISMOLOGISTS ARE SURVEYING AREA AROUND MAMMOTH LAKES, CALIF, IN EFFORT TO ASSESS CHANCES THAT CONTINUING EARTHQUAKES THERE MAY TRIGGER MAJOR VOLCANIC ERUPTIONS; ILLUS. (M), JA 11, 3:1
MOUNT ST. HELENS, WASHINGTON STATE, EXPLODES TWICE, SPREADING ASH UP TO 100 MILES AWAY AND SENDING MUD DOWN SLOPES TO SPIRIT LAKE (S) F 4, I, 10:6 SCIENTISTS AT WASHINGTON UNIV. AND US GEOLOGICAL SURVEY SAY THEY EXPECT MOUNT ST. HELENS TO ERUPT AGAIN WITHIN 2 WEEKS. (S), F 7, I, 10:1

CAN YOU...

NAME THE HEADING THAT LISTS AN ARTICLE ON CYNTHIA VOIGT?

GIVE BOTH DATES OF THE ARTICLES ON MOUNT ST. HELENS?

FIND THE ONLY ARTICLE OF MEDIUM LENGTH?

IF NOT...ASK FOR HELP

Directions:

Establishing the Need for an Index:

- Shortly after you post the learning center discuss the *New York Times* with the class.

- Have them compare the information in a newspaper with that in a magazine. If you can, bring in a copy of the *New York Times* or a major newspaper in your area and a news magazine such as *Time* or *Newsweek*. The class will then be able to see the difference more clearly.

- Have students suggest report topics where newspaper articles would be helpful.

- Ask them how they would locate the article they would need for those report topics. If students are familiar with a periodical index, they will guess that an index exists.

Getting into the Index:

- Explain that the *New York Times* compiles and publishes its own index. In many libraries the *New York Times* is readily available on microfilm, which can be used to read the articles previously located in the *Index*.

- Introduce the structure of *The New York Times Index* using the permanent transparency of the sample entry.

- Go through the entries explaining the parts. Stress that, unlike the *Readers' Guide*, the *Times Index* does not give the year of the article, presuming that the user is aware that the year is the one appearing on the cover of the *Index*.

- Be sure to point out that the "(S)" and "(M)" in the sample indicate the length of the article. *The New York Times Index* uses S, M, and L to alert users as to how long articles run. This is not explained in the abbreviations key.

- Show students the sample page and tell them they will use that page to answer the task cards when they work at the center.

Follow Up:

Be sure to reinforce the unit by requiring newspaper articles as part of students' research papers. Students should also be informed as to the bibliographic citation that you prefer for newspaper articles.

Figure 7-16.

Task Card 1

Use the sample page of *The New York Times Index* to answer these questions:

1. What is the heading for SNOW removal?
2. What is the heading for SMOKE?
3. What is the preferred heading for SOAP?
4. For information on Snail Darters, what heading should be searched? Under what date will there be a story?
5. What office is held by Richard A. Snelling? Use the information given to guess the state in which he holds this office.

Task Card 2

Use the sample page of *The New York Times Index* to answer these questions:

1. If you are looking for articles on the effects of snow and snowstorms on travel, which of the references should you check?
2. To whom will Smith College grant an honorary degree in absentia?
3. If you are looking for information on the smuggling of guns, which "see" reference should you check?
4. Smith International, Inc. has a new president. Who is he?

Task Card 3

Use the sample page of *The New York Times Index* to answer these questions. Look under the heading SOCCER.

1. At a soccer game in Amsterdam, two homemade bombs exploded. What issue of the *Times* contains the article? In what section of the *Times* and on what page will you find it?
2. Three articles are about Don Popovic. Find the entries and answer the following questions:
   a. Where would you find the article on Popovic's resignation? (Include date, section, page, and column in your answer.)
   b. Where would you find information on his successor? (Include date, section, page, and column in your answer.)
3. You are doing a report on Team America. What three articles will you need to read? (Give complete citations.)
4. You are doing a report on the 1986 World Cup Soccer Tournament. There are four articles listed on the subject. Find them and answer the following:
   a. What three countries are still vying to be host country for the tournament?
   b. Which article presents possible U.S. sites for the World Cup? (Give complete citation.)

Task Card 4

Use the sample page of *The New York Times Index* to answer these questions. Look under the heading SMOKING.

1. Find the articles that discuss which company is number one in sales. (Give complete citation.)
2. Which article discusses cigarettes as a drug dependency? (Give complete citation.)
3. You are doing a report on "Modern Trends in the Cigarette Industry." The articles on female-oriented cigarettes, generic cigarettes, self-extinguishing cigarettes, and the drop in number of available low-tar cigarettes are a good beginning. Where will you find these articles? (Give complete citations.)
4. Find the two articles that discuss the implications of cigarette smoke on nonsmokers. (Give complete citations.)

Figure 7-17.

Answers to Task Cards

Card 1

1. Snow and Snowstorms
2. Air Pollution, Fires
3. Cleansers
4. Fish — February 23, 1983
5. Governor — Vermont

Card 2

1. Airlines, January 10, 13; Autos — U.S., January 16; Roads — U.S., January 27; Ships, February 13
2. Jeane J. Kirkpatrick, U.S. Ambassador to the U.N.
3. Firearms, January 15 and January 28
4. Fred J. Barnes

Card 3

1. January 10, section III, page 11
2. a. February 22, section II, page 11, column 4
   b. March 1, section II, page 7, column 1
3. a. January 21, section I, page 19, column 4
   b. January 26, section II, page 8, column 5
   c. March 15, section IV, page 2, column 5
4. a. U.S., Mexico, and Canada
   b. March 11, section I, page 27, column 5

Card 4

1. "Philip Morris Inc. is closing in on R. J. Reynolds Tobacco Co . . ." January 17, section IV, page 1, column 3
2. "U.S. Office on Smoking and Health, in pamphlet . . ." March 7, section II, page 9, column 5
3. a. January 6, section IV, page 17, column 1
   b. January 16, section III, page 4, column 3
   c. February 15, section I, page 22, column 4 and March 1, section I, page 22, column 5
   d. March 29, section I, page 14, column 1
4. a. January 9, section I, page 33, column 1 (Parodi case)
   b. January 18, section III, page 2, column 1 (Cleveland Metropolitan General Hospital study)

Chapter 8

ONE-VOLUME REFERENCE WORKS

BACKGROUND INFORMATION

Developing a command of reference tools beyond the basics of dictionaries, encyclopedias, atlases, and almanacs gives students a wider variety of resources from which to draw information as well as the skills they need to gain access to the more sophisticated sources they will use as they advance through secondary school and college. Each new reference book they learn to use expands their knowledge of different indexes and entry words. The similarities and dissimilarities help them acquire a sense of the logic underlying each tool and the best ways to approach reference problems.

The three one-volume reference books explored in this section are complicated to use but provide information that is difficult to locate elsewhere. Fortunately, the results of their searches are so interesting that it is not difficult to motivate students to use these tools.

Bartlett's Familiar Quotations

Bartlett's Familiar Quotations (14th edition, Little, Brown, 1968) has been in publication since 1855 when John Bartlett first published his descriptively titled *Familiar Quotations: A Collection of Passages, Phrases, and Proverbs Traced to Their Sources in Ancient and Modern Literature*. The original was a 258-page paperback leaning heavily on the Bible, Shakespeare, and the major English poets. Bartlett, the owner of the University Book Store in Cambridge, Massachusetts, had a reputation among Harvard students and professors for knowing quotations, along with their authors and sources. The book was a natural result of this ability and was an instant and continuing success according to the prefatory material in the current edition. Each subsequent edition has not only been an invaluable aid, but the inclusions and omissions are a fascinating reflection on the changing taste of the times.

Bartlett's is arranged in chronological order. While it is interesting to discover which noted persons are contemporaries, the structure requires that there be an alphabetical index of authors. Check the table of contents to find the list. It exists, although people tend to miss it because of the overwhelming enormity of the "Index to the Quotations."

The prefatory material contains a "Guide to the Use of *Familiar Quotations*" which you can read if you feel you need detailed direction. A companion volume by John Mersand entitled *A Guide to the Use of Bartlett's Familiar Quotations* (3rd edition, Little, Brown, 1969) has projects, quizzes, and lesson plans mostly geared to high school, although some are suitable for grades 6 to 8 as well. It is available in some elementary media centers and you might want to look at it for further ideas.

In general, you need to know that the quotations are indexed under all key words that appear in the citation. To minimize the amount of time spent looking through the index when searching for the source of a quotation, choose its most unusual word. For example, to locate the author of "Beauty is in the eye of the beholder," it is far simpler to look under "beholder" where there is only the single listing (which, incidentally, gives two sources—Lew Wallace and Margaret Wolfe Hungerford). Entries under "beauty" take up nearly three columns, and "eye" is almost as lengthy.

Once you and your students are comfortable with *Bartlett's*, use the book in a variety of ways. Mark the birthdays of historic figures by having students find some of their famous lines. Choose a quotation as a topic. Students can analyze it and perhaps find a citation by the same writer or another to substantiate their views. Encourage students to use a quotation as an effective technique for beginning or ending a composition. The teaching unit given in this section will show you how to get started with any of these plans.

Facts About the Presidents

Joseph Nathan Kane has compiled this invaluable reference work on the presidents. The first part is arranged in chronological order. The first segment under each president gives basic biographical data such as: birth date and place, political party, age at inauguration, age at death (years and days), and place of death. Similar information is then given for the presidents' parents, siblings, children, and wives. The elections that placed them in office are briefly described, complete with electoral college votes, the cabinets, the congresses, and Supreme Court appointments. There is also a chronological listing of important dates in the presidents' administrations and lives. This is followed by information on the vice-presidents and short pieces described as "Additional Data." These are often fascinating sidelights on what occurred during a particular president's term. The last segment is devoted to the activities of the first ladies.

The second part of *Facts About the Presidents* (4th edition, H. W. Wilson Co.) consists of comparative data. To fully appreciate the scope you need to page through this section. The occupations of presidents before and after serving their country are listed and so are their last words. Physical characteristics of each president are given as well as the names of any books they have written. Although there are entries for these compilations in the index, you probably would not dream of checking for some of the information unless you already knew it would be included. The teaching unit gives your students experience in locating many of these unusual listings.

Famous First Facts

Famous First Facts by Joseph Nathan Kane (4th edition, H. W. Wilson Co.) is a compendium of more than 9,000 firsts in American history. Four complicated indexes lead the user to the body of the work—718 pages that describe the historical occurrences in alphabetical order. The first is an "Index by Years," 171 pages chronologically arranged from 1007 (yes, there is an American history "first" that goes back that far) to 1980. The second index of 163 pages is by day of the month, from January 1 to December 31. An alphabetical "Index to Personal Names" is the third entry approach. The fourth index is geographical and alphabetically lists the fifty states with subheadings for the cities in those states. The four indexes do not give the full information but indicate in boldface type the entry that should be checked in the main body of the text.

Although students at first find this reference tool difficult to use the facts they uncover are often so unusual and unexpected that they continue to check the indexes and text for other oddities. As they use the book often enough students become quite comfortable with its idiosyncracies. The teaching unit will get them started and you can add to the questions to expand the center as you want.

TEACHING UNIT 1: JUST THE FACTS

Combine the two reference works by Joseph Nathan Kane into one learning center. The two books occasionally duplicate information, such as when a presidential act is also a "first" or when some first event is politically relevant and is included in *Facts About the Presidents* under "Administration—Important Dates." Despite the duplication, the books are different in organization and central focus, and yet, perhaps because they are the work of the same person or are both concerned with American historical facts, there seems to be a similarity. Teaching them together serves to improve student skills just as learning how to use one reinforces knowledge of the other.

You do not have to give a lesson on the books since the learning center is almost self-teaching. The introductory card prepares students for the questions by having them familiarize themselves with the organization of the two reference books.

Objectives:

At the conclusion of this unit students will be able to:
- use a reference book with multiple indexes
- extract information on a specified subject from a detailed listing
- use a reference book to locate specific information on the presidents of the United States

Materials:

5 pieces of light blue posterboard 6" × 9"

5 pieces of white posterboard 6" × 9"

2 pieces of red posterboard 6" × 9"

18" × 24" sheet of oaktag

1 6" × 9" piece of white drawing paper

2 9" × 12" manila envelopes

clear self-stick vinyl

red and blue felt markers

tape

Preparation:

1. Copy the five task cards for *Famous First Facts* (see Figure 8-1) onto light blue posterboard and cover with clear self-stick vinyl.

2. Prepare the answer card (see Figure 8-2) on one piece of red posterboard. Only one of the five cards has an answer key. The other cards will produce different responses. Have one of your better students check other students' answers.

Figure 8-1.

Task Card 1

Use *Famous First Facts* to find the dates of these "firsts":

1. the first ice cream cone
2. the first chop suey
3. the first popcorn
4. the first lollipop machine
5. the first bicycle factory in the United States
6. the first crossword puzzle book
7. the first umbrella
8. the first electric toaster
9. the first book matches
10. the first safety pin patented

Task Card 2

Use the year index in *Famous First Facts*. Go back 100 years.

1. Find one "first" related to a modern invention and give its date and location. Example: first interstate telephone call.
2. Find one sports "first."
3. Find one transportation "first."
4. Find one strange or humorous "first."

Task Card 3

Use the day index in *Famous First Facts*. Check under your birthday. (Give the day in your answer.)

1. What is the oldest event listed? What happened?
2. What is the most recent event listed? What happened?
3. What funny or very special event happened? What year?

Task Card 4

Use the geographical index in *Famous First Facts*. Look up our state. Find five "firsts" that occurred in our state that you think are funny or important.

Task Card 5

This is a special task card. Use *Famous First Facts* to make a calendar.

1. Choose a month and make a calendar for that month.
2. Find an interesting fact for each day of the month.
3. Print the fact and date on the calendar.
4. Choose one fact and illustrate it to accompany your calendar.

Figure 8-2.

Answers to Task Cards

Card 1

1. 1904
2. August 29, 1896
3. February 22, 1630
4. 1908
5. 1878
6. April 18, 1924
7. 1740
8. June, 1926
9. 1896 (patent granted September 27, 1892)
10. April 10, 1849

---

3. Copy the five task cards for *Facts About the Presidents* (see Figure 8-3) on-to white posterboard. Cover with clear self-stick vinyl. Use the remaining red posterboard for the answer key (see Figure 8-4). You will need both sides of the card.

4. Print "JUST THE FACTS" across the top of the oaktag in red and blue felt markers. (See Figure 8-5.)

5. Use the marker to print the following directions on the white drawing paper:

1— —2— —3— —(GO!)

BEFORE you begin the question cards—

(1.) LOOK at the Table of Contents in both books.

(2.) FIND the different sections into which the books
        are divided.

        FACTS ABOUT THE PRESIDENTS has two parts
        FAMOUS FIRST FACTS has a main section and
            four indexes

(3.) TURN to the different sections and look at
        the information given.

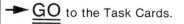 **GO** to the Task Cards.

Figure 8-3.

Task Card 1

Use *Facts About the Presidents* to answer these questions:

1. What was the date of John Adams' death? What was the date of Thomas Jefferson's death? Who was older?
2. Look under Zachary Taylor. What was his political party? What happened in his administration on April 10, 1849? Where was his horse pastured?

Task Card 2

Use *Facts About the Presidents* to answer these questions:

1. Who was the vice-president under Harry S. Truman?
2. In the 1948 election, who were the Republican candidates for president and vice-president?
3. What was the name of Truman's wife? Give her maiden name (before marriage).
4. How many children did Truman have?

Task Card 3

Use *Facts About the Presidents* to answer these questions:

1. Where was William McKinley born?
2. Who was McKinley's vice-president during his second term?
3. How many political parties nominated presidential candidates in the election of 1900?
4. Who assassinated McKinley? When? Where?

Task Card 4

Use the comparative data in *Facts About the Presidents* to answer the following questions on presidential wives:

1. How many wives lived to be over 80 years old? Who were they?
2. Who was the first presidential wife to regularly attend school?
3. Who was the first wife of a president to graduate from college?
4. How many presidential wives had fathers who were planters or farmers? Who were they?

Task Card 5

Use the comparative data in *Facts About the Presidents* to answer these questions:

1. How many presidents did not attend college? Name them.
2. How many presidents were under 5'7" tall? Name them.
3. How many presidents were 6'0" tall or taller? Name them.
4. Name the presidents who died in office.
5. What were the last words of James Madison?
6. Which president had 15 children?

Figure 8-4.

Answers to Task Cards

Card 1

1. July 4, 1826; July 4, 1826; Adams
2. Whig; safety pin patented; White House lawn

Card 2

1. Alben William Barkley
2. Thomas Edmund Dewey and Earl Warren
3. Elizabeth Virginia Wallace; she was known as Bess
4. One daughter, (Mary) Margaret Truman

Card 3

1. Niles, Ohio
2. Theodore Roosevelt
3. Eleven
4. Leon Czolgosz; September 6, 1901; Pan American Exposition, Buffalo, New York

Card 4

1. Nine. Mary Harrison; Edith Wilson; Anna Harrison; Sarah Polk; Edith Roosevelt; Lucretia Garfield; Frances Cleveland; Helen Taft; Dolley Madison. Bess Truman, born 1885, was past 80 when she died, but was still living in 1981 when the 4th edition of *Facts About the Presidents* was compiled.
2. Anna Harrison (Mrs. William Henry Harrison)
3. Lucy Hayes
4. Nine. Martha Washington; Martha Jefferson; Dolley Madison; Letitia Tyler; Sarah Polk; Margaret Taylor; Lucretia Garfield; Bess Truman; Claudia "Lady Bird" Johnson.

Task Card 5

1. Nine. Washington; Jackson; Van Buren; Taylor; Fillmore; Lincoln; A. Johnson; Cleveland; Truman
2. Three. Madison, Van Buren, and Benjamin Harrison. John Adams, John Quincy Adams, and McKinley were all exactly 5'7".
3. Sixteen. Washington; Jefferson; Monroe; Jackson; Tyler; Buchanan; Lincoln; Garfield; Arthur; Taft; Harding; Franklin D. Roosevelt; Kennedy; Lyndon Johnson; Ford; Reagan
4. William Henry Harrison; Zachary Taylor; Abraham Lincoln; James Abram Garfield; William McKinley; Warren Gamaliel Harding; Franklin Delano Roosevelt; John Fitzgerald Kennedy
5. "I always talk better lying down."
6. John Tyler

Figure 8-5.

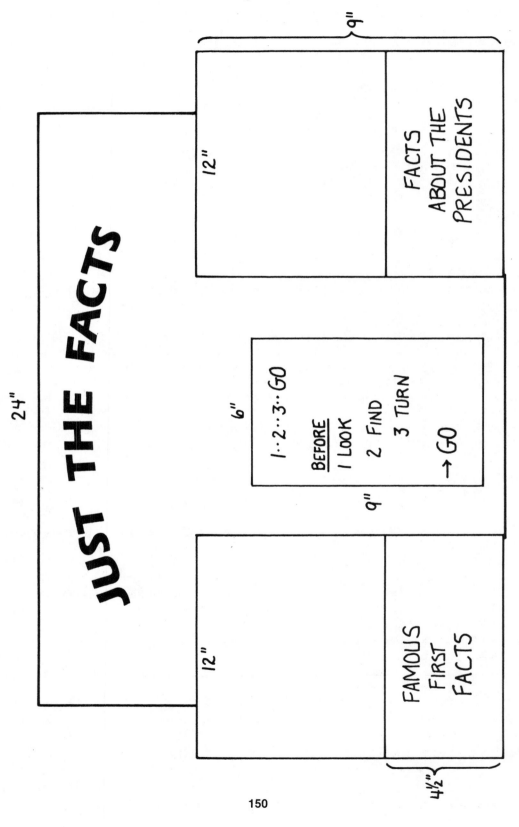

6. Paste the directions onto the lower center section of the oaktag.

7. Cut the manila envelopes to form pockets with a 4½ " high front. (See the illustration here.)

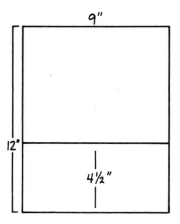

8. Put the blue posterboard cards into a manila envelope labeled *Famous First Facts* and the white posterboard cards into the other manila envelope labeled *Facts About the Presidents.* Attach them to the oaktag with part of each envelope extending over the left and right edges of the oaktag.

9. Keep the answer key at your desk.

TEACHING UNIT 2: BOOKMARKS FROM *BARTLETT'S*

Just before vacation or in celebration of Children's Book Week in November, or National Library Week in April, have students in grades 5 to 8 make bookmarks using quotations from *Bartlett's* as a theme.

Objectives:

At the conclusion of this unit students will be able to:

• use a key word to find a suitable listing in *Bartlett's Familiar Quotations*

• find the quotation from location information given in the index

Materials:

Bartlett's Familiar Quotations

two permanent transparencies (Figures 8-6 and 8-7)

a sample bookmark (Figure 8-8) on 7 " × 2½ " oaktag

7 " × 2½ " pieces of oaktag in sufficient quantities for the class

fine-tip felt marker

Procedure:

1. Open *Bartlett's* and show the students a sample page. Acknowledge that the format does not seem especially unusual. Then flip to the index. Let the students see how small the type is and then hold together all of the pages that comprise the index so that they can appreciate what a large proportion of the book is devoted to the index. The reason for this long index (the key word entry of the book) is what makes *Bartlett's* unusual.

2. Tell the class that there are several ways to use *Bartlett's*. The simplest way is to open to any page and browse through the quotations. A more difficult way is to find quotations by famous people such as Benjamin Franklin.

   • Explain that *Bartlett's* is not arranged in alphabetical order, but in chronological order. (A brief digression is necessary to remind the group that they know what alphabetical order and numerical order mean. Ask if anyone knows what chronological order is. If no one can explain this term, define it yourself.)

   • Show the class that there is an alphabetical index of authors just before the quotation index. Look up "Franklin" in the author index; then turn to the proper page and read some of his quotations.

3. Inform the students that although these two ways of using *Bartlett's* are enjoyable, they are too easy for them. What you have in store for them is the third and most difficult way of using this reference book. They will be using the main index to look up specific quotations.

Figure 8-6.

Readiness is all, 266b
Reading, affect you agreeably in r., 469b

    after r. your work, 417b
    contemplation more than r., 364b-365a
    cursed hard r., 482a
    digressions sunshine of r., 437b
    English dictionary best r., 916a
    I prefer r., 878a
    maketh a full man, 209b
    overset mind with r., 816b
    peace makes poor r., 783b
    to mind as exercise is to body, 395b
    write things worth r., 421b

Readings, our r. secret, 951b
Read, all he r. assails, 404a
    nothing but detective stories, 999b

Figure 8-7.

ADDISON - STEELE

a

We are always doing some-
thing for Posterity, but I would
fain see Posterity do something
for us.

   Ib. 587 (August 20, 1714)

See in what peace, a Christian
can die.

   Dying words (1719)
   From Young, Conjectures on
   Original Composition (1759)

SIR RICHARD STEELE
(1672 – 1729)

I am come to a tavern alone
to eat a steak, after which
I shall return to the office.
   Letters to His Wife
   (October 28, 1707)

b

A little in drink, but at all
times yr faithful husband.
   Ib. (September 27, 1708)

Though her mien carries
much more invitation than
command, to behold her is
an immediate check to
loose behavior.
   Tatler No. 49 (1709-1711)

Reading is to the mind what
exercise is to the body.
   Ib., No. 147

When you fall into a man's conversation, the first thing you
should consider is, whether
he has a greater inclination
to hear you or that you
should hear him.
   The Spectator No. 49 (April 26, 1711)

Figure 8-8.

4. Put the transparency of the excerpt from the index (see Figure 8-6) on the overhead projector. Explain the following points:
   - the index is alphabetical.
   - The first quotation for a word is given alongside the word; subsequent listings are indented and follow in alphabetical order.
   - The page references are followed by *a* or *b*.
   - When the entry word is within the body of the quotation, just an initial is used to identify it. If the initial does not appear, the entry word comes first in the quotation.
   - Plurals and other forms of a word have separate listings.
5. Read the quotation you have chosen for your bookmark and have a student find the page reference.
6. Put the transparency of the page on which the quotation appears (see Figure 8-7) on the overhead projector.
   - Have the students explain what *a* and *b* mean. (They can figure this out easily.)

- Show how to skim the page to find the quotation you want; run your finger across the words until you come to a word beginning with the right letter.

- Ask the class who is being quoted. Someone will figure out how to discover this.

- Now remind them that who said it is not enough; they must discover where it was said. There will be dead silence, or someone will suggest it was "Ib."

- Explain the meaning of "Ib." (It is *Bartlett's* shorter version of "Ibid.," the Latin word used to indicate that the source is the same as the one listed before.) Then point to another quotation that is followed by "Ib." and ask the students to locate its source.

7. Tell the class that instead of completing ditto sheets or task cards that require them to look up certain words, they will participate in an art activity.

8. Produce your sample bookmark (see Figure 8-8) and explain that the children will be using *Bartlett's* to produce their own bookmarks.

- They will use the index in *Bartlett's* to find a quotation.

- They will write down the complete quotation, the person who said it, and where it was said.

- They will print the information on precut oaktag and draw an appropriate illustration.

- Although you may suggest entry words such as books, reading, library, and learning, allow students to choose quotations about anything that interests them.

9. As a general precaution, all quotations should be shown to you before the art work begins.

10. You can display the student bookmarks in a variation of the bulletin board "To Mark It, to Mark It" found in Part Three.

Chapter 9

INDEXES TO COLLECTIONS OF SHORT WORKS

BACKGROUND INFORMATION

You may think you can find any information about books in the card catalog, but when you are looking for a poem in a poetry anthology or a very brief biography, few catalogs will help you find the individual sections that are incorporated within a book. For this type of information you will need to use special indexes.

Poetry Index

Hunting for a half-remembered poem may seem fruitless because you have forgotten the title or where you first saw it. Yet, if you know how to find and use a poetry index you can make your search quickly and effortlessly.

A poetry index lets you gain access to many different collections by giving you the locations in which you can find a particular poem. No poems are printed in the index itself. It is a very useful tool, but one that is underutilized because many people are unaware of its existence. Students will enjoy looking up favorite poems or finding new ones on specific topics once the unusual characteristics of this index are explained to them.

Unfortunately, a poetry index is useful only if a good number of the collections it indexes are available. There is nothing more frustrating than checking citations for the poem you want and finding that the media center or public library has none of the collections cited.

In putting together a poetry index, compilers select a number of anthologies published within a certain range of years, give each anthology a symbol, and place each poem in each collection under its title, its author, one or more subjects, and its first line in one comprehensive index or separate indexes within the book. Next to each title the anthology's symbol is listed so that users will know in which anthology to find each poem.

To allow for the most efficient use, the library purchasing the poetry index should note in pencil next to the listing of books indexed at the front of the volume how many of those collections it actually owns. If the call number is also placed next to the titles, anyone can find the anthology needed without any problems.

Many of these indexes are compiled specifically using collections for children and young people. *Index to Poetry for Children and Young People, 1970–1975*, compiled by John E. Brewton, G. Meredith Blackburn III, and Lorraine A. Blackburn (H. W. Wilson, 1978) indexes 110 collections published between 1970 and 1975, containing over 10,000 poems listed under 2,000 subjects. In this instance, all the listings (author, title, first line, and subject) are together in one 469-page alphabetical index. The key to symbols for the books indexed is at the front of the book. This is the fifth index compiled by John Brewton for H. W. Wilson—the first one was published in 1942.

Suppose you need a poem about beavers. Turn to "Beavers" in the comprehensive index of the Brewton work and you will find two poems listed:

"The Beaver" by Jack Prelutsky in PrT, which stands for *Toucans Two and Other Poems* by Jack Prelutsky (Macmillan, 1970), and

"The Beaver's Lesson" from "The Hunting of the Snark" in JoA-4 which is an *Anthology of Children's Literature*, 4th revised edition, edited by E. Johnson and others (Houghton Mifflin, 1970).

If either of the collections mentioned is available in your media center or public library, you will have no trouble finding the poems.

A different index is *Granger's Index to Poetry*, 7th edition, edited by William Jones Smith and William F. Bernhardt for Columbia University Press, 1982, which covers anthologies published from 1970 through 1981. *Granger's* has been a standard reference work since 1904 when the first edition compiled by Edith Granger was published. This 7th edition indexes 248 volumes. The key to symbols comes first, followed by a combined title and first line index of 952 pages, a three-column-per-page author index of 214 pages, and a subject index of 160 pages.

Once you have looked over the available poetry indexes and tried to find a specific poem, or something on a particular subject, or different poems by a favorite author, you will feel more at ease demonstrating the usefulness of this tool to your students. They, in turn, will learn a valuable skill that will help them throughout their schooling and on into adulthood.

Collective Biography Index

Students often need information on a famous person from a source other than an encyclopedia. Often they don't have to read a whole biography or the person they are seeking has not been the subject of a full-length biography. In this case, where can they turn? Most media centers have available a variety of collective biographies (books discussing groups of people in a specific field such as scientists, baseball pitchers, presidents, ice skating champions, and so forth, devoting several pages or a chapter to each person). The problem is, how do you know who is covered where without going through each book individually?

A simple way to find out is by using a book such as an *Index to Young Readers' Collective Biographies* by Judith Silverman (2nd edition, R. R. Bowker, 1975). This book lists over 5,800 people appearing in 720 collective biographies both alphabetically (from Hank Aaron to Vladimir K. Zworykin) and then by subject, giving the fields in which they belong (from Abolitionists to Zoologists). At the end of the book is an "Indexed Books by Title" section listing all the notables presented in each book. A "Key to Symbols" at the beginning of the volumes gives the three- or four-letter symbols that stand for specific titles and are used in the two main listings. If your media center or public library contains such an index and the list has been checked against its holdings, the book is much more valuable than if you must look up each reference in the card catalog when it appears to see whether or not the book is one that the library owns.

This index is relatively easy to use and the technique is similar to the one used with the poetry index. Suppose you want to find out where to get information on Sir Edmund Hillary, the New Zealand mountain climber. The first step is to look in the alphabetical listing under "Hillary." There you will find five listings: BAB; COLA; KEH; MOB; PRC. You next turn to the front of the book to the "Key to Symbols." The BAB refers to Bernadine Bailey's *Famous Modern Explorers* (Dodd, 1963). The COLA denotes Joseph Cottler and Haym Jaffe's *More Heroes of Civilization* (Little, 1969). KEH stands for Colman Kerr's *Great Adventurers* (Follett, 1967), while MOB is Patrick Moore's *Exploring the World* (Watts, 1966). PRC is Patrick Pringle's *They Were the First* (Roy, 1965). If the symbols have been checked to denote those available in the media center, you will know at once if any of these volumes are in the collection. Otherwise you will have to check the card catalog to get that information. If you find any of the titles you need only look at the table of contents to see on which pages to find the information about Sir Edmund Hillary.

Students who are sports fans will be especially attracted to collective biographies and to this index which will let them find more about their favorite athletes. The index is also helpful when you assign research on people associated with the subject matter you are teaching. Thus, when all the full-length biographies have been borrowed, there is still another source for finding material in the collective biography section.

TEACHING UNIT 1: INTRODUCING THE POETRY INDEX

Check the reference collection of your media center for a poetry index. If there is a choice, use the one with the most recent copyright date. Turn to the page entitled "Key to Symbols for Books Indexed." You should find a penciled-in check mark and/or a call number of those anthologies listed that the media center owns.

If no one has marked the index previously you will have to do it yourself or give the task to a few of the better students in grades 6 to 8. Working directly with the card catalog will improve their skills, so it is not a waste of time for them to do this.

Instruct those doing the job to sit down in front of the card catalog with a pencil and open the poetry index to the "Key to Symbols for Books Indexed." Have them write the call number of the books owned by the media center next to the titles listed in the index. Since the list is alphabetical by author, the job proceeds very systematically. Once this is done, it is simple to tell which volumes referred to in the poetry index are actually available and where they are located.

Use a little creativity to tie this lesson in with a regular class activity. For example, if your class is learning to do calligraphy as an enrichment project, have students write poems as their culminating activity.

Take the class to the media center or bring your examples to your room. You might be using the *Index to Poetry for Children and Young People, 1970–1975,* compiled by John E. Brewton and others (Wilson, 1978). If several older poetry index volumes are available, distribute them, too, so that students can get an idea of the format. An opaque projector can be used to show students a page from the index. If that is not available pass the index around frequently.

You will have to tell students what a poetry index does. This will probably be the first time they are faced with an index that does not refer them to a page in only one book or volume. Therefore, explain that a poetry index helps them gain access to the collection of poetry anthologies in the media center, and that no poems are printed in the index; only their location is given.

Show students that an individual poem in a collection is alphabetically listed by its author, title, subject line, or first line. Special features will also need to be called to the students' attention. Mention that the authors' full names and the first word of titles and subject headings are all in boldface type. Point out that the first lines of poems are enclosed in quotation marks and that they have their first words printed in boldface type.

Using the Index:

Finding Poems Arranged by Author: To give your students an example of how to locate poems arranged by author, turn to the listing under Silverstein, Shel. There you will find approximately two-and-a-half columns of his poems arranged alphabetically by their titles.

If no one in the group asks about the three or four code letters after each title, call the letters to their attention. Explain that they inform a person about which anthology contains a particular poem.

Turn to the page titled "Key to Symbols for Books Indexed" where students will find that the letters SiW stand for *Where the Sidewalk Ends* by Shel Silverstein (Harper and Row, 1974) and that the letters CoOh stand for *Oh, How Silly* by William Cole (Viking, 1972). If you have marked your index with call numbers, students will know where to find these books if they are in the collection.

You can then go to the shelf and remove these books or you may show them the ones you brought to class. Read a few more titles aloud and send one or two students to find them. When they return ask them to turn to a poem by Shel Silverstein.

These students will find they have yet another step to follow—they must check the anthology index under the author's name to find the page on which the poem is printed.

Finding Poems Arranged by Title: To demonstrate how to find poems that are listed by title, select a poem with which most students are familiar, such as "Arithmetic." Ask someone to locate the title in the index and to read aloud the name of the author and the name of the anthology in which this poem can be found.

Students will find that two anthologies are listed: SaT, which is Carl Sandburg's own *Sandburg Treasury: Prose and Poetry* (Harcourt, 1970), and MaFw, which is David MacKay's *Flock of Words* (Harcourt, 1970). Again, students will have to use the indexes of the anthologies to find the pages on which the poems are printed.

Finding Poems Arranged by Subject: Students will probably find it most useful to locate poems that are arranged by subject. To demonstrate how they can do this, turn to a subject that lists many books in your school's collection. Have some students study the titles until they find something they would like to read.

Then have the students locate the book on the shelves, bring it back, and show it to the rest of the class. Make sure they can find the poem in the anthology by using the index or the table of contents.

If you have other indexes this is a good time to have the students look at them. Point out any differences between the indexes and make sure that the class has grasped the essentials of finding special poems.

Conclude the lesson by devising an activity that will combine the students' newly acquired skill with their ability to do calligraphy. Display their work on a bulletin board.

TEACHING UNIT 2: BIOGRAPHIES IN BRIEF

The reasons for authoring a book that includes the lives of several famous people rather than writing a full-length biography vary. The subjects may be chosen to show different paths to similar careers, to illustrate common strengths or virtues, to provide brief overviews of very famous people for those who do not have time to read many full-length works, or to record the life histories of the not-so-famous, which might not otherwise be available.

Students often are unaware that these collective biographies exist. Even when they know the books are there, it does not follow that they can find the lives of those they seek. By teaching students in fifth grade and above how to locate a biography within a volume of collective biographies you will make them aware of resources they may never have found on their own.

Launch this learning center before you assign any biographical readings. For example, when doing a science unit on electricity you may want students to learn about those who contributed to its discovery and use. Full-length biographies are too time-consuming for them to read under the circumstances and many of these people have not been the subject of long works. Collective biographies are the ideal solution.

Setting up the center will take little time and almost no space. Once your students are accustomed to using *Index to Young Readers' Collective Biographies*, they will have a ready source for enriching their study in many subject areas.

Note that the questions and answers used on these cards are based on the *second* edition of the Silverman index. There is also a third edition published in 1979 which includes all the titles in the second edition plus an additional 222 books. Since you may have access to any one of the three editions be aware that your answer key may have to be changed accordingly.

Objective:

At the conclusion of this unit students will be able to:

- use the symbols to identify the titles of biography collections indexed
- use the listings for general information about the lives of the people indexed
- locate biographies by category

Materials:

> 8 pieces of 6″ × 9″ posterboard
>
> clear self-stick vinyl
>
> 9″ × 12″ manila envelope
>
> felt markers
>
> tape
>
> scissors

Preparation:

1. Copy the two instruction cards (Figures 9-1 and 9-2) and the four task cards (Figure 9-3) onto posterboard. Cover with self-stick vinyl.
2. Use the two remaining pieces of posterboard for an answer key (Figure 9-4).
3. Cut the manila envelope to make a pocket with a 4″ front.
4. Print "BIOGRAPHIES IN BRIEF" on the pocket.
5. Place the task cards and the instruction cards inside the pocket.
6. Attach the envelope to a wall or a bulletin board.

LEARNING CENTER: THE VERSE SEARCH

Set up a year-long poetry learning center to reinforce students' skills. Call it "The Verse Search" and have cards that ask them to complete the following activities:

- Given the first line of a poem, find the last line.
- Given the title of a poem, find the first line.
- Given an author, find the first four lines of a poem written by that poet.
- Given a subject, find either the whole poem if it is short, or the first verse.

For the first two activities you will have to research the answers possible. For the last two activities you can check the accuracy of the responses by looking at the results.

Change the subject in the learning center to reflect the changing of seasons. Students will then gain an even better understanding of the purpose and usefulness of a poetry index.

Figure 9-1.

Instruction card — 1

TWO DEFINITIONS

    1. BIOGRAPHY IS THE STORY OF SOMEONE'S LIFE

    2. COLLECTIVE BIOGRAPHY IS ONE BOOK WITH SEVERAL BIOGRAPHIES

TWO LOCATIONS

    1. BIOGRAPHY IS GIVEN A CALL NUMBER OF "B" AND THE NAME OF THE PERSON THE BIOGRAPHY IS ABOUT

EXAMPLE
```
  B
ADAMS
```
  OR SOMETIMES
```
 B
ADA
```

    2. COLLECTIVE BIOGRAPHY IS USUALLY FOUND IN 920. THE LETTERS UNDERNEATH ARE THE FIRST LETTERS OF THE AUTHOR'S LAST NAME

EXAMPLE
```
920
YOS
```

Figure 9-2.

Instruction card — 2

FINDING COLLECTIVE BIOGRAPHIES
USING

AN <u>INDEX TO YOUNG READERS'
COLLECTIVE BIOGRAPHIES</u>

1. LOOK AT THE BOOK

2. TURN TO -- BOTH "KEYS"
   SECTION I
   SECTION II
   AND BOTH INDEXES

3. BECOME FAMILIAR WITH THE WAY THE
   BOOK IS ARRANGED

4. ANSWER THE 4 TASK CARD
   QUESTIONS

Figure 9-3.

Task Card 1

1. LET SUE WED ROB — What four books are indicated by those symbols? Give authors and titles.
2. What was the occupation of Oliver Wendell Holmes, Jr.?
3. What is the real name of Mata Hari and what two occupations are listed for her.
4. What dates are given for Stephen, King of England?

Task Card 2

1. If you are looking for a biography of Edward Teach, under what heading should you look?
2. Under what heading are biographies of Leonardo da Vinci listed?
3. Frederick North, a key figure in the history of the U.S. Revolutionary War, held two noble titles. What were they?
4. Which of the three books listed on Albert Bruce Sabin contains the *least* information? How do you know?

Task Card 3

1. Name a Dutch botanist listed in the *Index*.
2. If you are looking for information on "Farmers," under what heading would you check?
3. In addition to those listed under "Explorers and Discoverers," what other headings would give biographies of explorers?
4. How many Chinese emperors have biographies listed?

Task Card 4

1. Look under a nationality that is part of your ethnic background and name three people who have biographies listed.
2. Check under "Immigrants to U.S." and find the section listing people with your ethnic background. Name two.
3. Select a career you might consider for yourself and find biographies of two people in that field.
4. You are planning a major report on "Cowboys and Indians" and are looking for biographies that will add to your report. What headings will prove helpful?

Figure 9-4.

Answers to the Task Cards

Card 1

1. LET — Levitan, Tina. *The Laureates: Jewish Winners of the Nobel Prize*
   SUE — Sullivan, Navin. *Pioneer Astonomers*
   WED — Weisberger, Bernard A. *Captains of Industry*
   ROB — Robinson, Ray. *The Greatest Yankees of Them All*
2. Supreme Court Justice
3. Gertrud Margarete Zelle — Dutch dancer/spy
4. 1097?–1154

Card 2

1. Blackbeard
2. Leonardo da Vinci (under "L")
3. Second Earl of Guilford and Eighth Baron North
4. CHE — Caroline A. Chandler's *Famous Men of Medicine.* The dagger symbol indicates that it has less than a full page of information.

Card 3

1. Beijerinck, Martinus Willem
2. Agriculturists
3. Astronauts; Geographers; Pioneers and Frontiersmen; Travelers; Underwater Explorers
4. Seven

Card 4

1–3. Answers will vary
4. Six headings: Cowboys; Law Enforcers; Pioneers and Frontiersmen; Ranchers and Cattlemen; Indians, American; Indian Captives

Chapter 10

THE RESEARCH PAPER

BACKGROUND INFORMATION

Research papers were once exclusively a requirement of college courses. Term papers were assigned in high school and occasionally in junior high, and elementary school students prepared reports. Today, children routinely do research papers in the fourth grade and many begin as early as second grade. In essence, the finished product is similar to the report of yesteryear, but the name change is not merely an attempt to enhance the importance of an elementary school assignment. It represents a shift in the way students are required to organize and present the paper. From the earliest grades students mimic in a simplified form the process that they will repeat and expand throughout their school years.

The research paper is a chance for students to apply all their library skills in one project. They need to use encyclopedias and the card catalog, understand shelf arrangement, and consult indexes. Depending on the topic, they may need more specialized reference books as well.

In order to present the information in final written form students must know how to prepare a bibliographic citation, write an outline, take notes, and write a rough draft and final copy. The combination of reading, writing, and information-gathering skills into one final product makes the assignment of a research paper an ideal method for helping students put these skills to a practical purpose.

The teaching units in this chapter are designed to instruct students in the library skills they need beyond those covered in the previous chapters. Before you assign a paper make sure that the class understands the basic information-gathering process.

As you help students learn how to assemble a research paper it is important for you to train them in time management as well. Invariably, students underestimate the time it takes to translate notes into a rough draft. They also assume they can make the final copy in one or two nights. Physically, they can rarely transcribe more than four pages in a night if they are to pay attention to spelling and neatness. Too often, time pressure causes them to leave out words and even whole sentences. The end product is a disappointment because so much effort invested should produce a better-looking result. Even students using word processors at home need the extra time to properly proofread their work. The solution is to build in deadlines along the way. Figure 10-1 is one way to help

Figure 10-1.

Student Work Record Sheet

Name _____ Room No. _____

Topic selected _____

_____

_____ Approved on: _____
                                                      Date

ASSIGNMENT	DATE DUE	DATE COMPLETED	APPROVED
1. Preliminary research (encyclopedias)			
2. Rough outline			
3. Bibliographic search (card catalog and shelves)			
4. Notes			
5. Formal outline			
6. Rough draft			
7. Bibliography			
8. Final paper			

students pace themselves. Simplify the form for use in lower grades and you will get students started on the proper technique for managing long-term projects. If you guide them through all the steps, the completed paper will prove to be worth all their time and yours as well.

The following three books are helpful for providing students with more detailed descriptions on how to write papers. They are listed in ascending order of difficulty:

James, Elizabeth and Carol Barkin. *How to Write a Great School Report.* Lothrop, 1983, 79 pp.

James, Elizabeth and Carol Barkin. *How to Write a Term Paper.* Lothrop, 1980, 94 pp.

Turabian, Kate L. *Student's Guide for Writing College Papers.* 3rd ed. University of Chicago Press, 1976, 256 pp.

TEACHING UNIT 1: PREPARING A BIBLIOGRAPHY

Research papers must include a bibliography. In the lower grades students use few sources and can prepare simple citations to become accustomed to the requirement and the process. (See Chapter 4's Teaching Unit 1, or use Figure 10-2.) Students in grades 5 to 8 are expected to use more sources and need to learn to prepare a more sophisticated bibliographic citation.

Surprisingly, there is no standard bibliographic form although certain constants do exist:

- The list is always arranged in alphabetical order.
- When the author's name is known, citations begin with the author's last name followed by a comma and then the first name.
- When the author is unknown, entry is by the title of the article or book.
- Titles of books and long works are underlined.
- Articles in encyclopedias and magazines are put in quotation marks.
- Second and succeeding lines of the entry are indented.
- Publisher and copyright date are always included.

Punctuation marks are used to separate author from title and title from publisher but they are not standard. The place of publication is not always given. Pages are given when only a portion of the text is used. Even the titles cited at the end of the background information do not agree in all aspects in their bibliographic citations.

The important lesson students should learn is to follow a required format. You can establish how your citations should be written, that is, the form they should use for the year. In essence, this is similar to college professors informing their classes what particular style manuals should be followed in preparing papers. It is helpful to students if all the teachers in a school or a district can agree on one style of citations.

Handing out copies of the bibliographic form you require is not enough. Students find it difficult to translate their sources into proper citations. An intensive period of drilling, separate from the actual research paper, is helpful. If you teach this unit at the beginning of the year your students will have a sound

Figure 10-2.

BIBLIOGRAPHY FORM
(second grade)

For a BOOK

Author's last name, author's first name. *Title.*

Example:

Zim, Herbert S. *The Great Whales.*

For an ENCYCLOPEDIA

"Title of Article," *Name of encyclopedia*, volume number, pages.

Example:

"Whales," *The New Book of Knowledge*, v 20, 147–158.

For a MAGAZINE ARTICLE

"Title of Article," *Name of magazine*, date, pages.

Example:

"An Incredible Feasting of Whales," *National Geographic*, January 1984, 88–93.

---

base for their research projects throughout the year. You may choose to limit the unit to print materials, but in today's multi-media world it is advantageous to alert students to the feasibility of obtaining information from nonprint sources as well.

Objectives:

At the conclusion of this unit students will be able to:

- extract bibliographic data from a variety of sources
- write a bibliographic citation in acceptable form
- arrange citations in alphabetical order
- prepare a bibliography on a given topic (optional)

Preparation:

1. Make a ditto master (or stencil if you want to use this over several years) of the bibliographic form of your choice or use Figure 10-2 or Figure 10-3.
2. Run off sufficient copies for the entire class.
3. Have a sample of each of the different types of sources students will learn to cite.
4. Have many examples of each source for student use. If you have a paperback collection in your class, students can use these to prepare their citation of books. Avoid textbooks because they usually have editors and multiple authors, which present problems for beginners. There are often classroom encyclopedias available for that segment of the bibliographic citations. You may need to borrow another set so that each student can have a volume. Magazines can be obtained from the media center or brought from home. Obviously, study prints and filmstrips can only be included if you have samples for students to use.

Figure 10-3.

BIBLIOGRAPHIC FORM

For a BOOK

Author. Title. City of publication: Publisher, Copyright.

Example:

Sperry, Armstrong. *All About the Arctic and the Antarctic.* New York: Random House, 1975.

For a book with two authors:

Author (last name, first name) and second author (first name, last name). Title. City of publication: Publisher, Copyright.

Example:

Murphy, Barbara Beasley and Norman Baker. *Thor Heyerdahl and the Reed Boat Ra.* New York: Lippincott, 1974.

For an ENCYCLOPEDIA ARTICLE

"Article." Encyclopedia name. Most recent copyright. Volume number, Pages.

Example:

"Ethiopia." *The New Book of Knowledge.* 1978. 5, 296–301.

For a MAGAZINE ARTICLE

Author (if known). "Article," *Magazine.* Date, Page.

Example:

Cumming, Joseph E., Jr. "Terrible Twists of Fate," *National Wildlife.* June/July 1980, p. 29.

For a FILMSTRIP

"Title of Strip," *Title of Series* (filmstrip). Producer, Copyright (if available).

Example:

"Keeping Well," *Good Health Habits* (filmstrip). Coronet Instructional Media, 1968.

For a STUDY PRINT

"Title of Print," Name of Series (study print). Producer, Copyright.

Example:

"Rain," *Weather Phenomena* (study print). Instructional Aids, 1968.

---

5. Have several packs of 3″ × 5″ cards—you need 30 to 50 per student. If they are unavailable, lined paper cut in half will do.

Optional:

6. Prepare a list of topics that will be covered during the year. Include anticipated units in science, social studies, health, and holidays.

Procedure:

1. Discuss with the class the need for bibliographic citations in research papers.

2. Distribute the form sheet.

3. Make sure students know where to find the required information. For example, some know where the copyright date is given; others do not.

4. Show the book you have chosen as a sample and go through the process of writing the citation. Have students tell you where to look for each piece of information that you need. Be sure they understand what to do if a book has two authors. (In the form shown, the second author's name is *not* inverted.) Call their attention to the way the bibliographic citations are indented. You can describe this as the opposite of paragraph form. Instead of the first line being indented and subsequent lines starting at the left hand margin, the first line of a bibliographic entry begins at the margin and subsequent lines are indented.

5. Distribute 10 3″ × 5″ cards or 10 half sheets of paper to each student.

6. Instruct the class to prepare citations for 10 books, one to a card or piece of paper.

7. Students are to alphabetize the completed citations and transcribe them onto a sheet of paper or papers which you will collect.

8. The next day go through the steps for preparing a citation for an encyclopedia article. Students need to be told that the copyright date they should use is the most recent one given. Remind them that the "v" for volume is always in lower case. Pagination in encyclopedias may cause a problem. Publishers' policies of continuous revision mean that some articles are expanded from one edition to the next. Rather than change all page numbers, added pages are indicated by letter supplements to the page numbers. You may find page 331 followed by 331a, 331b, and so on. It is quite possible for the citation to show that an article runs from pp. 250–250h.

9. Distribute 10 blank cards or papers. Each student begins with a volume of an encyclopedia and selects an article within it. You can have them use two articles from one volume and then switch encyclopedias with someone else. Have students alphabetize citations and prepare the list as before.

10. On the third day go through the process for writing citations for magazine articles. The only difficulty usually encountered is the inconsistency of authorship. Sometimes there is an author; sometimes there isn't. In the form shown no volume number is required for magazines. Although the volume number is called for in many recommended citations students do not need to locate it at this time.

11. Distribute 10 blank cards or papers and hand out the magazines. Again have students alphabetize citations and prepare their lists.

12. If you have filmstrips and study prints available continue the unit on subsequent days, distributing more cards or papers for student use. Finding the copyright date on filmstrips is sometimes difficult. Usually the frame after the title frame includes the information, occasionally in the form of a Roman numeral as the date. If the filmstrip set has a teacher's guide you may find the copyright date there.

Optional:

13. Now that students have a solid foundation in writing bibliographic citations, have them prepare one. Bibliographies of units that are to be studied

during the year are excellent choices. This will prepare students for future assignments.

14. Assign each student a topic to search. Require three to five books, two encyclopedia articles, three magazine articles, and one filmstrip or study print, if they were included.

15. Make blank cards or sheets of paper available as needed.

16. Students are to hand in a properly alphabetized list of bibliographic citations using correct forms under their topic.

TEACHING UNIT 2: THE FIRST RESEARCH PAPER

For second graders, the introduction to research explained in Chapter 4's Teaching Unit 1 may be more than adequate. If the class becomes enthusiastic about the process, however, expand on their experience with this teaching unit. If you want more control, instead of giving each student a separate topic, prepare a single research paper and have students work on the parts as individuals or in groups. For example, you can do a paper on "Eagles." Work can be assigned on the following subtopics:

• What do eagles look like?

• Where in the world are eagles found?

• How do they build their nests and raise their young?

• What do eagles eat? How do they locate and get food?

• What are some different types of eagles?

• Why is the eagle the national bird of the United States?

• What are the ecological problems faced by eagles?

Each group prepares its own bibliography and the lists are combined by one group when the report is put together. One or two students draw the cover design while two other students put the parts together in logical order (this can be a class decision) and write the table of contents. The completed research paper can be kept on display for class visitors to see.

Topics for students to research should be closely related to the curriculum. If you are studying animals in science have students select one animal for their paper. Try to keep them from choosing a domestic animal because they have been developed into a large number of breeds so their size and coloring vary greatly within the species and their habitat is among humans. Although you could require the topic to be narrowed down to one breed, there may still be too little information available at this level.

Objectives:

At the conclusion of this unit students will be able to:

• formulate a plan for beginning a research paper

• locate material on a given topic

• take notes from their reading

• prepare a bibliography of sources used according to the form required

• write a rough draft

• complete a research paper with all required parts

Materials:

> copy of the bibliographic form students are to use (fourth graders might use the more complex form)
>
> copy of the instructions for the paper (Figure 10-4)
>
> one large sheet of construction paper (18″ × 24″) for each student
>
> lined paper

Preparation:

1. Run off copies of both forms.
2. Prepare a list of topics from which students may choose the subject of their report.

Figure 10-4.

RESEARCH PAPER
FORM TO FOLLOW

1. COVER

   Use oaktag or construction paper.
   Include a picture, the title, and your name.

2. TITLE PAGE

   Print the title in the center of the page.
   Put your name and the date in the bottom right-hand corner.

   > *Title*
   >
   > Name
   > Date

3. TABLE OF CONTENTS

   List all sections of your paper, including the bibliography and give the page where they begin.

4. THE PAPER

   Use your best handwriting. Be sure to watch your margins.
   Number all pages in the upper right-hand corner.

5. BIBLIOGRAPHY

   Follow the form you were given. Be sure to include all the books you used.
   List them in alphabetical order.

Procedure:

1. Discuss the overall topics (such as animals) with the class, pointing out that while their science text is very general, individual animals have special

characteristics. Inform them that you will give them a chance to learn more about some animals. At this grade level (2–4) your news should be greeted with enthusiasm.

2. Present your list of topics and have students make their selections. One or two will ask if they can investigate a topic not on your list. Unless there is a good reason not to (such as researching a domestic animal as explained earlier), let them have the subject of their choice.

3. Prepare students for research. The lesson should be given a few days before they go to the media center or public library.

   Words to Work With. Have students make lists of words associated with their topic. They need to think of their subject as singular or plural. It helps if they can come up with more general words for their topic. For example, whales are mammals. They are also sea creatures (MARINE ANIMALS in the card catalog). Lions are mammals, too, but they are also cats. Preparing the list helps them think about their subject and suggest possible entry words for research.

   Questions to Answer. Each student prepares a list of five or six questions to be answered by the research paper. (There were seven in the suggested class paper on eagles.) These questions structure the research and help maintain continuity in the organization of the final paper. The same thought processes involved in preparing the questions will be used by upper grade students to formulate an outline as their preparation to research. As an added benefit, the question approach reduces and often eliminates copying from a book. When students locate answers, they write their notes in terms of the question rather than lifting the language entirely from the source. Have them add as a final query, "What are some interesting facts about _____ (topic)?" to allow for some unexpected discoveries during research. Distribute six or seven sheets of paper per student so they can write their questions one on each sheet.

   Getting Organized/Staying Neat. Distribute large sheets of construction paper to each student. Have them fold the 24″ width in half to make a booklet. Open the booklet and fold the bottom up 4″ to make a folder. (See the illustration.) On the outside of the folder they are to write their name, the topic they are researching, and the phrase "Work Papers." The list of words they prepared is to be kept in the folder along with the papers containing their questions. Have them hand in the folders with their final papers.

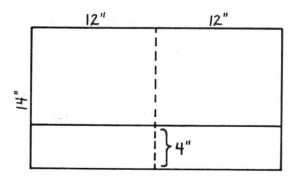

4. The day before students go to the media center or public library, prepare them for the actual process of searching and notetaking.

Likely Locations to Start. Have students take out their work papers folders. Ask where they plan to look for the answers to their questions. Encyclopedias are one of the first sources mentioned. Students beyond grade 2 should be reminded again about the index volume. The card catalog is next, and it is assumed they have had enough experience so they can use this tool. If they have had the appropriate teaching unit in Chapter 7 they may know about the magazine index as well. Remind them to use their list of words as they consult these tools.

Bibliography Begins Immediately. Ask the class what they will do when they find an answer to one of their questions. The usual response is that they will write it down or take notes. Caution them to write the bibliographic information first. If the citation is not copied immediately students tend to forget it, and then must search frantically for it at a later date. Distribute the form you prepared and review it. Students should keep this form in their folders also.

Painless Notetaking. Students copy information not because they willfully wish to plagiarize but because they are unsure of themselves. Explain that they should only write down the answers to the questions they have and not worry about other information. If they can't read something, they should ask an adult or older student to read that section to them. They should never use information they don't understand. Once they know they have an answer to a question and have copied the bibliographic information, they remove the sheet containing that question from their folders and write the answer as briefly as possible. Full sentences are to be avoided. It helps if they number their answers. For example, for the question "What do eagles look like?" they may make the following notes:

a. eyes in front, not at side like other birds

b. strong claws called talons

Skipping lines between notes helps keep information orderly.

Inform students that you will be looking at their notes in the next two or three days. At that time you can see how well they are doing and make suggestions. Of course, if you can take the class to the media center and work with them as they begin the project the results will be even better. Students tend to over-write their notes. Learning to be succinct takes time and practice. Try to evaluate their progress by looking for their growing abilities to keep notes brief, limited to one idea, and related to the question. If you can go to the media center schedule several periods over a period of two weeks to allow students to work on their papers. Be sure they keep their bibliographies up to date.

5. Once students are well into notetaking, set the due date for their rough drafts and hand out the instructions for the final paper (Figure 10-4). At this grade level students need your corrections in order to prepare a final copy. The rough draft does not need a cover or table of contents but should include a title page and the bibliography. No matter how often you have explained the need for arranging the latter in alphabetical order or told the fourth graders how to indent, students make errors.

6. The final paper should be due one week after the rough drafts are returned. Students need time to recopy and make a neat cover. Display the final papers in the hall. If you can, time the project to be completed shortly before a parent conference period or visitation time. In this way, you will give the children the adult appreciation such an effort deserves.

TEACHING UNIT 3: THE RESEARCH PAPER

In the intermediate grades 5–8, students are capable of writing research papers of ten or more pages. They build on their previously acquired skills: using reference tools, taking notes, and organizing their papers much as they did in the lower grades. The quality of the writing improves as does the information itself, since they can read books with more detailed information. The new skill to be learned at this level is outlining coupled with notetaking on $3'' \times 5''$ cards. For some fifth graders the cards are still too difficult, so you can have them use the separate sheet of paper method described in Teaching Unit 2. Instead of questions heading the papers, they should use the subdivisions of their outline. Before you begin the unit accustom students to preparing outlines by reviewing Teaching Unit 3 in Chapter 4.

The major problem that students encounter arises from the need to integrate information from many sources. Some facts they find are repetitive, others are contradictory, and still others overlap. Using an outline and the $3'' \times 5''$ cards will help students control the data, but you will need to supervise their work regularly. It can prove overwhelming.

Students still need you to assign deadlines within the overall project. They cannot cope with an assignment that is due in five to six weeks unless the various steps to be completed are checked by you at scheduled intervals. A typical plan might require the rough outline to be due three days after the topic is approved and the preliminary bibliographic search to be completed approximately one week later. Three weeks is the maximum time needed for notetaking. This allows time for you to teach a lesson, correct the students' attempts, and monitor progress along the way. The remaining week and a half is for completing the formal outline if you want it, writing the rough draft, and doing the final paper. You must have a due date for the rough draft or students will skip that step. This requirement also solves the problem of whether or not to permit parents to type the final paper. If you have seen the rough draft, you know how the student is doing and can easily determine if the final product is mainly the work of the parents.

This teaching unit does not include a lesson on footnotes, which are normally not required until high school. In the lower grades it is not advisable to suggest ways of copying directly from a source. You work too hard to teach students how to paraphrase and restate, and the concept of footnotes is apt to confuse. If you really want a bright group of seventh or eighth graders to learn the rudiments of footnotes, use one of the texts suggested in the background information, select a simple form, and give students their own copy.

Objectives:

At the end of this unit students will be able to prepare a complete research paper:

- using a variety of sources
- written in their own words
- following an organized plan
- including a bibliography

Materials:

copy of the bibliographic form

copy of the student worksheet

transparency of one or two paragraphs from the textbook

overhead projector

acetate sheets

transparency markers

Procedure:

1. Hand out copies of the worksheet. Schedule the first and final due dates. Add interim due dates as the project continues.
2. Have students select a topic. Try to help them avoid one that is too broad or too narrow.
3. To prepare their rough outline, students can consult encyclopedias. This gives them an overview of the topic and may encourage some of them to expand or contract their subject. In some cases, students may decide to alter their topic as a result of this preliminary exploration.

   Extra sets of encyclopedias are vital. Despite your efforts to keep the topics diverse, there will be much overlapping. Students may share a book if there is no other recourse.

   The major points to be covered in this lesson include the following:

- Students should begin their research plan only after they are familiar with the scope of their topic.
- Encyclopedias provide an overall view of a subject.
- The index to an encyclopedia should always be consulted first to be sure that all possible supporting areas will be covered.
- Cross-references at the end of the articles give further clues to related subjects, which may be helpful avenues to explore or may be even more interesting than the original topic.
- In an encyclopedia, the use of different type sizes and the positioning of headings give an outline of the article.
- Students may or may not take notes from the encyclopedia, but they must record information for their bibliography.

If you taught outlining earlier in the year, you may want to remind students of the proper form. In this first draft the outline should conform to the numbering system commonly used, that is, Roman numerals for the major headings, capital letters for prime subdivisions, and Arabic numerals for subsets as in the following:

> I. Major Heading
>   A. Prime Subdivision
>   B. Prime Subdivision
> II. Major Heading
>   A. Prime Subdivision
>   1. Subset
>   2. Subset
>   B. Prime Subdivision

Remind them that every "I" must have at least a "II" and every "A," a "B." At this stage, the outline should only have Roman numerals and capital letters. Anything further would be premature.

For the rough outline students can use one heading that is a participial phrase and another that is an infinitive phrase or a complete sentence. This draft serves to organize thoughts and enables students to structure their research. Before the rough draft is written the outline must be refined, and at that time, you may want them to use a formal outline.

4. Now that students have a good idea of what they will research, they should start locating available resources. They need to begin with the card catalog and, depending on their topic, possibly a magazine or newspaper index as well. It is helpful if they write their anticipated sources on separate 3" × 5" cards.

5. When they start taking notes, students check off the bibliography card, indicating the source was used and must be listed in the final bibliography. At that time, they will add any bibliographic data (such as pages used) that they did not include in the initial survey of the resources.

Getting to Work. Taking notes is the central activity of a research paper. Students inevitably find it difficult to paraphrase and to select the essential facts from a large body of information. The use of 3" × 5" cards is more than a convenience. It is an aid to paraphrasing.

Using an overhead projector with a prepared transparency, or using an opaque projector, show the class one or two paragraphs from their textbook. On a 3" × 5" card or on an acetate facsimile, prepare an acceptable note. Point out that complete sentences are unnecessary and that words should be changed to keep the note as brief as possible. Since there is not much room on a 3" × 5" card, students will not be able to copy word for word.

Make several more notes based on the transparency. Just list these; it isn't necessary to fit them onto the 3" × 5" shape. Stress the need to keep notes to a single idea. As students acquire information they may complain about duplication. Encourage them to copy anything as long as there is some additional information given. Eventually, the facts will be combined when they prepare their final paper.

Contradictory information can be verified by consulting a third source. Students can also make a note that some sources say, "...." while other sources say "...." Caution them not to use pronouns in notes. "It" is a confusing term when they are writing the paper and are no longer sure what "it" refers to. Proper nouns and unusual words should be carefully printed to avoid spelling errors when the paper is written.

To make the writing of the paper simpler students can add special references to the note cards by putting a code or phrase referring to their rough outline in the upper left-hand corner of their card. The code can be "II.A.," indicating that the note deals with that part of the outline.

In the lower left-hand corner students put the last name of the author and a shortened title to show the source of their note. They can also complete the bibliographic citation (publisher, copyright date, and pages) since they have now used the book or magazine.

Preparing the final outline and getting note cards in order does not take very long but you need to help students get organized. By now, students can see where their research has led and they can polish and refine their rough outlines. Further subdivision, using lower-case letters and circled numbers and letters, can be made.

Once the outline is set and checked the note cards can be assembled according to the code previously placed in the upper right-hand corner. With their outlines complete, students may want to move notes to other locations or assign a more specific code. Note cards are now combined and/or discarded as the structure of the emerging paper dictates. At least ten percent of the cards should be eliminated as the notes are arranged in the final sequence. When all the cards are in order students number them, putting another number in the upper right-hand corner. Thus, if the cards are accidentally dropped they can easily be resequenced.

Finishing the Project. Although the students will most probably write their rough draft at home it is best to give them some idea of how to write it before they begin. Few students prepare a rough draft unless they are compelled to do so, yet no paper has polish without it. First, instruct them to sit down with their completed outline, note cards, and scrap paper. Next, recommend that in writing the rough draft they skip lines so that they will have room to include additions and corrections.

The introductory paragraphs, usually written in the students' own words, present the objective and viewpoint of the paper. The students will be relieved to know that they do not need to recopy their notes into the draft. When they must cite their first note remind them to refer to the number they assigned to that card. For example, ask them to write "Card 1" on their rough draft.

At this time, they should also check the note to see if it needs any corrections in phrasing or spelling. This procedure of correcting the cards and incorporating them into the draft is continued until all the cards are used and the conclusion is written. It is advisable for the students to read their work and to make changes as needed before recopying or typing the paper.

The form of the final bibliography is your decision. The required arrangement may be strictly by alphabetical order; by type of material, such as books, periodicals, nonprint sources, etc.; or by primary and secondary sources. Again, explain the use of inverted indentation for each entry. If typing is required, the class should be told how to space within and between entries.

All that remains to be done is the final paper. Since students have been led through all the basic steps the actual writing is almost an anticlimax. After all, the outlines, note cards, and rough draft are already done.

The students' satisfaction in accomplishing a difficult task and the pride in knowing that the job was well done will be apparent in the completed papers. Because they are made to understand what is required of them, students will be able to master the successive steps.

In the future, they will confidently approach research knowing that they have an understanding of the parts that contribute to the whole. Whether it is for a college assignment or a business need, they will be able to logically gather data.

PART
TWO

Puzzles, Games,
and
Reference Questions

Please note that the following activities originally appeared in various issues of *The School Librarian's Workshop* by Library Learning Resources, Inc., Box 87, Berkeley Heights, New Jersey 07922. © by Hilda K. Weisburg and Ruth Toor.

HAPPY THANKSGIVING DAY

grades 1–3—coordinates with Chapter 1

A simple crossword puzzle for the youngest students carries a holiday message and reviews the basics of library terminology. If you want to use this puzzle with first graders write the answers in random order on the puzzle page before making copies. Second and third graders should be able to solve the puzzle on their own.

Answers to "Happy Thanksgiving Day!"

1. author	5. easy
2. spine	6. card
3. title	7. illustrator
4. fiction	8. biography

A DOT-TO-DOT IN ALPHABETICAL ORDER

grades 3–9—coordinates with Chapter 1

Save this game for Halloween week. Promise students that if they solve the puzzle an appropriate surprise will be revealed. Meanwhile, you can test two skills—arranging things in alphabetical order and following directions—by having students work on this complex dot-to-dot puzzle. Not only must they put a long list of authors' names in alphabetical order, they must also transfer the numbers preceding the names and then follow the dots in that sequence rather than in numerical order!

You can use this pencil game for grade 3, but do it as a class activity. Make a permanent transparency of the list of authors and of the puzzle, then go through it with the class, presenting it as a group lesson about alphabetical order.

Answers to "A Dot-to-Dot in Alphabetical Order"

29. Agle	34. Farley	45. Norton
13. Aiken	23. Field	16. O'Dell
7. Avi	17. Fitzhugh	19. Peck
33. Bach	57. Fleischman	38. Raskin
35. Beatty	15. Gardner	25. Rinkoff
46. Blume	6. Greene	22. Robertson
40. Bond	18. Haywood	5. Sachs
24. Bulla	27. Heide	56. Sharmat
36. Cameron	1. Henry	47. Slobodkin
10. Christopher	49. Hildick	12. Speare
52. Cleary	37. Hurwitz	4. Taylor
44. Coatsworth	39. Key	53. Todd
21. Conford	3. Konigsburg	28. Turkle
4. Curry	20. Lawson	43. Uchida
51. Dahl	31. Lenski	9. Udry
26. DuBois	42. Levitin	2. Van Leeuwen
41. Eager	14. Lindgren	54. White
11. Embry	30. MacGregor	32. Wilder
50. Erickson	55. Mendoza	8. Williams

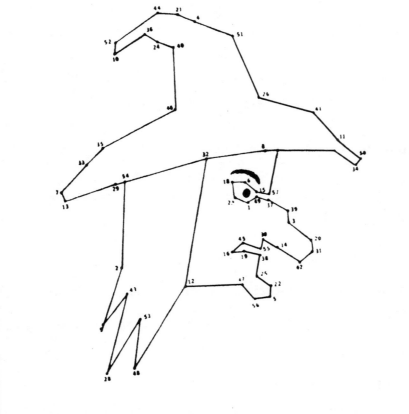

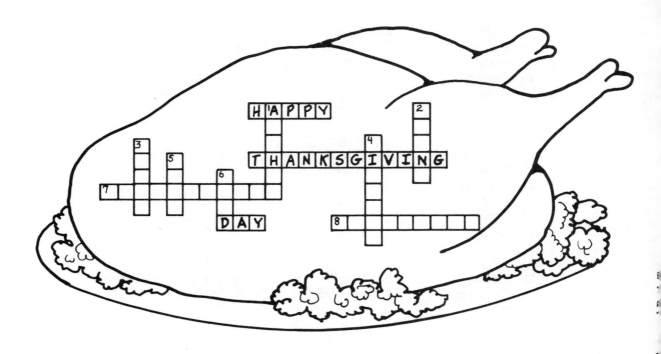

HAPPY THANKSGIVING DAY!

1. A person who writes a book is called the _____.

2. The part of the book that holds the front and back covers together is called the _____ .

3. A book's name is its _____.

4. Books that are not true are called _____.

5. If you have a beginning reader section, the "E" stands for the word _____.

6. When you check out a book, you must write your name on the book _____.

7. A person who draws the pictures for a book is called the _____.

8. A story about a person's life is called a _____.

A DOT-TO-DOT
IN ALPHABETICAL ORDER

Directions: 1. Put the following list of authors in alphabetical order.
2. Write the numbers and names in the spaces provided.
3. Connect the dots in the order in which the numbers now appear.

Example: 7. Avi   29. Agle
13. Aiken   becomes   13. Aiken
29. Agle   7. Avi

Therefore, you will connect the first three dots in this order: number 29 to number 13 to number 7.

TIP: First, make a separate list of all the authors whose names begin with "A." Put those names in alphabetical order and write them in the spaces. Repeat these steps for authors whose names begin with "B," "C," etc.

1. Henry _____
2. Van Leeuwen _____
3. Konigsburg _____
4. Curry _____
5. Sachs _____
6. Greene _____
7. Avi _____
8. Williams _____
9. Udry _____
10. Christopher _____
11. Embry _____
12. Speare _____
13. Aiken _____
14. Lindgren _____
15. Gardner _____
16. O'Dell _____
17. Fitzhugh _____
18. Haywood _____
19. Peck _____
20. Lawson _____
21. Conford _____
22. Robertson _____
23. Field _____
24. Bulla _____
25. Rinkoff _____
26. DuBois _____
27. Heide _____
28. Turkle _____
29. Agle _____

30. MacGregor _____
31. Lenski _____
32. Wilder _____
33. Bach _____
34. Farley _____
35. Beatty _____
36. Cameron _____
37. Hurwitz _____
38. Raskin _____
39. Key _____
40. Bond _____
41. Eager _____
42. Levitin _____
43. Uchida _____
44. Coatsworth _____
45. Norton _____
46. Blume _____
47. Slobodkin _____
48. Taylor _____
49. Hildick _____
50. Erickson _____
51. Dahl _____
52. Cleary _____
53. Todd _____
54. White _____
55. Mendoza _____
56. Sharmat _____
57. Fleischman _____

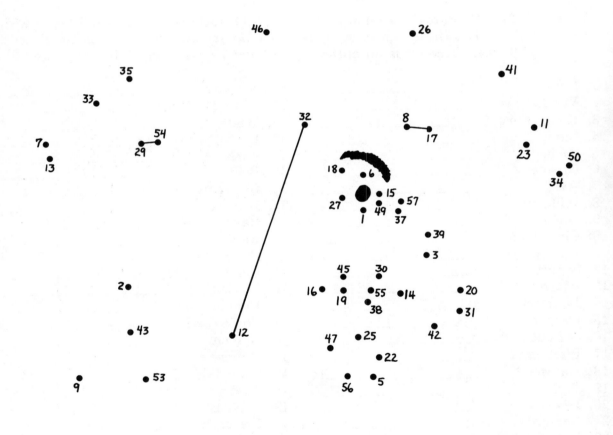

A NONFICTION DOT-TO-DOT
grades 5–8—coordinates with Chapter 1

This pencil game is a double tribute—first to the Brooklyn Bridge in New York and then to those nonfiction authors whose works can be found in virtually all collections serving children and young adults. The puzzle is in three parts. Part 1 is the alphabetical arrangement of authors; Part 2 is the alphabetical arrangement of eleven titles by Irving and Ruth Adler; and Part 3 requires students to name the bridge they made.

You can use the pencil game as the introduction to a unit on nonfiction for fifth grade and up. As a follow-up students can find the first name of the authors included and/or some of the titles they have written. The game can also be used as a brief reference activity on the Brooklyn Bridge. Have students put their names on the completed puzzle and fill in one fact about the bridge below its name. Put all the finished work on display and salute the Brooklyn Bridge.

Answers to "A Nonfiction Dot-to-Dot"

Part 1:

9.	Adler	30.	Nourse
39.	Aliki	8.	Paradis
16.	Asimov	53.	Parish
20.	Beame	4.	Patent
46.	Bendick	33.	Podendorf
12.	Berger	51.	Poole
37.	Bleeker	11.	Pringle
25.	Branley	23.	Rockwell
40.	Carpenter	49.	Schwartz
18.	Cobb	5.	Selsam
43.	Colby	7.	Showers
31.	Cole	21.	Shuttlesworth
13.	Conklin	29.	Silverstein
14.	Earle	1.	Simon
3.	Epstein	10.	Sootin
28.	Farb	41.	Sterling
47.	Freeman	26.	Tunis
50.	Gallant	2.	Weiss
17.	Glubok	36.	White
34.	Goldreich	22.	Wyler
45.	Hofsinde	44.	Zim
24.	Hogner	35.	Zubrowski
48.	Hurd		
27.	Hutchins		
38.	Johnson		
42.	Kettelkamp		
6.	Lauber		
52.	Lavine		
15.	Leeming		
32.	Macauley		
19.	McClung		

Part 2:

H.	*Coal*
C.	*Color in Your Life*
D.	*The Earth's Crust*
I.	*Electricity*
F.	*Evolution*
B.	*Machines*
E.	*Magic House of Numbers*
A.	*Magnets*
G.	*The Story of Light*
J.	*Taste, Touch, and Smell*

Part 3:

This is the Brooklyn Bridge

© 1983 by Hilda K. Weisburg and Ruth Toor

Name _____   Date _____

A NONFICTION DOT-TO-DOT

Directions: This puzzle is in three parts.

Part 1:   1. Put the following list of nonfiction authors in alphabetical order.
          2. Write the numbers and names in the spaces provided.
          3. Connect the dots in the order the numbers now appear.

Example: three authors' names begin with "A"

so	9. Adler	in correct order become:	9. Adler
	16. Asimov		39. Aliki
	39. Aliki		16. Asimov

Therefore, connect the first three dots in this order: 9 to 39 to 16

Part 2   1. Arrange the list of titles by Irving and Ruth Adler in alphabetical order.
         2. Write the letters and titles in the spaces provided.
         3. Connect the dots in the order the letters now appear.

Part 3   Identify the drawing you made. Give its full name.

Clues
Part 1—Authors

1. Simon	_____	28. Farb	_____
2. Weiss	_____	29. Silverstein	_____
3. Epstein	_____	30. Nourse	_____
4. Patent	_____	31. Cole	_____
5. Selsam	_____	32. Macauley	_____
6. Lauber	_____	33. Podendorf	_____
7. Showers	_____	34. Goldreich	_____
8. Paradis	_____	35. Zubrowski	_____
9. Adler	_____	36. White	_____
10. Sootin	_____	37. Bleeker	_____
11. Pringle	_____	38. Johnson	_____
12. Berger	_____	39. Aliki	_____
13. Conklin	_____	40. Carpenter	_____
14. Earle	_____	41. Sterling	_____
15. Leeming	_____	42. Kettelkamp	_____
16. Asimov	_____	43. Colby	_____
17. Glubok	_____	44. Zim	_____
18. Cobb	_____	45. Hofsinde	_____
19. McClung	_____	46. Bendick	_____
20. Beame	_____	47. Freeman	_____
21. Shuttlesworth	_____	48. Hurd	_____
22. Wyler	_____	49. Schwartz	_____
23. Rockwell	_____	50. Gallant	_____
24. Hogner	_____	51. Poole	_____
25. Branley	_____	52. Lavine	_____
26. Tunis	_____	53. Parish	_____
27. Hutchins	_____		

Name _____   **Date** _____

A NONFICTION DOT-TO-DOT

Part 2—Titles

A. *Magnets*

B. *Machines*

C. *Color in Your Life*

D. *The Earth's Crust*

E. *Magic House of Numbers*

F. *Evolution* _____

G. *The Story of Light* _____

H. *Coal* _____

I. *Electricity* _____

J. *Taste, Touch, and* _____
   Smell

Part 3—This is

A DOT-TO-DOT OF SUMMER READING

grades 6–9—coordinates with Chapter 1

Students' love for complex puzzles can be used to reinforce alphabetizing skills while providing a suggested list of authors for middle and junior high school readers. This pencil game is fairly difficult and should provide a challenge. As their reward for a correct solution, students will find a rose in the dot-to-dot game. Save this as a June reading list, as the rose is also the flower associated with June.

Answers to "A Dot-to-Dot of Summer Reading"

29. Alexander, Lloyd	11. Gault, William Campbell	2. O'Brien, Robert
20. Armstrong, Robert	6. Girion, Barbara	35. Orgel, Doris
25. Arthur, Ruth M.	19. Hautzig, Deborah	32. Peyton, K.M.
7. Bethancourt, T. Ernesto	8. Hinton, S.E.	14. Rockwell, Thomas
17. Bridgers, Sue Ellen	22. Keller, Beverly	23. Rodgers, Mary
24. Collier, James Lincoln	27. Kerr, M.E.	5. Schlee, Ann
4. Cooper, Susan	1. Levy, Elizabeth	9. Steele, Mary Q.
15. Corbett, Scott	33. Lewis, C.S.	30. Terris, Susan
26. Corcoran, Barbara	10. Lipsyte, Robert	28. Wells, H.G.
34. Dickinson, Peter	3. Lowry, Lois	12. Westall, Robert
21. Duncan, Lois	18. McHargue, Georgess	16. Wibberley, Leonard
31. Dygaard, Thomas J.	13. Miles, Betty	

BEAR FACTS

grades 2–4—coordinates with Chapter 2

The ever-popular teddy bear is featured in this simple crossword puzzle suitable for grades 2–4. The titles are found in most media centers. Students should check the card catalog. If some books are not part of the collection standard bibliographies such as *The Elementary School Library Collection* (Bro-Dart) should list them.

Answers to "Bear Facts"

Name _____   **Date** _____

A DOT-TO-DOT OF SUMMER READING

Directions: 1. Put the following list of authors in alphabetical order.
2. Write the numbers and names in the spaces provided.
3. Connect the dots in the order in which the numbers now appear.

Example: 20. Armstrong, Robert   29. Alexander, Lloyd
25. Arthur, Ruth M.   becomes   20. Armstrong, Robert
29. Alexander, Lloyd   25. Arthur, Ruth M.

Therefore, you will connect the first three dots in this order: number 29 to number 20 to number 25.

TIP: First make a separate list of all the authors whose names begin with "A." Put those names in alphabetical order and write them in the spaces. Repeat these steps for authors whose names begin with "B," "C," etc.

1. Levy, Elizabeth	_____	19. Hautzig, Deborah	_____
2. O'Brien, Robert	_____	20. Armstrong, Robert	_____
3. Lowry, Lois	_____	21. Duncan, Lois	_____
4. Cooper, Susan	_____	22. Keller, Beverly	_____
5. Schlee, Ann	_____	23. Rodgers, Mary	_____
6. Girion, Barbara	_____	24. Collier, James Lincoln	_____
7. Bethancourt, T. Ernesto	_____	25. Arthur, Ruth M.	_____
8. Hinton, S.E.	_____	26. Corcoran, Barbara	_____
9. Steele, Mary Q.	_____	27. Kerr, M.E.	_____
10. Lipsyte, Robert	_____	28. Wells, H.G.	_____
11. Gault, William Campbell	_____	29. Alexander, Lloyd	_____
12. Westall, Robert	_____	30. Terris, Susan	_____
13. Miles, Betty	_____	31. Dygaard, Thomas	_____
14. Rockwell, Thomas	_____	32. Peyton, K.M.	_____
15. Corbett, Scott	_____	33. Lewis, C.S.	_____
16. Wibberley, Leonard	_____	34. Dickinson, Peter	_____
17. Bridgers, Sue Ellen	_____	35. Orgel, Doris	_____
18. McHargue, Georgess	_____		

A DOT-TO-DOT OF SUMMER READING

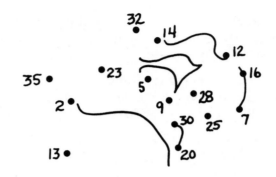

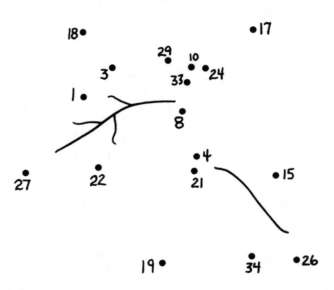

BEAR FACTS

Name _____ Date _____

ACROSS

1. The author of *The Biggest Bear* is Lynd _____.

4. *Big Bad Bruce* is about a bear who learns his lesson. It is by Bill _____.

6. Don Freeman's lovable bear named _____ needs a button.

7. The author of *The Smartest Bear and His Brother Oliver* is Alice _____.

11. Stan and Janice _____ are the authors of *The Bear's Vacation* and *The Big Honey Hunt*.

13. Don Freeman wrote the story of a wind-up bear named _____.

14. _____ visited the home of the three bears.

15. William Lipkind and Roger Duvoisin wrote _____ Bear.

DOWN

2. The author of *The Bear Party* is William Pene _____.

3. Else Minarik writes about *Little* _____.

4. Michael Bond's famous bear is called _____.

5. Martha Alexander's _____ Bear is drawn with chalk.

8. Gahan Wilson wrote _____ *the Fat Bear Spy.*

9. A.A. Milne's well-known teddy bear is called _____-the-Pooh.

10. Ormondroyd's _____ loves being dirty.

12. The author of *Grizzwold* is Syd _____.

193

MAGIC IN THE AIR

grades 3–5—coordinates with Chapter 2

There is always magic in books, but some books put magic in their titles. Have students locate the missing words in the pencil game to complete the "magic." The circled letters will spell a magical answer. If your school's media center does not have some of the titles, ask the students to refer to any bibliographic sources that are on hand.

Answers to "Magic in the Air"

1. *The MAGICian and the Petnapping*
2. *Big Anthony and the MAGIC Ring*
3. *The MAGICian's Nephew*
4. The MAGIC Summer
5. *The MAGIC Grandfather*
6. *MAGIC in the Alley*
7. *Barney Bipple's MAGIC Dandelion*
8. *A MAGIC Eye for Ida*
9. *Fog MAGIC*
10. *The MAGIC Fishbone*
11. *The Trouble with MAGIC*
12. *MAGICal Changes*
13. *A Certain MAGIC*
14. *MAGIC Michael*
15. *A Touch of MAGIC*
16. *Black and Blue MAGIC*

MAGICal answer: PRESTIDIGITATION

COLORFUL READING

grades 3–5—coordinates with Chapter 2

Give your students a pencil game containing most of the colors of the rainbow. The card catalog or a standard bibliography can be used to locate the titles.

Answers to "Colorful Reading"

1. *Ha(r)old and the Purple Crayon*
2. *Little Black, (a) Pony*
3. *When Violet D(i)ed*
4. *The Golden Ve(n)ture*
5. *The Blue(b)erry Collection*
6. *Brown C(o)w Farm*
7. *Blue-Nosed (W)itch*
8. *The City (o)f Gold and Lead*
9. *Ru(f)us, Red Rufus*
10. *The (G)reat Green Turkey Creek Monster*
11. *Blue M(o)ose*
12. *The Gray Gh(o)st of Taylor Ridge*
13. *The White Car(d)inal*
14. *The (B)ig Orange Splot*
15. *Six Blue H(o)rses*
16. *Mystery (o)f the Golden Horn*
17. *The S(k)y was Blue*
18. *Is It Red? I(s) It Yellow? Is It Blue?*

Mystery Message: RAINBOW OF GOOD BOOKS

Name _____ Date _____

MAGIC IN THE AIR

Directions: Read the clues and fill in the answers, which all have the word "magic" in them. Then copy the circled letters on the spaces below to find out the magical answer.

1. A picture book by David McKee   _ _ _ MAGIC_ _ _ _ _ _ _ _ _

        Ⓞ_ _ _ _ _ _ _ _ _

2. A picture book story by Tomie de Paola that takes place in Italy   _ _ _ _ _ _ _ _ _ _ _

        _ _ _ MAGIC Ⓞ_ _ _

3. One of the Narnia series by C.S. Lewis   _ _ _ MAGIC_ _ _'_ _ _ _ _ _Ⓞ_

4. A mystery and adventure story by Noel Streatfeild that takes place in Ireland   _ _ _ MAGIC Ⓞ_ _ _ _ _

5. A book by Jay Williams   _ _ _ MAGIC _ _ _ _ _ _ _Ⓞ_ _ _

6. A book by Mary Calhoun   MAGIC Ⓞ_ _ _ _ _ _ _ _ _

7. A picture book by Carol Chapman   _ _ _ _ _ _ _ _ _ _ _ _'_ MAGIC

        Ⓞ_ _ _ _ _ _ _ _

8. A picture book by Kay Chorao   _ MAGIC _ _ _ _ _ _ Ⓞ_ _

9. A book by Julia L. Sauer set in Nova Scotia   _ _Ⓞ MAGIC

10. A picture book fairy tale by Charles Dickens   _ _ _ MAGIC _Ⓞ_ _ _ _ _ _

11. A story by Ruth Chew   _ _ _ Ⓞ_ _ _ _ _ _ _ _ _ MAGIC

12. A wordless book of changing pictures by Graham Oakley   MAGIC_ _ _ _Ⓞ_ _ _ _

13. A novel by Doris Orgel   _ _ _ _Ⓞ_ _ _ MAGIC

14. A picture book by Louis Slobodkin   MAGIC _Ⓞ_ _ _ _ _

15. A historical fiction book by Betty Cavanna about the Revolution   _ _Ⓞ_ _ _ _ _ MAGIC

16. A book by Zilpha Keatley Snyder   _ _ _ _ _ _Ⓞ_ _ _ _ _ MAGIC

MAGICal answer: _ _ _ _ _ _ _ _ _ _ _ _ _ _ _ _ _

(Definition: sleight of hand or legerdemain, the MAGICal arts practiced by MAGICians)

COLORFUL READING

Find the missing words in these colorful titles. When you fill in the circled letters, you will see a mystery message.

1. _ _◯_ _ _ _ _ _ _ _ _ Purple _ _ _ _ _ _
by Crockett Johnson

2. _ _ _ _ _ _ Black, ◯ _ _ _ _ by Walter Farley

3. _ _ _ _ Violet _◯_ _ by Mildred Kantrowitz

4. _ _ _ Golden _ _◯_ _ _ by Jane Flory

5. _ _ _ Blue◯ _ _ _ _ _ _ _ _ _ _ _ _ _ _ by Ann Waldron

6. Brown _◯_ _ _ _ _ by Dahlov Ipcar

7. Blue-_ _ _ _ _ ◯_ _ _ _ by Margaret Embry

8. _ _ _ _ _ _ _ _ _ Gold _ _ _ _ _ _ _ by John Christopher

9. _ _◯_ _, Red _ _ _ _ _ _ by Patricia Beatty

10. _ _ _ ◯_ _ _ Green _ _ _ _ _ _ _ _ _ _ _ _ _ _ _ _ _
by James Flora

11. Blue _◯_ _ _ by Daniel M. Pinkwater

12. _ _ _ Gray _ _◯_ _ _ _ _ _ _ _ _ _ _ _ _ _ by Mary
Francis Shura

13. _ _ _ White _ _ _◯_ _ _ _ by Griffing Bancroft

14. _ _ _ ◯_ _ Orange _ _ _ _ _ _ by Daniel M. Pinkwater

15. _ _ _ Blue _◯_ _ _ _ by Yvonne Escoula

16. _ _ _ _ _ _ _ ◯_ _ _ _ Golden _ _ _ _ by Phyllis A. Whitney

17. _ _ _ _◯_ _ _ _ Blue by Charlotte Zolotow

18. _ _ _ _ Red? _◯_ _ Yellow? _ _ _ _ Blue? by Tana Hoban

MYSTERY MESSAGE: Read these books and you will have a

_ _ _ _ _ _ _ _ _ _ _ _ _ _ _ _ _ _

ANAGRAM

grades 3–6—coordinates with Chapter 2

By completing this pencil game students will demonstrate their awareness of authors' names. To fill in the blanks they can either use the card catalog or depend on their own knowledge. When they finish, the first letter of each last name will spell the full name of a famous librarian.

Answers to "Anagram"

1. Merrill
2. Emberley
3. Lawson
4. Van Leeuwen
5. Irving
6. London
7. Delton
8. Erickson
9. Williams
10. Estes
11. Yashima

Mystery Librarian: MELVIL DEWEY

SCRAMBLED PICTURE BOOK TITLES

grades 3–6—coordinates with Chapter 2

Challenge students with this scrambled words game. If they cannot decipher the titles on their own, students can look under the author's name in the card catalog. The titles should prove nostalgic for students in the upper grades.

Answers to "Scrambled Picture Book Titles"

1. Corduroy
2. Owliver
3. George and Martha
4. Curious George
5. The Three Robbers
6. Strega Nona
7. Caps for Sale
8. Mr. Gumpy's Outing
9. Spectacles
10. The Amazing Bone
11. The Lorax
12. Petunia
13. Titch
14. Swimmy
15. The Plant Sitter

Name _____   Date _____

Directions: Fill in the blanks with the last names of the authors of the books listed below. If you need help, check your card catalog. The first letter of each last name will spell the name of a famous librarian who in 1876 developed a system for classifying books.

ANAGRAM

A-AL	C-CHE	EN-EZ	GO-GZ
AM-AQ	CHI-COI	F-FE	H-HE
AK-AZ	COJ-CZ	FI-FOK	HI-HORR
B-BE	D-DOF	FOL-FOR	HORS-HZ
BI-BZ	DOG-EM	FOS-GI	I-J

ANAGRAM

1. *The Pushcart War*   _ _ _ _ _ _

2. *Drummer Hoff*   _ _ _ _ _ _ _ _

3. *Ben and Me*   _ _ _ _ _ _

4. *The Great Cheese Conspiracy*   _ _ _ _ _ _ _ _ _ _ _

5. *The Legend of Sleepy Hollow*   _ _ _ _ _ _ _

6. *Call of the Wild*   _ _ _ _ _ _

7. *Two Good Friends*   _ _ _ _ _ _

8. *A Toad for Tuesday*   _ _ _ _ _ _ _ _

9. *Danny Dunn and the Homework Machine*   _ _ _ _ _ _ _ _

10. *The Moffats*   _ _ _ _ _

11. *Crow Boy*   _ _ _ _ _ _ _

Mystery Librarian: _ _ _ _ _ _ _ _ _ _ _

198

SCRAMBLED PICTURE BOOK TITLES

Can you find the titles of some favorite picture books from the scrambled words below? If you have any problems, use the card catalog to look up the authors' names.

1. ORORCYDU _____
   by Don Freeman

2. WLIREVO _____
   by Robert Kraus

3. OEGGER NAD ATRMAH _____
   by James Marshall

4. URCSOIU RGEOEG _____
   by H.A. Rey

5. HTE REEHT BEBRSOR _____
   by Tomi Ungerer

6. RGSATE ONNA _____
   by Tomie de Paola

7. ACSP RFO LASE _____
   by Esphyr Slobodkina

8. RM PMGUYS TUOGIN _____
   by John Burningham

9. APCLSESECT _____
   by Ellen Raskin

10. HTE MGIANZA OBEN _____
    by William Steig

11. HTE XROLA _____
    by Dr. Seuss

12. TIAPUNE _____
    by Roger Duvoisin

13. HICTT _____
    by Pat Hutchins

14. WIYMSM _____
    by Leo Lionni

15. HTE LTPAN TTISRE _____
    by Gene Zion

ILLUSTRIOUS ILLUSTRATORS

grades 3–6—coordinates with Chapter 2

Although students in grades 3–6 have outgrown picture books, they can still be challenged by this pencil game. Use it not only to reinforce card catalog skills, but also as an introduction to the Caldecott Medals. Many of the illustrators included in this puzzle have been honored with this award.

Answers to "Illustrious Illustrators"

1. Aliki
2. Robert McCloskey
3. Tomi Ungerer
4. Hoff
5. Uri Shulevitz
6. Remy Charlip
7. Raskin
8. Arnold Lobel
9. Crosby Bonsall
10. Kay Chorao
11. H.A. Rey
12. Ardizzone
13. Maurice Sendak

Mystery Illustrator: ARTHUR RACKHAM

IN LIKE A LION

grades 3–6—coordinates with Chapter 2

Be prepared for all kinds of weather from sun to fog, from thunder to snow, and from wind to hail in these book titles. Students can fill in the missing word in the titles by using various bibliographic tools. They should then transfer the circled letters to spell out the mystery word, a term related to weather forecasting, at the bottom of the sheet.

Answers to "In Like a Lion"

1. Meatballs
2. Blew
3. Thunder
4. Fine
5. Snowy
6. Hurricane
7. Hailstones
8. Loved
9. Fog
10. Magic
11. Wind
12. Sunshine
13. Wet

Mystery Word: METEOROLOGIST

Name _____   Date _____

ILLUSTRIOUS ILLUSTRATORS

Directions: Fill in the blanks with the illustrators of the books listed below. (Sometimes they are the authors, too.) Use the card catalog for help. The first letters of the illustrators' names will spell out the name of a famous illustrator.

1. *Keep Your Mouth Closed, Dear*   O_ _ _ _

2. *Lentil* (entire name)   O_ _ _ _ _ _ _ _ _ _ _

3. *Allumette* (entire name)   O_ _ _ _ _ _ _ _ _

4. *Julius* (last name only)   O_ _ _

5. *The Fool of the World and the Flying Ship* (entire name)   O_ _ _ _ _ _ _ _ _ _ _ _

6. *Thirteen* (entire name)   O_ _ _ _ _ _ _ _ _ _

7. *Spectacles* (last name only)   O_ _ _ _ _ _

8. *Lucille* (entire name)   O_ _ _ _ _ _ _ _ _ _

9. *And I Mean It, Stanley* (entire name)   O_ _ _ _ _ _ _ _ _ _

10. *Albert's Toothache* (entire name)   O_ _ _ _ _ _ _ _

11. *Curious George* (first two initials and last name)   O _ _ _ _ _

12. *Little Tim and the Brave Sea Captain* (last name only)   O_ _ _ _ _ _ _ _ _

13. *Where the Wild Things Are* (entire name)   O_ _ _ _ _ _ _ _ _ _ _ _

MYSTERY ILLUSTRATOR: _ _ _ _ _ _ _ _ _ _ _ _ _ _

IN LIKE A LION

The following titles all deal with different types of weather. Complete these titles by using the card catalog or other sources suggested by your teacher. Write in the spaces at the bottom of the page the letters that are placed in circles. They will spell out a word that has something to do with the weather.

1. Cloudy with a Chance of ◯_ _ _ _ _ _ _ _   by Judi Barrett

2. The Wind _ _◯_   by Pat Hutchins

3. Roll of ◯_ _ _ _ _ _, Hear My Cry   by Mildred Taylor

4. One _ _ _◯ Day   by Nonny Hogrogian

5. The _ _◯_ _ Day   by Ezra Jack Keats

6. The Day the _ _◯_ _ _ _ _ Happened   by Lonzo Anderson

7. _ _ _ _ _ _◯_ _ and Halibut Bones   by Mary O'Neill

8. The Girl Who ◯_ _ _ _ the Wind   by Jane Yolen

9. Hide and Seek _◯_   by Alvin Tresselt

10. Fog _ _◯_ _   by Julia L. Sauer

11. _◯_ _ in the Willows   by Kenneth Grahame

12. Days of ◯_ _ _ _ _ _ _, Days of Rain   by Dean Frye

13. A _ _◯ and Sandy Day   by Joanne Ryder

MYSTERY WORD: _ _ _ _ _ _ _ _ _ _ _ _ _ _

APRIL SHOWERS

grades 3–6—coordinates with Chapter 2

"April showers bring May flowers." Part of this saying is the secret message that will be spelled out by working this pencil game. If your school's card catalog does not contain all the books mentioned in the answer key, let students use any bibliographic source that is available, such as *Children's Books in Print* (Bowker).

Answers to "April Showers"

1. *Mushroom in the Rain*
2. *And It Rained*
3. *Rainy Rainy Saturday*
4. *So What If It's Raining?*
5. *The Rain Cloud*
6. *Rain Drop Splash*
7. *Rain, Rain Don't Go Away*
8. *Rain Makes Applesauce*
9. *Where Does All the Rain Go?*
10. *Rainbow in the Sky*

Mystery Message: MAY FLOWERS

FAMOUS SLEUTHS

grades 3–6—coordinates with Chapter 2

Mystery and detective stories are always popular with students. Let them solve this puzzle by filling in the blanks, which will complete the names of some popular sleuths. The circled letters should also be copied onto the spaces at the bottom of the sheet to form the mystery word, which is an adjective describing a quality of both real and fictional mysteries. If students encounter problems have them check the card catalog or *Children's Books in Print* (Bowker).

Answers to "Famous Sleuths"

1. Emil
2. Desmond
3. Sherlock
4. Encyclopedia
5. Freddy
6. McGurk
7. Nate
8. Watson
9. Basil
10. Spotlight
11. Mole

Mystery Word: INSCRUTABLE

WHAT'S IN A NAME?

grades 5–8—coordinates with Chapter 2

This pencil game is a crossword puzzle that spotlights book titles familiar to students in the middle and upper grades. Each blank represents a first name that appears in the title.

Unfamiliar titles provide students with an ideal opportunity to reinforce skills in using author cards in the card catalog. Answers might even be the stimulus for something new to read just for fun.

Answers to "What's in a Name?"

Across		Down	
2. Harriet	18. Alice	1. Charlie	14. Teddy
6. Jonathan	19. Julie	3. Sheila	15. Stuart
8. Felicia	20. Ramona	4. Matthew	16. Elizabeth
9. Peter	21. Rebecca	5. Emily	22. Henry
10. Danny	22. Homer	6. James	23. Pippi
11. Isabelle	24. Charlotte	7. Johnny	25. Tom
14. Trissy	26. Maggie	12. Ben	27. Anne
17. Alvin	28. Veronica	13. Margaret	

Name _____   Date _____

APRIL SHOWERS

Directions: The following books all contain the word "rain" in their titles. See if you can complete these book titles by using the card catalog or other sources suggested by your teacher. Write in the spaces at the bottom of the page the letters that are placed in circles. They will spell out something you can look forward to.

1. ◯_ _ _ _ _ _ _ _ _ _ _ _ Rain   by Mirra Ginsburg

2. ◯_ _ _ _ Rain_ _   by Ellen Raskin

3. Rain_ Rain_ _ _ _ _ _ _ _◯   by Jack Prelutsky

4. _ _ _ _ _ _ _◯ _ _'_   by Miriam Young

   Rain_ _ _?

5. _ _ _ Rain _◯_ _ _   by Mary Rayner

6. Rain _ _◯_, _ _ _ _ _ _   by Alvin Tresselt

7. Rain, Rain _ _ _'_ _ _ _◯_ _   by Shirley Morgan

8. Rain _ _ _ _ _

   _ _ _ _◯_ _ _ _ _   by Julian Scheer

9. _ _ _◯_ _ _ _ _ _ _ _ _ _ _   by Margaret Farrington Bartlett

   Rain _ _?

10. Rain_ _ _ _ _ _ _ _ ◯_ _   by Louis Untermeyer

MYSTERY MESSAGE: _ _ _ _ _ _ _ _ _ _ _

205

FAMOUS SLEUTHS

Directions: This puzzle contains the names of some popular sleuths from mystery and detective stories. Solve the puzzle by filling in the blanks, which will complete the detectives' names. Transfer to the bottom of the sheet each letter that is circled and you will spell the mystery word. If you need help check the card catalog.

1. _ _O_   _____ *and the Detectives*, by Erich Kastner

2. _ _ _ _ _O_   _____ *the Dog Detective*, by Herbert Best

3. O_ _ _ _ _ _ _   _____ Holmes, the eminent detective in the stories by Arthur Conan Doyle

4. _ _O_ _ _ _ _ _ _ _   _____ Brown, the police chief's son in the series by Donald J. Sobol

5. _O_ _ _ _   _____, the pig who became a detective in the book by Walter R. Brooks

6. _ _ _O_ _   Jack P. _____, head of an organization of sleuths created by E.W. Hildick

7. _ _O_   _____ *the Great*, by Marjorie Weinman Sharmat

8. _O_ _ _ _   Holmes's assistant, Dr. _____, from the stories by Arthur Conan Doyle

9. O_ _ _ _   _____, the mouse who lived in the basement on Baker Street in the series by Eve Titus

10. _ _ _ _O_ _ _ _   _____ Club Detectives, Jay and Cindy Temple and Dexter Tate in a series by Florence Parry Heide and Rosanne Heide

11. _ _ _O   *Detective* _____, by Robert Quackenbush

MYSTERY WORD: _ _ _ _ _ _ _ _ _ _ _

DEFINITION: mysterious, incomprehensible

WHAT'S IN A NAME?

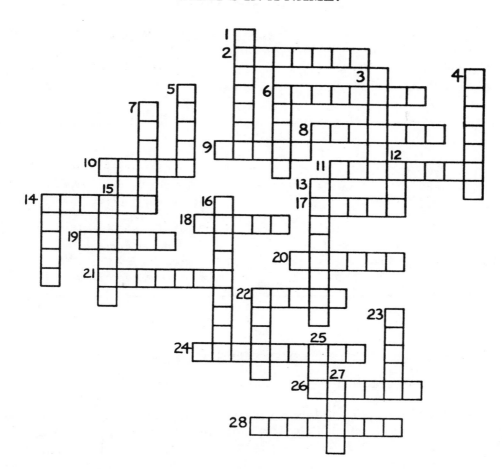

Across

2. ____ *the Spy* by Fitzhugh
6. ____ *Livingston Seagull* by Bach
8. ____ *the Critic* by Conford
9. ____ *Pan* by Barrie
10. ____ *Dunn, Time Traveler* by Williams
11. ____ *the Itch* by Greene
14. *I* ____ by Mazer
17. ____ *Fernald Superweasel* by Hicks
18. ____ *in Wonderland* by Carroll
19. ____ *of the Wolves* by George
20. ____ *the Pest* by Cleary
21. ____ *of Sunnybrook Farm* by Wiggin
22. ____ *Price* by McCloskey
24. ____ *'s Web* by White
26. ____ *Marmelstein for President* by Sharmat
28. *Peter and* ____ by Sachs

Down

1. *A Boy Named* ____ *Brown* by Shulz
3. *Otherwise Known as* ____ *the Great* by Blume
4. ____ *Looney & the Space Pirates* by Beatty
5. *Jane* ____ by Clapp
6. ____ *and the Giant Peach* by Dahl
7. ____ *Tremain* by Forbes
12. ____ *and Me* by Lawson
13. *Are You There, God? It's Me,* ____ by Blume
14. *Don't Take* ____ by Friis-Baastad
15. ____ *Little* by White
16. *Jennifer, Hecate, Macbeth, William McKinley and Me,* ____ by Konigsburg
22. ____ *Huggins* by Cleary
23. ____ *Longstocking* by Lindgren
25. ____ *Sawyer* by Twain
27. ____ *Frank: Diary of a Young Girl*

MIXED-UP LOVE

grades 5–8—coordinates with Chapter 2

Love is everywhere, especially in the titles of this pencil game! Many of the titles are in the *Elementary School Library Collection* as well as in the *Junior High Catalog*, and there are enough clues for adept students to unscramble the titles even without a bibliography or card catalog.

Answers to "Mixed-Up Love"

1. *Like Everybody Else*
2. *The Crime of Martin Coverly*
3. *Calico Captive*
4. *Silver on the Tree*
5. *Across Five Aprils*
6. *Prove Yourself a Hero*
7. *Tunnel Vision*
8. *The Lotus Caves*
9. *The War on Villa Street*
10. *Julie of the Wolves*
11. *National Velvet*
12. *The Devil on the Road*
13. *The Forever Formula*
14. *Coming Back Alive*
15. *Seven Spells to Sunday*

DOT-TO-DOT WITH TITLES

grades 5–9—coordinates with Chapter 2

This dot-to-dot puzzle reinforces the complex alphabetizing skills necessary to locate titles in the card catalog. The books listed present problems in alphabetical sequence, such as *Ellen Grae* filed under "E"; "Mr." filed as Mister; *No Time for Tears* filed before *Nobody Has to Be a Kid Forever* and other confusions, including dropping "The" when it is the first word and including it in the alphabetical sequence when it appears within the title.

The picture that emerges when students complete the task is a frog, chosen to celebrate the annual frog jumping contest held each May in California in tribute to Mark Twain's short story, "The Celebrated Jumping Frog of Calaveras County."

Answers to "Dot-to-Dot with Titles"

51. *About the B'nai Bagels*
47. *Alan and the Animal Kingdom*
21. *And You Give Me a Pain, Elaine*
57. *The Best Bad Thing*
59. *Call Me Moose*
35. *The Carousel Horse*
11. *The Cartoonist*
20. *The Case of the Felon's Fiddle*
38. *The Case of the Silver Skull*
49. *The Chicken Pox Papers*
52. *The Computer That Said Steal Me*
19. *Do Bananas Chew Gum?*
28. *The Dog Days of Arthur Cane*
58. *The Edge of the World*
33. *The 18th Emergency*
43. *Ellen Grae*
24. *Emma's Dilemma*
50. *Felicia the Critic*
 1. *Finding Fever*
 8. *Fox Farm*
 3. *Growing Anyway Up*
10. *The Hoboken Chicken Emergency*
37. *Home Before Dark*
14. *I and Sproggy*
53. *In Summertime, It's Tuffy*
41. *Incident at Hawk's Hill*
23. *Incognito Mosquito, Private Detective*
12. *Just Between Us*
44. *Just the Beginning*
13. *The Late Great Me*
32. *The Law of Gravity*
 2. *Little Little*
15. *Lucy Makes a Match*
48. *Midnight Is a Place*
26. *Mr. McFadden's Hallowe'en*

36. *My Twin Sister Erika*
 4. *Mystery at St. Martin's*
 7. *No Applause, Please*
60. *No Time for Tears*
42. *Nobody Has to Be a Kid Forever*
25. *On the Ropes*
31. *One to Grow On*
39. *Out of Love*
40. *Philip Hall Likes Me, I Reckon Maybe*
17. *Pinch*
29. *Queen of Hearts*
34. *Run, Westy, Run*
45. *The Runaway Summer*
54. *A Solitary Blue*
16. *A Summer to Die*
22. *A Tangled Web*
56. *The Telltale Summer of Tina C.*
46. *That Julia Redfern*
30. *The Trouble with Thirteen*
 6. *Tunnels of Terror*
27. *The Westing Game*
18. *What Are Friends For?*
 5. *The Winter Hero*
55. *The Wolves of Aam*
 9. *Working Trot*

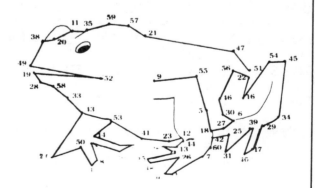

Name _____   Date _____

MIXED-UP LOVE

Directions: 1. Put LOVE back in and unscramble the words to find the titles.
2. These clues will help you:
  • The author's name is one point of reference.
  • The numbers in parentheses are the number of letters in each word of the title.
  • All titles are listed in the *Junior High Catalog* (4th edition) and supplements.

Example: LOVE DIDA__ FPRIDCEP__ __ __ by Charles Dickens
(5, 11) becomes DAVID COPPERFIELD

1. LOVE KEI__ EREYDBY__ __ SEL__ by Barbara Girion (4, 9, 4)

2. LOVE HET MIRC__ FO RAMNIT CREY__ __ __ by Leonard Wibberley (3, 5, 2, 6, 7)

3. LOVE CAIC__ __ TACPI__ __ by Elizabeth George Speare (6, 7)

4. LOVE RISE__ __ N__ HET TER__ by Susan Cooper (6, 2, 3, 4)

5. LOVE CRASS__ IF__ __ SPAIR__ by Irene Hunt (6, 4, 6)

6. LOVE ROPE__ SEROUFY__ A RH__ __ by K.M. Peyton (5, 8, 1, 4)

7. LOVE NUNT__ __ INIS__ __ by Fran Arrick (6, 6)

8. LOVE HET SUT__ __ SAC__ __ by John Christopher (3, 5, 5)

9. LOVE HET RAW N__ LIE__ __ TREST__ by Harry Mazer (3, 3, 2, 5, 6)

10. LOVE IJU__ __ FO HET SLEW__ __ by Jean Craighead George (5, 2, 3, 6)

11. LOVE TINANA__ __ VELT__ __ by Enid Bagnold (8, 6)

12. LOVE HET DI__ __ __ NO HET DAR__ by Robert Westall (3, 5, 2, 3, 4)

13. LOVE HET REFOR__ __ FARUM__ __ by Frank Bonham (3, 7, 7)

14. LOVE MINCG__ KABC AI__ __ __ by Dennis J. Reader (6, 4, 5)

15. LOVE NES__ __ SLEPS__ T__ DUNAYS by Andre Norton (5, 6, 2, 6)

© 1984 by Hilda K. Weisburg and Ruth Toor

Name _____   Date _____

DOT-TO-DOT WITH TITLES

Directions: 1. Put the following list of titles in alphabetical order. (Remember, the order is word by word, not letter by letter.)
2. Write the numbers and titles in order on a separate sheet.
3. Connect the dots in the order the numbers now appear.

Example: Three titles begin with "A"

21 *And You Give Me a Pain, Elaine*
47 *Alan and the Animal Kingdom*
51 *About the B'nai Bagels*

in correct order, they become:

51 *About the B'nai Bagels*
47 *Alan and the Animal Kingdom*
21 *And You Give Me a Pain, Elaine*

Clues

1. *Finding Fever*
2. *Little Little*
3. *Growing Anyway Up*
4. *Mystery at St. Martin's*
5. *The Winter Hero*
6. *Tunnels of Terror*
7. *No Applause, Please*
8. *Fox Farm*
9. *Working Trot*
10. *The Hoboken Chicken Emergency*
11. *The Cartoonist*
12. *Just Between Us*
13. *The Late Great Me*
14. *I and Sproggy*
15. *Lucy Makes a Match*
16. *A Summer to Die*
17. *Pinch*
18. *What Are Friends For?*
19. *Do Bananas Chew Gum?*
20. *The Case of the Felon's Fiddle*
21. *And You Give Me a Pain, Elaine*
22. *A Tangled Web*
23. *Incognito Mosquito, Private Detective*
24. *Emma's Dilemma*
25. *On the Ropes*
26. *Mr. McFadden's Hallowe'en*
27. *The Westing Game*
28. *The Dog Days of Arthur Cane*
29. *Queen of Hearts*
30. *The Trouble with Thirteen*
31. *One to Grow On*
32. *The Law of Gravity*
33. *The 18th Emergency*
34. *Run, Westy, Run*
35. *The Carousel Horse*
36. *My Twin Sister Erika*
37. *Home Before Dark*
38. *The Case of the Silver Skull*
39. *Out of Love*
40. *Philip Hall Likes Me, I Reckon Maybe*
41. *Incident at Hawk's Hill*
42. *Nobody Has to Be a Kid Forever*
43. *Ellen Grae*
44. *Just the Beginning*
45. *The Runaway Summer*
46. *That Julia Redfern*
47. *Alan and the Animal Kingdom*
48. *Midnight Is a Place*
49. *The Chicken Pox Papers*
50. *Felicia the Critic*
51. *About the B'nai Bagels*
52. *The Computer That Said Steal Me*
53. *In Summertime It's Tuffy*
54. *A Solitary Blue*
55. *The Wolves of Aam*
56. *The Telltale Summer of Tina C.*
57. *The Best Bad Thing*
58. *The Edge of the World*
59. *Call Me Moose*
60. *No Time for Tears*

DOT-TO-DOT WITH TITLES

AUTHOR, AUTHOR

grades 6–10—coordinates with Chapter 2

Once students in junior and senior high school have solved the crossword puzzle they can use the answers as a reading list. This will encourage your students to make use of the facilities at the public library or the school library.

Answers to "Author, Author"

DEVELOP YOUR WORD POWER

grades 3–6—coordinates with Chapter 3

Skill in using the dictionary is not enough. Students need to develop the habit of using this tool. To make dictionary use habit-forming you must reinforce the practice in pleasant ways. Games offered throughout the year establish a behavior pattern and this word game provides one good start. (The definitions are based on *The American Heritage Dictionary*.)

NOTE: This word game goes with the "Develop Your Word Power" bulletin board in Part Three.

Answers to "Develop Your Word Power"

1. habit
2. tack
3. continue
4. void
5. account
6. fast
7. buckle
8. fine
9. engage
10. hold

CROSSWORD PUZZLE CLUES FOR AUTHOR, AUTHOR

Across

4. Author of *A Portrait for Margarita* and *An Old Magic*, Ruth M. _____

6. Author of *Summer of Fear* and *A Gift of Magic*, Lois _____

8. Author of *A Summer to Die* and *Anastasia Krupnik*, Lois _____

10. Author of *The High King* and *The Book of Three*, Lloyd _____

13. Author of *The Westing Game* and *Figgs and Phantoms*, Ellen _____

14. First two initials of the author of the *Chronicles of Narnia* and *Out of the Silent Planet*

15. Author of *I, Robot* and *Foundation*, Isaac _____

17. Short for Deborah, or a girl in her coming out year

19. Author of *A Pocket Full of Seeds* and *Dorrie's Book*, Marilyn _____

21. Author of *A Girl Called Al* and *Beat the Turtle Drum*, Constance _____

22. Author of *The Court of the Stone Children* and *A House Made of Windows*, Eleanor _____

24. Author of *The Pigman* and *My Darling, My Hamburger*, Paul _____

25. Author of *Dinky Hocker Shoots Smack*, M.E. _____

27. Author of *Warrior Scarlet* and *Eagle of the Ninth*, Rosemary _____

32. Nothing, or dog hero in Cresswell's Bagthorpe saga

33. Author of *White Fang* and *Call of the Wild*, Jack _____

34. Author of *The Hobbit* and *The Lord of the Rings*, J.R.R. _____

35. Creator of Sherlock Holmes, Arthur Conan _____

37. Author of *A Light in the Forest* and *The Town*, Conrad _____

38. Author of *The Slave Dancer* and *The Stone-Faced Boy*, Paula _____

39. Author of *The Zero Stone* and *Uncharted Stars*, Andre _____

41. Author of *From the Mixed-up Files of Mrs. Basil E. Frankweiler* and (*George*), E.L. _____

45. Author of *Toby Lived Here* and *Introducing Shirley Braverman*, Hilma _____

48. Author of *Durango Street* and *Cool Cat*, Frank _____

50. Author of *Mrs. Frisby and the Rats of NIMH*, Robert _____

51. Author of *Leave Well Enough Alone* and *None of the Above*, Rosemary _____

54. Author of *Then Again Maybe I Won't* and *It's Not the End of the World*, Judy _____

55. Author of *Dolphin Crossing* and *Huffler*, Jill Paton _____

56. Author of *The Cay* and *Teetoncy*, Theodore _____

58. Author of *20,000 Leagues Under the Sea* and *Journey to the Center of the Earth*, Jules _____

59. Author of *The Egypt Game* and *Below the Root*, Zilpha Keatley _____

60. Author of *Chloris and the Freaks* and *The Boy Who Could Make Himself Disappear*, Kim _____

214

Down

1. Author of *Who Killed Cock Robin?* and *Julie of the Wolves*, Jean Craighead _____
2. Author of *Across Five Aprils* and *Up a Road Slowly*, Irene
3. Author of *18th Emergency* and *The Pinballs*, Betsy _____
5. Author of *The Adventures of Huckleberry Finn*, Mark _____
7. Authors of *Me, Too!* and *Ellen Grae*, Vera and Bill
9. Author of *Ordinary Jack* and *Absolute Zero*, Helen
11. Author of *Black Hearts in Battersea* and *Nightbirds in Nantucket*, Joan
12. Author of *Jonathan Livingston Seagull*, Richard
13. Author of *Freaky Friday* and *A Billion for Boris*, Mary
14. Author of *The Chocolate War* and *I Am the Cheese*, Robert
16. Author of *The Cat Ate My Gymsuit* and *Can You Sue Your Parents for Malpractice?* Paula _____
19. Homonym for sew
20. Author of *The Outsiders* and *That Was Then, This Is Now*, S.E. _____
22. Author of *And This Is Laura* and *Anything for a Friend*, Ellen _____
23. Author of *Berries Goodman* and *It's Like This Cat*, Emily Cheney _____
26. Author of *Mom, The Wolf Man and Me*, and *What's It All About?* Norma _____
28. Author of *Snow Bound* and *The War on Villa Street*, Harry _____

29. Author of *A Wizard of Earthsea* and *The Tombs of Atuan*, Ursula K.
30. Author of *A Dance to Still Music* and *Winds of Time*, Barbara _____
31. Author of *The Ghost Belonged to Me* and *Dreamland Lake*, Richard
34. Author of *The Great Quillow* and *Many Moons*, James
36. Author of *Beware of This Shop* and *I Will Make You Disappear*, Carol _____
38. Author of *Harriet the Spy* and *Nobody's Family Is Going to Change*, Louise
40. Author of *Animal Farm* and *1984*, George _____
42. Author of *The King's Fifth* and *Island of the Blue Dolphins*, Scott _____
43. Author of *Land's End* and *By the Highway Home*, Mary
44. Author of *Devil in Vienna* and *A Certain Magic*, Doris
46. Not off
47. Author of *Prince Caspian* and *The Magician's Nephew*, C.S.
49. Author of *The Trouble with Thirteen* and *The Real Me*, Betty _____
52. Abbreviation for Los Angeles
53. Abbreviation for steamship
57. Author of *Child of the Owl* and *Dragonwings*, Lawrence _____

215

AUTHOR, AUTHOR

Fill in the crossword puzzle with the surnames of the authors referred to in the clues.

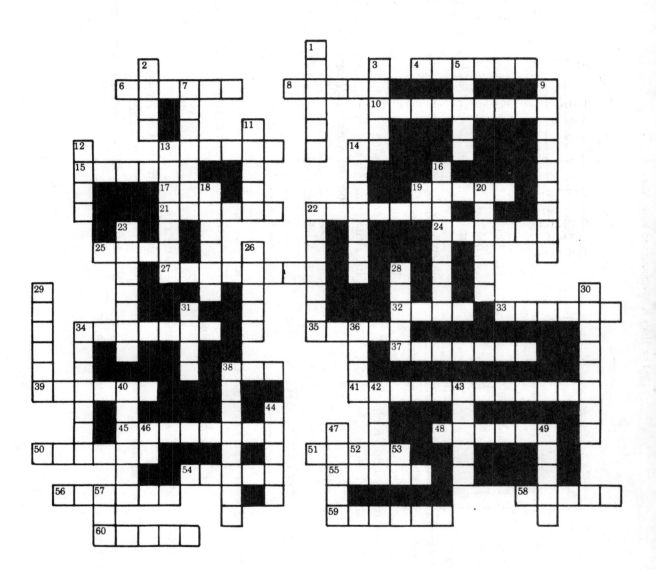

Name _____   Date _____

DEVELOP YOUR WORD POWER

Directions: 1. Use the dictionary to help you.
2. The words here have at least two different meanings. Match them to the two definitions shown in the weights.
3. Put the correct answer in the bar.

FAST	FINE
BUCKLE	CONTINUE
ACCOUNT	TACK
ENGAGE	HOLD
HABIT	VOID

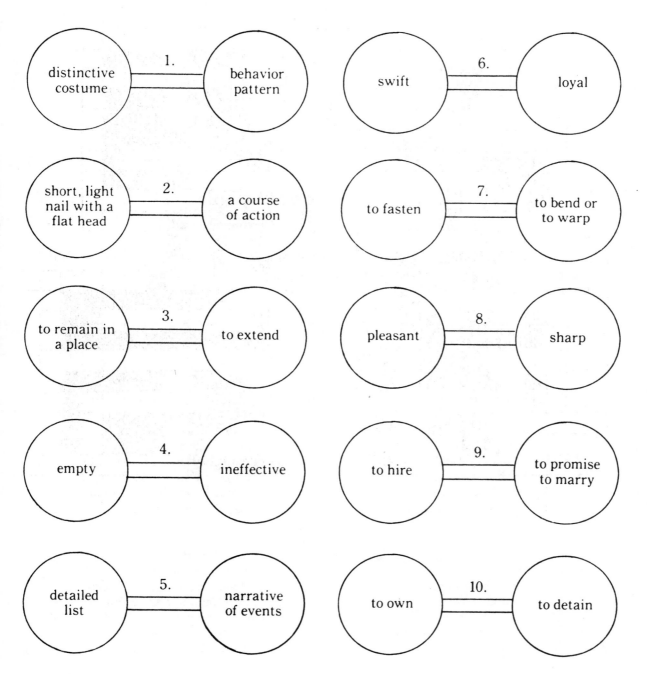

1. distinctive costume — behavior pattern

2. short, light nail with a flat head — a course of action

3. to remain in a place — to extend

4. empty — ineffective

5. detailed list — narrative of events

6. swift — loyal

7. to fasten — to bend or to warp

8. pleasant — sharp

9. to hire — to promise to marry

10. to own — to detain

DEFINING POWER

grades 4–7—coordinates with Chapter 3

There are many titles given to those who have the power to rule, but often they have only slightly different meanings. Have the students use a dictionary (or several dictionaries) to match each definition to the correct term for the ruling power. (These definitions are taken from *World Book Dictionary* and *Random House Dictionary*.)

		Answers to "Defining Power"					
a.	15	f.	10	k.	2	p.	4
b.	5	g.	18	l.	13	q.	20
c.	9	h.	11	m.	3	r.	14
d.	17	i.	1	n.	19	s.	16
e.	7	j.	8	o.	12	t.	6

OUR NATIONAL TREASURE

grades 5–8—coordinates with Chapters 4 and 5

Have your students think about great places to visit while still practicing reference skills. Encyclopedias and atlases are good sources for answers. There are also many excellent books on national parks that could be helpful.

Answers to "Our National Treasure"

1. Yellowstone National Park; Old Faithful
2. Everglades National Park; Florida
3. Carlsbad Caverns National Park
4. Acadia National Park; Maine
5. Death Valley National Monument; Petrified Forest National Monument (the Painted Desert portion)
6. Denali National Park (formerly Mount McKinley National Park), Alaska; Mount McKinley is 20,320 feet above sea level
7. Cape Hatteras National Seashore; Cape Cod National Seashore
8. Mesa Verde National Park, Colorado
9. Devils Tower National Monument; Wyoming
10. Grand Canyon National Park; Arizona
11. Navajo National Monument (Arizona); Canyon de Chelly National Monument (Arizona)
12. Rocky Mountain National Park
13. Craters of the Moon National Monument (Idaho); Mount Rainier National Park (Washington); Crater Lake National park (Oregon); Lassen Volcanic National Park (California); Hawaii Volcanoes National Park (Hawaii)

Name _____   Date _____

DEFINING POWER

Directions: Using one or more dictionaries suggested by your teacher, match each definition to the correct term for the ruling power.

1. Emperor   _____ a.   One of a small number of persons holding the ruling power in a state.

2. Shah   _____ b.   A male ruler of a nation.

3. Satrap   _____ c.   The highest executive officer of a republic.

4. Czar   _____ d.   A feudal overlord.

5. King   _____ e.   An emperor in ancient Rome.

6. Pharaoh   _____ f.   A person who rules when the regular ruler is absent, unfit or temporarily disqualified.

7. Caesar   _____ g.   A German emperor.

8. Dictator   _____ h.   A tyrant; oppressor; a monarch having unlimited power; absolute ruler.

9. President   _____ i.   A ruler of an empire.

10. Regent   _____ j.   A person exercising absolute authority, especially a person who, without having any claim through inheritance or free popular election, seizes control of a government.

11. Despot   _____ k.   Former title of the sovereign of Iran.

12. Sovereign   _____ l.   A member of a wealthy ruling class.

13. Plutocrat   _____ m.   A ruler, often a tyrant, who is subordinate to a higher ruler.

14. Prime Minister   _____ n.   The chief of an Arab family or tribe.

15. Oligarch   _____ o.   The supreme ruler of a people or nation under monarchical government; a king or queen.

16. Khan   _____ p.   An emperor; title of the former emperors of Russia.

17. Suzerain   _____ q.   The former ruling prince in India, especially of one of the major states.

18. Kaiser   _____ r.   The chief minister of government who is head of the cabinet and chief of state.

19. Sheik   _____ s.   The medieval ruler of Tartar and Mongol tribes.

20. Maharajah   _____ t.   A king of ancient Egypt.

© 1983 by Hilda K. Weisburg and Ruth Toor

Name _____   Date _____

OUR NATIONAL TREASURE

1. Two hundred geysers are a feature of one of our national parks. What is the name of the park and of its most famous geyser? _____

2. In which national park could you expect to see alligators, and in what state is it located? _____

3. The world's largest cave is found in a national park in New Mexico. What is the name of the park? _____

4. Which national park in which state is located mostly on Mount Desert Island and partially overlooks the Atlantic Ocean? _____

5. Two of the national monuments in the southwest are either completely or partially located in deserts. Name them. _____

6. Which national park contains the tallest mountain on the North American continent and how tall is it? _____

7. Two of our national seashore areas are located in North Carolina and Massachusetts. Name them. _____

8. Which national park contains remains of cliff dwellings built by prehistoric Indians?
_____

9. The first national monument, created in 1906, was featured in the movie *Close Encounters of the Third Kind*. What is its name and where is it located? _____
_____

10. This famous national park is one mile deep. At the bottom, the Colorado River runs and the best way to get down to the river is by mule. You can read about these mules in a book by Marguerite Henry. Name the park and the state where it is located.
_____

11. Two national monuments preserve the ancient dwellings of the Navajo Indians. What are they? _____

12. Only 80 miles from Denver, Colorado, this national park contains 65 mountains all over 10,000 feet high. Name it. _____

13. Idaho, Washington, Oregon, California, and Hawaii all have a national park or monument created by or containing volcanoes. Name them all. _____
_____

14. Is there any area of your state that is part of the National Park System? Can you name it? _____

FRANKLIN D. ROOSEVELT

grades 5–8—coordinates with Chapters 4 and 8

Franklin Delano Roosevelt, born on January 30, 1882, was one of the most influential presidents in our national history. Although this puzzle's questions do not fully explore his accomplishments, they serve as a general introduction to his life and require students to use a variety of reference sources for their answers. A good starting place is *Facts About the Presidents*. Encyclopedias are also helpful.

Answers to "Franklin D. Roosevelt"

1. Alfred Lando(n)
2. (W) oman
3. Poli(o)myelitis
4. Dem(o)cracy
5. De(p)ression
6. Firesi(d)e chats
7. F(i)fteen
8. Warm Sprin(g)s
9. Decembe(r) 7, 1941
10. Brain Tru(s)t

Roosevelt family home: SPRINGWOOD

UNDER THE JOLLY ROGER

grades 5–8—coordinates with Chapters 4 and 8

Although pirates no longer sail the Spanish Main looking for ships laden with booty, and sailors do not worry about sighting a ship flying the Jolly Roger, a fascination with real and fictitious pirates remains to this day.

For these questions students will need the index volumes of encyclopedias, *Bartlett's Familiar Quotations*, and perhaps some books on pirates. A good one is American Heritage's *Pirates of the Spanish Main* (Harper, 1961).

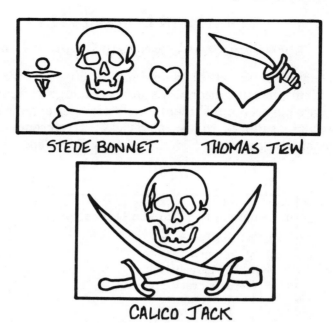

STEDE BONNET   THOMAS TEW

CALICO JACK

Answers to "Under the Jolly Roger"

1. (See the illustrations.)
2. Mary Read and Anne Bonny dressed as men, and although "Calico Jack" knew they were women, the rest of the crew thought they were men.
3. The Spanish Main is the mainland of Central and South America and the Barbary Coast is Mediterranean Africa around Algeria.
4. Kidd was hanged on May 23, 1701. Morgan was brought to England as a prisoner, but was instead knighted, returned to Jamaica, and died in bed, a wealthy planter, in 1688. Blackbeard was killed as he tried to take a ship commanded by Lieutenant Maynard of the Royal Navy in 1718.
5. Spanish coins—the treasure captured by many pirates.
6. They are fictitious pirates. Hook appears in James Barrie's *Peter Pan* and Blood in Sabatini's story of *Captain Blood*.

7. Davy Jones is the spirit of the sea and those who die at sea are said to have gone to his locker.
8. Freebooters, Buccaneers, Corsairs, Privateers, and to be technical, Vikings.
9. Teach was known as Blackbeard and Roberts was called "Black Bart."
10. Blackbeard's Castle.
11. Blackbeard tied colored ribbons in his beard for shore wear, and in battle he wore lighted matches in his hat and carried six loaded pistols, as well as a cutlass, over his shoulder.
12. Fourteen wives.
13. "Drink and the Devil had done for the rest—Yo-ho-ho and a bottle of rum."
14. An island visible between St. John and Tortola in the Virgin Islands.
15. Pyle was an American illustrator (1853-1911) who was famous for his paintings of pirates and their adventures.

© 1982 by Hilda K. Weisburg and Ruth Toor

Name _____   **Date** _____

FRANKLIN D. ROOSEVELT

Directions: Fill in the blanks.

1. The Republican candidate that Roosevelt overwhelmingly defeated was

   _ _ _ _ _ _   _ _ _ _ _Ⓞ

2. When Roosevelt revealed his choice for his first Secretary of Labor he created a stir because it was the first time that a cabinet post would be held by a

   Ⓞ_ _ _ _

3. If Roosevelt had lived after Jonas Salk and Albert Sabin had made their discoveries he would not have been stricken with

   _ _ _ _Ⓞ_ _ _ _ _ _ _ _

4. Roosevelt said the United States must be "the great arsenal of

   _ _ _Ⓞ_ _ _ _ _"

5. In his second inaugural address, Roosevelt said that one-third of the nation was "ill-housed, ill-clad, ill-nourished." This condition was caused by the great

   _ _Ⓞ_ _ _ _ _ _

6. Roosevelt's radio broadcasts were known as

   _ _ _ _ _ _Ⓞ_ _ _ _ _ _

7. In an attempt to make the Supreme Court more modern, Roosevelt asked Congress to increase the number of justices from nine to

   _Ⓞ_ _ _ _ _

8. Roosevelt exercised often in the naturally heated waters of Georgia called

   _ _ _ _ _ _ _ _ _Ⓞ_

9. According to Roosevelt, the "Date which will live in infamy" was Sunday,

   _ _ _ _ _ _ _Ⓞ _, _ _ _ _

10. The team of bright people who were assembled to give Roosevelt ideas and advice that would help him win the 1932 election was called the

    _ _ _ _ _ _ _ _Ⓞ_

Write the 10 circled letters here:

_ _ _ _ _ _ _ _ _ _

Rearrange them to spell the name of the Roosevelt family home in Hyde Park.

_ _ _ _ _ _ _ _ _ _

UNDER THE JOLLY ROGER

Directions: Using the books suggested by your teacher, find the answers to the following questions.

1. The Jolly Roger is the term used to describe the pirate flag, but there were many variations. See how many different ones you can locate and draw. (HINT: Check Stede Bonnet, "Calico Jack" Rackham, and Thomas Tew.)

2. Who were the two unusual crew members who served with "Calico Jack" Rackham?

3. Pirates sailed the Spanish Main and the Barbary Coast. Where are these places?

4. Captain Kidd, Henry Morgan, and Blackbeard were famous pirates who met very different ends. How did each one die?

5. What are "doubloons," "pieces of eight," and "picayunes"?

6. What do Captain Hook and Captain Blood have in common?

7. Who was Davy Jones and what is his "locker"?

8. Find at least four other names for pirates.

9. By what nicknames were Edward Teach and Bartholomew Roberts known?

10. What landmark on Charlotte Amalie on St. Thomas in the Virgin Islands remains as a memory of the days when it was a pirate port?

11. Blackbeard chose an unusual style of dress when he went ashore and a frightening style when he was in battle. Describe them.

12. According to legend, how many wives did Blackbeard have?

13. Complete the famous verse:
"Fifteen men on the Dead Man's Chest—Yo-ho-ho and a bottle of rum."

14. What is the "Dead Man's Chest" referred to in question 13?

15. What connection is there between Howard Pyle and pirates?

NATIONAL SYMBOLS AND EMBLEMS

grades 4–7—coordinates with Chapter 4

This is a simple reference exercise to introduce students to the living symbols used by states and countries. Two books that will help students in addition to the encyclopedia are:

Earle, Olive L. *State Trees*, rev. ed. Morrow, 1973, unpaged.

Simon, Hilda. *Bird and Flower Emblems of the United States*. Dodd, 1978, 128 pp.

Answers to "National Symbols and Emblems"

1. Cardinal—Illinois, Indiana, Kentucky, North Carolina, Ohio, Virginia, West Virginia
2. Virginia; North Carolina
3. Maine; pine cone and tassel
4. Kiwi
5. Sacred ibis
6. Laurel leaves
7. The rose
8. Maple leaf
9. Bald eagle; turkey
10. New York; Vermont; West Virginia; Wisconsin
11. Arizona; Saguaro blossom and Cactus wren
12. Dove; olive branch

AN AMAZING WORLD

grades 6–8—coordinates with Chapter 5

Have fun with a most "a-MAZE-ing" puzzle. As you can see from the directions, there are three required solutions. Students must use the atlas to find each correct route, since it is quite possible for them to go from Kabul to Lake Margherita and exit at Venezuela, which is completely incorrect.

Print the directions on the chalkboard or make copies for students. After they have completed the maze you can use a permanent transparency of the puzzle to show the correct routes to the class.

Directions:

1. Choose one of the three ovals with a capital city printed inside.
2. Check the index of an atlas to find out in what country that city is located.
3. Look at the map to see which of the three countries shown at the exits of the maze is the one you want. Label the country underneath the outline.
4. Look up the three geographic features shown in the square boxes and find out which one is found in the country you are going to.
5. Now trace a path from START to the capital city, then to the geographic feature, and finally exit at the correct country.
6. Repeat the above steps for the other two capitals.

Answers to "An Amazing World"

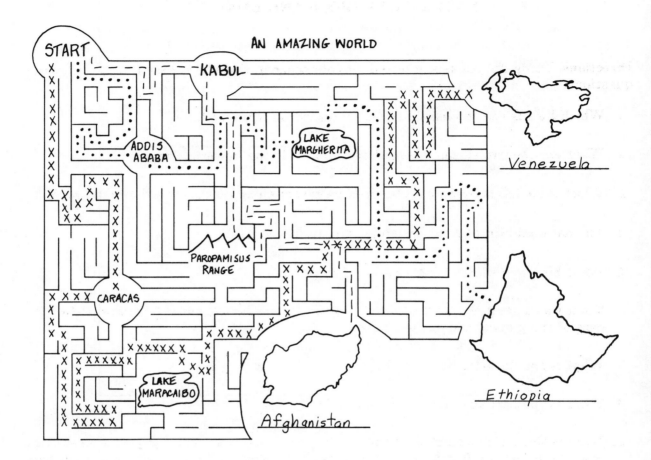

NATIONAL SYMBOLS AND EMBLEMS

Directions: Using the books suggested by your teacher, find the answers to the following questions.

1. Which bird is the emblem of seven states in the United States?

2. What are the two states whose floral emblem is the flowering dogwood?

3. Which state has chosen for its floral emblem something that is not a flower? What is it?

4. The national bird of New Zealand can't fly. What is it?

5. What bird was sacred to the ancient Egyptians?

6. What was a symbol of victory and honor first given by the ancient Greeks to the winners of the games held at Delphi?

7. What is the national flower of England?

8. What is the national symbol of Canada?

9. What is the national emblem of the United States? It was chosen despite a suggestion made by Benjamin Franklin to use another symbol which he thought was a more useful one. What had Benjamin Franklin suggested?

10. Four states have chosen the sugar maple for their state tree. Which are they?

11. Which state has chosen both a cactus flower and a cactus bird as its emblem? Name the flower and the bird.

12. What bird and tree were chosen as the emblem of the United Nations?

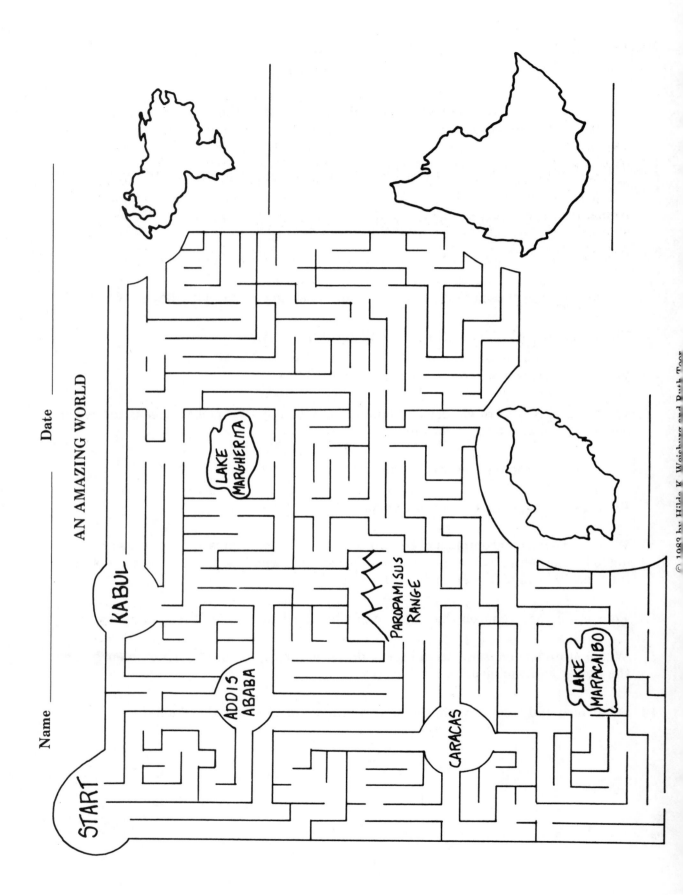

START

KABUL

ADDIS ABABA

LAKE MARGHERITA

PAROPAMISUS RANGE

CARACAS

LAKE MARACAIBO

ATLAS EXPLORATION

grades 6–up—coordinates with Chapter 5

The only way to learn to use an atlas effectively is by practicing regularly. This activity is one of five worksheets developed by Darlene J. Shiverdecker (Librarian/Media Specialist at Aiken High School, Cincinnati, Ohio). She creates new ones by repeating the same format. For example, the first question on another worksheet is, "What is the air distance from Panama City, Panama to Nome, Alaska?" (answer 5,541 miles) Another question 3 type is, "What is the steamship distance from Manila to New York City?" (answer 13,086 miles) You can use this pattern to develop your own series of worksheets.

Answers to "Atlas Exploration"

1. 8,088 miles
2. 850 miles
3. 11,047 miles
4. 10,439 miles
5. 1,850 feet above sea level
6. 40 feet below sea level
7. Jordan
8. Poland
9. Turkey
10. Ethiopia
11. South Africa
12. the Zambezi
13. the Tigris
14. the Lena
15. Berkeley
16. Owyhee
17. Cochise
18. San Francisco—9 a.m.; Athens —7 p.m.
19. Vancouver—northwest; Casablanca—east
20. (a) Africa; (b) Europe; (c) South America; (d) North America; (e) Asia

---

READERS' GUIDE WORKSHEET

grades 6–up—coordinates with Chapter 7

Reinforce your students' skills in using the *Readers' Guide* and give them the head start they need on research assignments early in the year by using this worksheet created by Darlene J. Shiverdecker (Librarian/Media Specialist at Aiken High School, Cincinnati, Ohio). If your school uses the *Abridged Readers' Guide*, the worksheet is easily adapted to use this.

Answers to "*Readers' Guide* Worksheet"

1. Foreign Aff
2. cont
3. Jl
4. por
5. ed
6. tr
7. Curr Hist
8. w
9. q
10. My
11. Ag
12. il
13. Ja
14. Sci Am
15. Good Housekeep

16. S
17. v
18. Read Dig
19. Ap
20. Mr
21. this answer varies by student
22. pseudonym (pen name)
23. 175 (58 in the *Abridged Readers' Guide*)
24. (a) Between the pigs and the swill
　　(b) *Time*
　　(c) 111
　　(d) March 13, 1978
　　(e) a portrait is included in the article
　　(f) 22

HAPPY BIRTHDAY, HARRY S.

grades 5–8—coordinates with Chapter 8

The birthday of President Harry S. Truman on May 8 is an opportunity to acquaint students with a generally unfamiliar time period. The questions include highlights of Truman's administration as well as minor facts about his life. In the first case, students' knowledge of history will increase if you are willing to follow-up on the questions. The lesser details allow students to explore the complexities of using *Facts About the Presidents*.

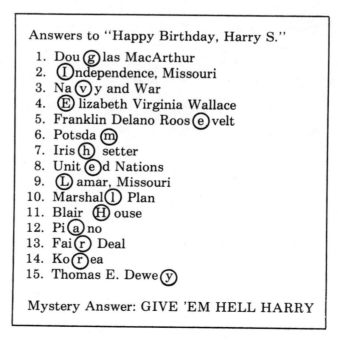

Answers to "Happy Birthday, Harry S."

1. Dou(g)las MacArthur
2. (I)ndependence, Missouri
3. Na(v)y and War
4. (E)lizabeth Virginia Wallace
5. Franklin Delano Roos(e)velt
6. Potsda(m)
7. Iris(h) setter
8. Unit(e)d Nations
9. (L)amar, Missouri
10. Marshal(l) Plan
11. Blair (H)ouse
12. Pi(a)no
13. Fai(r) Deal
14. Ko(r)ea
15. Thomas E. Dewe(y)

Mystery Answer: GIVE 'EM HELL HARRY

Name _____ Date _____

ATLAS EXPLORATION

Use an atlas to answer the following questions:

1. What is the air distance between Calcutta, India and Washington, D.C.? _____

2. What is the air distance between Oslo, Norway and Vienna, Austria? _____

3. What is the steamship distance between Halifax, Canada and Singapore? _____

4. What is the steamship distance between New Orleans, Louisiana and Yokohama, Japan?

_____

5. What is the altitude of Interlaken, Switzerland? _____

6. What is the altitude of Baku, Soviet Union? _____

7. In what country is Kufrinja located? _____

8. In what country is Wloszczowa located? _____

9. In what country is Unye located? _____

10. In what country is Thio located? _____

11. In what country is Reitz located? _____

12. Which river is longer, the Zambezi or the Ohio? _____

13. Which river is longer, the Tigris or the Snake? _____

14. Which river is longer, the Irrawaddy or the Lena? _____

15. In which county of South Carolina is Lake Moultrie located? _____

16. In which county is Grasmere, Idaho located? _____

17. In which county is Tombstone, Arizona located? _____

18. When it is noon, E.S.T. in New York City, what time is it in the following cities?

    San Francisco, California: _____ Athens, Greece _____

19. From Los Angeles, California, in which direction do you travel to get to the following

    cities? Vancouver, British Columbia _____ Casablanca, Morocco _____

20. Match the cities below to the continents on which they are located:

    (a) Algiers, Algeria _____   (d) Winnipeg, Manitoba _____

    (b) Tinto, Spain _____   (e) Bombay, India _____

    (c) Sao Paulo, Brazil _____

Name _____   Date _____

READERS' GUIDE WORKSHEET

Using a volume of the *Readers' Guide*, find the abbreviations which it uses for the following:

1. Foreign Affairs _____
2. Continued _____
3. July _____
4. Portrait _____
5. Editor _____
6. Translator _____
7. Current History _____
8. Weekly _____
9. Quarterly _____
10. May _____
11. August _____
12. Illustrations _____
13. January _____
14. Scientific American _____
15. Good Housekeeping _____
16. September _____
17. Volume _____
18. Reader's Digest _____
19. April _____
20. March _____

21. Name two of your favorite magazines that are indexed in the *Readers' Guide:*

_____

22. What does the abbreviation pseud. mean? _____

23. How many magazines are indexed in the *Readers' Guide*? _____

24. List the parts of the following entry:

Between the pigs and the swill. por Time 111:22 Mr 13 '78

a) Circle the title of the article.

b) What is the name of the magazine? _____

c) What is the volume number? _____

d) What is the date of the magazine? _____

e) What does the "por" stand for? _____

f) What is the page number for this article? _____

Name _____ **Date** _____

HAPPY BIRTHDAY, HARRY S.

Fill in the blanks with the answers to the questions. The letters inside the circles will spell out one of the better-known nicknames given to President Truman.

1. What is the name of the general dismissed by Harry S. Truman on April 11, 1951?
   _ _ _Ⓞ_ _ _   _ _ _ _ _ _ _ _

2. Where is Truman buried?
   Ⓞ_ _ _ _ _ _ _ _ _ _ _,   _ _ _ _ _ _ _ _

3. What two cabinet departments were combined under the Secretary of Defense in 1947?
   _ _Ⓞ_   and   _ _ _ _

4. What was the full maiden name of Harry S. Truman's wife?
   Ⓞ_ _ _ _ _ _ _ _   _ _ _ _ _ _ _ _   _ _ _ _ _ _ _

5. Upon whose death in 1945 did Truman say, "I felt like the moon, the stars, and all the planets had fallen on me"?
   _ _ _ _ _ _ _ _ _   _ _ _ _ _ _   _ _ _ _Ⓞ_ _ _ _

6. What conference was Truman attending when he received a secret message that told of the successful test of the atomic bomb?
   _ _ _ _ _ _Ⓞ

7. What breed was Mike, the Trumans' pet dog?
   _ _ _ _Ⓞ_   _ _ _ _ _ _

8. The charter of what international organization was signed in San Francisco in 1945?
   _ _ _ _Ⓞ_   _ _ _ _ _ _ _

9. Where was Truman born?
   Ⓞ_ _ _ _,   _ _ _ _ _ _ _ _ _

10. What program was devised by Truman's Secretary of State to help our allies recover from the effects of World War II?
    _ _ _ _ _ _ _Ⓞ_   _ _ _ _ _

11. In what Washington, D.C. building did Truman live during most of his administration?
    _ _ _ _ _Ⓞ_ _ _ _

12. What instrument did Truman play?
    _ _Ⓞ_ _

13. What was the name of the Truman program that extended Roosevelt's New Deal?
    _ _ _Ⓞ_   _ _ _ _ _

14. Into what country did the United States send troops in 1950 as a response to Communist aggression?
    _ _Ⓞ_ _

15. What was the name of the Republican candidate unexpectedly defeated by Truman in 1948?
    _ _ _ _ _ _ _   _ _ _ _ _Ⓞ

MYSTERY QUESTION: This was a popular nickname for President Truman:

_ _ _ _ ,_ _ _ _ _ _   _ _ _ _ _

MAY I QUOTE YOU?

grades 5–8—coordinates with Chapter 8

Although few media centers have classroom collections of *Bartlett's Familiar Quotations*, you can use this pencil game as an extra credit assignment to give students a chance to practice using that reference book. You might also use it with anyone who has finished making a quotation bookmark (see Chapter 8) before the rest of the class.

Answers to "May I Quote You?"

1. two	7. a
2. secret	8. them
3. if	9. may
4. of	10. are
5. three	11. keep
6. dead	

Mystery Quotation: Three may keep a secret, if two of them are dead.
Mystery Author: Benjamin Franklin
Book: *Poor Richard's Almanac* (for 1735)

FACTS ABOUT THE FIRST LADIES

grades 5–8—coordinates with Chapter 8

Although you may want to save this activity for May, traditionally associated with Mother's Day, this reference question can be used at any time during the school year. The answers can be found in the usual sources, such as encyclopedias, almanacs, and *Facts About the Presidents*. Enough information is given in each question to allow students entry into the reference sources, although in some cases careful reading of the question is required to find the clues. Two collective biographies that will help the students in addition to the reference books are:

Blumberg, Rhoda. *First Ladies*, updated ed. Watts, 1981.
Melick, Arden Davis. *Wives of the Presidents*. Hammond, 1972.

Answers to "Facts About the First Ladies"

1. Abigail Adams
2. Dorothea (Dolley) Madison
3. Eliza Johnson
4. Lucy Hayes, because she would not serve liquor in the White House
5. Frances Folsom Cleveland
6. Caroline Harrison
7. Helen (Nellie) Taft
8. Edith Wilson
9. Eleanor Roosevelt
10. Jacqueline Kennedy
11. Anna and William Henry Harrison
12. Louisa Adams
13. Claudia (Lady Bird) Johnson
14. Harriet Lane, James Buchanan's niece
15. Abigail Fillmore
16. Bess Truman
17. Lucretia and James A. Garfield
18. Abigail Smith Adams, Abigail Powers Fillmore, Jane Applegate Pierce, Caroline Scott Harrison, and Ellen Axson Wilson
19. Letitia Tyler, Caroline Harrison, and Ellen Wilson
20. Lucy Hayes graduated from Ohio Wesleyan University in 1850

IN THE MEDIA CENTER

grades 3–8—coordinates with Chapter 10

Use this word search as a warm-up to research. It serves to remind students of the many sources that can be used to locate information.

Answers to "In the Media Center"

```
V E R T I C A L F I L E C A B
F C E N C Y C L O P E D I A S
I A F E N L A D R O C E R S P
L R E N O I S I V E L E T N O
L E R O N A T C A S S E E G O
M D E F F I C T I O N F B L L
S S N F I T A I E C T I I O N
T K C E C O S O N S K O O B E
R C E J T E S N Y C E L G E W
S A T L I S E A C A L M R S S
E B T I O A T R L N O S A T P
S R E S N C T I O A U T P E A
A E L E R G E E P M S R H L P
L P S P I R T S M L I F Y E E
T A E A M A G A Z A N A C V R
A P S T A S E N I Z A G A M S
```

MAY I QUOTE YOU?

Directions: Use *Bartlett's Familiar Quotations* to fill in the missing words in these quotations. Then rearrange the missing words to form a quotation by a famous American. CAUTION: Look under the key word. The index does not always give a reference from all words in a quote. Try to find the most unusual word in the quotation. CLUE: Once you have several of the missing words, you might want to check the index.

1. . . . takes _____ to speak the truth.

2. Death . . . a _____ of Nature.

3. It is hard, _____ not impossible, to snub a beautiful woman.

4. Each page _____ them Quotations that this Bartlett man got out . . .

5. When shall we _____ meet again/In thunder, lightning or in rain?

6. Books are not absolutely _____ things.

7. I shot _____ poem into the air.

8. . . . "Let _____ eat cake."

9. For in that sleep of death what dreams _____ come.

10. Tale-bearers _____ as bad as the tale-makers.

11. Push on—_____ moving.

MYSTERY QUOTATION

_____

_____

AUTHOR OF MYSTERY QUOTATION

_____

BOOK IN WHICH QUOTATION APPEARED

_____

FACTS ABOUT THE FIRST LADIES

Directions: Using the books suggested by your teacher, find the answers to the following questions.

1. Which first lady was both the wife and mother of a president?

2. Which first lady, known as a great hostess, saved the original drafts of the Declaration of Independence and Constitution as well as Stuart's portrait of George Washington before the White House was burned by the British?

3. Which first lady taught her husband, who had never gone to school, to read and write? This president came into office in 1865.

4. Which first lady was known as "Lemonade Lucy"? Why?

5. Who became first lady, when at the age of 22, she married the president?

6. Which first lady had electric lights installed in the White House and began the tradition of having a White House Christmas tree?

7. Which twentieth-century first lady had 3,000 cherry trees shipped from Japan to Washington, D.C.? These trees beautify Washington, D.C. each spring.

8. Which twentieth-century first lady was the unofficial "acting president" while her husband recuperated from a stroke?

9. Which first lady became known as "First Lady of the World" because of her extensive travels during World War II and her appointment as a United States delegate to the United Nations General Assembly after her husband's death? She also wrote a newspaper column called "My Day."

10. Which first lady refurnished and redecorated the public rooms in the White House and then appeared on television as hostess for a guided tour of the mansion?

11. Which first lady and her husband had ten children, one of whom was the father of a future president?

12. Which first lady was not born in America?

13. Which first lady began a "beautification" program throughout the country in the 1960s?

14. Who filled the first lady's position as hostess for our only bachelor president?

15. Which first lady began the White House library?

16. Which twentieth-century first lady, referred to as "The Boss" by her husband, shunned the limelight, unlike her world-traveling predecessor?

17. Which first lady and her husband, who became president in 1881, were both school teachers when they married?

18. Which five first ladies were daughters of ministers?

19. Which three first ladies died while their husbands were in office?

20. Which first lady was the first to graduate from college?

IN THE MEDIA CENTER

Directions: Look at the words in the box. These words are located in the word search puzzle either horizontally, vertically, frontwards, or backwards. When you find the words, circle them.

```
V  E  R  T  I  C  A  L  F  I  L  E  C  A  B
F  C  E  N  C  Y  C  L  O  P  E  D  I  A  S
I  A  F  E  N  L  A  D  R  O  C  E  R  S  P
L  R  E  N  O  I  S  I  V  E  L  E  T  N  O
L  E  R  O  N  A  T  C  A  S  S  E  E  G  O
M  D  E  F  F  I  C  T  I  O  N  F  B  L  L
S  S  N  F  I  T  A  I  E  C  T  I  I  O  N
T  K  C  E  C  O  S  O  N  S  K  O  O  B  E
R  C  E  J  T  E  S  N  Y  C  E  L  G  E  W
S  A  T  L  I  S  E  A  C  A  L  M  R  S  S
E  B  T  I  O  A  T  R  L  N  O  S  A  T  P
S  R  E  S  N  C  T  I  O  A  U  T  P  E  A
A  E  L  E  R  G  E  E  P  M  S  R  H  L  P
L  P  S  P  I  R  T  S  M  L  I  F  Y  E  E
T  A  E  A  M  A  G  A  Z  A  N  A  C  V  R
A  P  S  T  A  S  E  N  I  Z  A  G  A  M  S
```

Almanacs	Loops
Atlases	Magazines
Biography	Nonfiction
Books	Paperbacks
Cassette	Record
Dictionaries	Reference
Encyclopedias	Vertical File
Fiction	Tapes
Filmstrips	Newspapers
Globes	Television

A MATTER OF STATE

grades 5–up—coordinates with Chapter 10

A cross-country look at historical happenings in the United States is the focus of this reference exercise. There are many sources for the answers, but your students might enjoy an unusual one—the National Geographic Society's "Historical Map of the Conterminous United States," 1967, available for a small fee from the National Geographic Society, Department 87, Washington, D.C. 20036.

Answers to "A Matter of State"

1. Kentucky
2. Florida; St. Augustine
3. Maryland
4. New Mexico
5. New York, Manhattan
6. Montana
7. Missouri
8. Georgia; Eli Whitney
9. Illinois
10. California; Sutter's Mill
11. Ohio
12. Delaware
13. Massachusetts
14. Pennsylvania; Gettysburg Address
15. Minnesota

EXPLORING REFERENCE BOOKS

grades 5–8—coordinates with Chapter 10

The subtle differences among many of the reference sources are often difficult for students to grasp. This reference activity, created by Barbara M. Collins (Media Specialist at Lightfoot Elementary School, Unionville, Virginia), presents a guided tour through several of these books that will help students become familiar with the distinctions. Since answers will depend on the specific reference books available, you will have to check them yourself before turning students loose. (You might want to use the first six questions for the holiday season and save questions seven through twelve for later in the school year.)

Answers (sources to check) for "Exploring Reference Books"

1. almanac
2. dictionary
3. *Webster's Biographical Dictionary* or encyclopedia
4. encyclopedia
5. *Webster's Geographical Dictionary*
6. periodical index
7. *Webster's Biographical Dictionary* or encyclopedia
8. *Webster's Geographical Dictionary*
9. periodical index
10. dictionary
11. almanac
12. encyclopedia

PERSONALITIES IN BLACK HISTORY

grades 5–8—coordinates with Chapter 10

Introduce students to leading figures, both black and white, who have advanced the cause or called attention to the plight of blacks in the United States. In solving these "puzzling" questions, the usual reference sources—almanacs, encyclopedias, and so forth—will be helpful, as well as books such as *Black Struggle: A History of the Negro in America* by Bryan Fulks, Delacorte, 1969.

Answers to "Personalities in Black History"

1. C(r)ispus Attucks
2. Benjamin B(a)nneker
3. William (L)loyd Garrison
4. Rosa (P)arks
5. (H)arriet Beecher Stowe
6. Jackie Ro(b)inson
7. Harriet T(u)bman
8. Marti(n) Luther King, Jr.
9. Dred S(c)ott
10. Thurgood Mars(h)all
11. James M(e)redith

Mystery Personality: RALPH BUNCHE

Name _____ Date _____

A MATTER OF STATE

Directions: Using the books suggested by your teacher, find the answers to the following questions.

1. In what state were the future President of the Confederate States of America and the future President of the United States of America born? The first was born in 1808 and the second in 1809.

2. In what state is the oldest city in the United States, founded by Spaniards in 1565? What is the name of the city?

3. In what state did Francis Scott Key write "The Star Spangled Banner" in 1814?

4. In what state was the first atomic bomb tested in 1945?

5. In what state is the island originally purchased by Peter Minuit from the Indians in 1624 for $24? What is the name of this island?

6. In what state were General Custer and his men killed at Little Big Horn in 1876?

7. In what state did Winston Churchill make his famous "Iron Curtain" speech in 1946?

8. In what state was the cotton gin invented in 1793? Who was the inventor?

9. From what state did the Lewis and Clark Expedition set out in May 1804?

10. In what state did James Marshall discover gold in 1848? Where did he find the gold?

11. In what state did Oliver Hazard Perry say, "We have met the enemy and they are ours"? This was said in 1813 at the end of a battle.

12. From what state did Caesar Rodney come? He had cast the decisive vote for the Declaration of Independence.

13. In what state did Alexander Graham Bell transmit the first message through his new invention, the telephone, in March 1876?

14. In what state did President Lincoln dedicate a cemetery in November 1863 with a short speech that was to become famous? What is the speech called?

15. In what state is the world's largest open-pit iron mine located?

EXPLORING REFERENCE BOOKS

Here are six reference sources that will help you find answers to the questions below. Give the answer and tell which book you used and the page where you found it.

World Almanac a periodical index   an encyclopedia
a dictionary   *Webster's Biographical Dictionary*   *Webster's Geographical Dictionary*

1. What other legal holidays, besides Christmas, are celebrated in our state?

    _____ _____ p. ____

2. How is the word "Noël" pronounced?

    _____ _____ p. ____

3. When did St. Nicholas live?

    _____ _____ p. ____

4. When did people first start celebrating Christmas?

    _____ _____ p. ____

5. Where is the North Pole? Is it on land or water?

    _____ _____ p. ____

6. What would tell you where to find some photographs of Bethlehem?

    _____ _____ p. ____

7. When did George Washington die?

    _____ _____ p. ____

8. How big is the District of Columbia? How much of that is water?

    _____ _____ p. ____

9. What would tell you where to find some photographs of the Vietnam Memorial in Washingon, D.C.?

    _____ _____ p. ____

10. The National Archives has an original copy of the Declaration of Independence. How is the word "Archives" pronounced?

    _____ _____ p. ____

11. How does Washington, D.C. rank in population among cities in the United States?

    _____ _____ p. ____

12. When was the Lincoln Memorial built?

    _____ _____ p. ____

Name _____   Date _____

PERSONALITIES IN BLACK HISTORY

Directions: Using the books suggested by your teacher, fill in the names on the spaces. Then write the circled letters at the bottom of the page to find another personality in Black History who was a winner of the Nobel Peace Prize in 1950 and an undersecretary of the United Nations from 1955 to 1971.

1. This black man was the first person to die during the Boston Massacre in 1770, a prelude to the American Revolution. _ O_ _ _ _ _   _ _ _ _ _ _ _

2. This black man, who argued for freedom throughout his life in the 1700s, invented the first wooden clock, published an almanac that greatly impressed Thomas Jefferson, helped survey and plan the site for the city of Washington, D.C., and became a noted astronomer. _ _ _ _ _ _ _ _   _ O_ _ _ _ _ _

3. A white man who helped publicize the abolitionist movement was the publisher of *The Liberator,* most of whose subscribers were blacks. He became a spokesman for the movement in 1831.

   _ _ _ _ _ _ _   O_ _ _ _   _ _ _ _ _ _ _ _ _

4. This seamstress began what was to become known as the Montgomery, Alabama bus boycott in late 1955. _ _ _ _   O_ _ _ _

5. A white woman wrote a famous book about slavery published in 1852. When she was presented to President Abraham Lincoln, he said, "So this is the little lady who started the big war!"

   O_ _ _ _ _ _   _ _ _ _ _ _ _ _   _ _ _ _ _ _

6. He was the first baseball player to break the color line in the major leagues, joining the Brooklyn Dodgers in 1947. He was elected to the Baseball Hall of Fame in 1962.

   _ _ _ _ _ _ _   _ _ O_ _ _ _ _

7. This lady, called "The Black Moses," helped over 300 slaves to freedom along the Underground Railroad. _ _ _ _ _ _ _   _ O_ _ _ _

8. This black man was the head of the Southern Christian Leadership Conference, believed in nonviolence, won the Nobel Peace Prize in 1965, and was assassinated in April 1968.

   _ _ _ _ _ O_   _ _ _ _ _ _ _ _   _ _ _ _ _,   _ _

9. In a famous 1857 case, U.S. Supreme Court Chief Justice Roger Taney ruled against this black man who had filed suit ten years earlier in Missouri claiming that, because his master took him to Illinois where slavery was forbidden, he should be free.

   _ _ _ _ _   _ O_ _ _

10. In 1967 he became the first black U.S. Supreme Court Justice, nominated by President Lyndon Johnson.

    _ _ _ _ _ _ _ _ _   _ _ _ _ O_ _ _

11. This Air Force veteran tried to enroll at the University of Mississippi in 1962. When he was refused admittance, President John F. Kennedy sent Federal marshals to the campus to enforce the court order admitting him. He later became the first black to graduate from the University of Mississippi.

    _ _ _ _ _   _ O_ _ _ _ _

Mystery Personality: _ _ _ _ _   _ _ _ _ _ _ _ _ _

FIND THE MISSING HEADLINE

grades 6–up—coordinates with Chapter 10

Keep reference skills sharp and help students find inventive ways to extract information by regularly presenting them with reference problems such as the one presented here that will creatively inform them about a historical occurrence while familiarizing them with the layout of a newspaper.

Background Information

On April 18, 1906, San Francisco experienced a massive earthquake. Set up a reference problem in the format of a newspaper, which students will follow daily to unearth the solution.

In place of a headline, you will put question marks across a banner. The students use clues to find the missing headline. If you use all of the clues listed here, the activity can continue for a month; if you prefer a shorter problem, eliminate or combine some clues.

To write the headline students will have to do research. Some clues lead to only part of the answer. Many clues need to be put together to arrive at a logical approach to investigation. By giving one clue a day you will stimulate the students' curiosity. Be sure not to comment on any guesses.

On the last day cover the question marks on the banner with the missing headline—"Quake Rocks San Francisco." Put the name of the winner in the box you have prepared. (see Step 3 in the section titled "Materials and Preparation").

Materials and Preparation:

1. To make a poster, see the sample for suggestions. You can draw the newspaper directly onto white posterboard, using a black marking pen, or use folded tissue paper to simulate a newspaper. Print the paper's name, question marks, and so on, on white drawing paper and paste them onto the tissue paper, and then paste the whole onto the posterboard.

2. Prepare and make copies of the card for recording guesses. (See the illustration here.)

Date _____

Name _____

Headline _____

_____

3. Use a small box, such as the type in which catalog cards come. Cover it with newspapers, and cut a slit in the top. Be sure you can open the box easily. Use this box for the students' guesses.

4. Print or type all the clues on separate pieces of white drawing paper. Number the clues on the back and put them in an envelope until you are ready to post them.

Procedure:

Put up the poster with the first clue. Be prepared to explain what is happening. After a day or so, word-of-mouth will make further explanations unnecessary.

- Keep copies of the "guess" forms at the desk next to the box you prepared.

- Empty the box daily.

- When the first correct guess is made, make a note to yourself. Keep the slip in a safe place—but don't announce the winner until all the clues have been posted.

- On the last day, cover the question marks with the correct headline: "Quake Rocks San Francisco."

- Post the name of the winner in the space provided.

- Depending on your financial resources, award the winner a paperback book or an ice cream cone, or just allow the glory of victory to be enough of a reward.

- If you had any unusual guesses you can post them too—but don't reveal the names of the students who made them.

USING LIBRARY SOURCES
grades 5–up—coordinates with Chapter 10

Concentrating on teaching students to use a particular reference tool is a good idea, but at some point students must learn to choose which of the many resources will best answer a specific question. This reference activity, created by Luann Moro (Elementary Library Media Specialist at the Randall and Virgil Schools, Cortland, New York), requires the use of six different resources to go from START to END. Students need only select ten questions. This gives them a choice and avoids the problem created when the whole class needs the same book.

Answers to "Using Library Sources"

00	Almanac	Washington
01	Atlas	41°N 112°W
02	Telephone book	
03	Encyclopedia	16
04	Card Catalog	
05	Dictionary	"a small bundle"
06	Dictionary	"prison toilet; expel from school"
07	Encyclopedia	inner bark of cinnamon tree, laurel grown in tropical regions
08	Encyclopedia, Almanac	Franklin Pierce
09	Card catalog	
10	Atlas	Water—straits, inlets, etc.
11	Almanac	April 7
12	Almanac	1928
13	Encyclopedia, Almanac	9 (Chief Justice and 8 Associate Justices)
14	Encyclopedia	terrier, collie, cocker spaniel, etc.
15	Almanac	99502
16	Atlas	See Tombouctou; Mali
17	Almanac	Baseball, Horse Racing
18	Atlas	Just over 800 miles
19	Card catalog	
20	Dictionary	"unruly"
21	Almanac, Encyclopedia	February 14, 1912
22	Almanac (78)	133,160 (1976)
23	Almanac	Washington, D.C., Monday-Friday every 30 minutes from 9–3:30 concourse

BONUS: Encyclopedia—False

The Examiner

Fill in the missing headline

? ? ? ?

Watch this box for the Winner

Name

_____

Room Number

_____
_____
_____
_____
_____
_____
_____
_____
_____
_____
_____

CLUES:

1. It happened in April.

2. First paper owned by Hearst is located where this event occurred.

3. John Barrymore, the actor, was there.

4. Enrico Caruso, famous opera singer, was there.

5. It happened on a Wednesday.

6. It began at 5:12 a.m.

7. Jack London, author, went to see it.

8. The first part lasted 2 minutes.

9. 497 city blocks were destroyed.

10. 28,000 buildings were destroyed.

11. Fires caused $500,000,000 worth of damage.

12. 52 fires started within half an hour.

13. 15 fires joined to become a solid sheet of flame.

14. 250,000 people were left homeless.

15. The Bank of America, world's largest, began because of it.

MORE CLUES:

16. A movie starring Clark Gable and Jeanette MacDonald was made about it.

17. Brigadier General Funston took charge.

18. It ended, at last, three days later on Saturday morning.

19. The year was 1906.

_____
_____
_____
_____
_____
_____
_____
_____

USING LIBRARY RESOURCES

Begin at "Start." Finish at "End."
Answer 10 questions by giving the answer
and the source.

START
00 Who won the Rose Bowl in 1960?

06 What are two slang versions of the word "can"?

10 Describe the terrain around Mackinaw, Michigan.

01 What are the latitude and longitude for Salt Lake City, Utah?

07 Where does cinnamon come from?

11 On what day and month will Easter fall in 1985?

12 When was Shirley Temple Black born?

02 Where can I have a TV repaired in _____?
(your town)

08 Give three facts about the 14th President of the U.S.

13 How many justices are there on the Supreme Court?

14 Name 15 kinds of dogs.

03 In the game of chess, how many men does each player have?

09 How many titles do we have by Donald Sobol?

15 What is the ZIP code for Anchorage, Alaska?

16 Is there such a place as "Timbuktu"? If so, where is it?

04 Give the call number for a book on Puppetry.

17 In what two sports are there Triple Crown winners?

18 What is the distance from Paris, France to Warsaw, Poland?

23 Where is the Pentagon and when could I take a tour of it?

05 What is a fascicle?

19 Give the author of a book on China.

22 How many telephones are there in Erie, Pa.?

20 Use the word "obstreperous" in a coherent sentence.

21 Give the exact date on which AZ became a state of the United States.

END
BONUS: A snake swallows its young in case of danger. True or False.

A TRIBUTE TO GEORGE WASHINGTON

grades 5–up—coordinates with Chapter 10

Test the research skills of your students with this monumental tribute to George Washington. Begin early in February, coordinate the activity with the "250+ Years of U.S. History" bulletin board in Part Three, and truly celebrate the birth of our first president.

There are several ways to organize the research. You need not use all 250 questions at one time so that you can vary the questions from year to year.

Method 1—Everywhere a Face

Make a copy of Washington's face on a ditto master. (Find your own portrait or use the one on the "250+ Years of U.S. History" bulletin board.) At the top of the ditto master leave space for each student's name and a question. Below the picture leave space for the answer. Run off as many copies as needed.

To begin, hand out one question per student. Have everyone verify answers with you first, so that once they know they have a correct answer they can write the questions and answers on the ditto. Mount completed dittos on red, white, and blue construction paper and hang in the hallway or around the classroom. After students have one portrait hanging they may try for another if they want.

Method 2—The Team Approach

Divide the class into teams of four. Assign 40 questions per team, giving the same number of difficult questions (starred) to each group. You can award small prizes to the team finishing first with the most correct answers.

Answers to "A Tribute to George Washington"

Family Relations

1. Augustine Washington
2. Mary Ball Washington
3. Jane Butler Washington
4. February 22, 1732
5. Six
6. Four
7. 11 years old
8. 81 years old
9. 6'2½"
10. His half-brother Lawrence
11. Westmoreland County, Virginia
12. Charles Washington —born May 2, 1738, died May 3, 1799
13. Martha Dandridge Custis Washington
14. 26 years
15. 27 years
16. Daniel Parke Custis
17. Four children (two died in infancy)
18. John "Jackie" Parke Custis and Martha "Patsy" Parke Custis
19. None, but he adopted his two step-grand-children
20. Children of Martha Washington's son John, who were adopted and raised by George Washington and his wife when their father died
21. June 21, 1731
22. New Kent County, Virginia
23. Planter
24. 1708
25. 1694
26. March 6, 1730
27. Tuberculosis
28. Smallpox
29. Mount Vernon
30. Colonel John Dandridge

31. Frances Jones Dandridge
32. Episcopalian
33. January 6, 1759; Kent County, Virginia
34. Younger
35. May 22, 1802
36. 70 years old
37. Sulgrave Manor
38. Place his father purchased when George was 7 years old
39. On the Rappahannock River
40. Wife of Lawrence Washington
41. Mount Vernon
42. She was the wife of Anne Fairfax's brother and may have been a secret love of George Washington
43. He was always considerate and dutiful, although modern historians note that there were strains on the relationship because she was selfish, inconsiderate, and ignorant
44. In 1752, England accepted the more accurate Gregorian calendar. All dates were put 11 days ahead. Washington seemed to have preferred February 11, which took the notation "o.s." or Old Style.
45. Beverly Whiting and Captain Christopher Brooks
46. Mrs. Mildred Gregory
47. About 49 years old
48. Sandy brown
49. Blue

Education

50. There are two stories: 1) his father hired an educated convict who had been transported to Virginia; 2) he went to a school run by clergy in Fredericksburg
51. Mathematics
52. Very poor, but not unusually so for the times

53. His mother refused to let him go
54. At Appleby in England
55. Between 7 and 8
56. His father's death and his mother's protectiveness kept him from leaving the farm

First Occupation

57. From his father
58. The county surveyor
59. 15 years old
60. Mapping the western lands of Lord Fairfax
61. Belhaven—later known as Alexandria
62. William and Mary College in Williamsburg
63. Culpeper County
64. 17 years old
65. 100 pounds

Early Military Career

66. Adjutant of Southern district of Royal Colony of Virginia; February 1, 1753; Major George Washington
67. To the French Commander at Fort LeBoeuf (now Waterford, Pennsylvania, near Erie)
68. Served as scout
69. Principal Chief of the Seneca Indians
70. January 16, 1754
71. The junction of the Monongahela and Allegheny Rivers; Pittsburg, Pennsylvania
72. Lieutenant Colonel
73. Fort Duquesne
74. The French seized it
75. George Washington and his men
76. Great Meadows (now Confluence, Pennsylvania) 50-60 miles from Fort Duquesne
77. He resigned it
78. Volunteer Aide
79. 1756–1763
80. Colonel in charge of the Colonial Armed Force
81. Brigadier General John Forbes
82. 1758

Plantation Life

83. Tobacco
84. Wheat
85. Considered to be one of the best
86. Potomac River
87. The Colonial Legislature of Virginia
88. 1758
89. Patrick Henry, Thomas Jefferson
90. He learned the workings of government
91. 15 years
92. Salt fish ("alewives" or herring)
93. Between 8,000 and 9,000 acres or 13 square miles

The Revolution

94. Seven
95. September, 1774
96. Philadelphia
97. May 1775
98. Battle of Lexington; Battle of Concord
99. John Adams
100. No salary, just his expenses
101. June 15, 1775
102. Boston/Cambridge, Massachusetts
103. July 3, 1775
104. George III
105. Prime Minister of Great Britain, from 1770–1782
106. Queen Charlotte
107. December 25, 1776
108. Battle of Trenton; Battle of Princeton
109. Hessians
110. Morristown, New Jersey
111. Spent the winter there, from 1777–1778
112. There was little food, little clothing, and very harsh weather
113. He taught soldiers vital lessons in drill
114. Lieutenant General John Burgoyne
115. Marquis de Lafayette
116. West Point
117. Major John Andre; he was hanged
118. He escaped and joined the British
119. General Lord Cornwallis

120. October 19, 1781
121. The end of the Revolutionary War
122. Paris, France
123. September 3, 1783
124. He said farewell to his troops
125. December 23, 1783
126. A spy recruited by George Washington
127. He told him about Trenton so that Washington could attack
128. Colonel Johann Rall

The Presidency: First Term

129. 69
130. John Adams
131. Alexander Hamilton
132. Henry Knox
133. John Jay
134. Frederick Augustus Conrad Muhlenberg
135. New York City
136. April 30, 1789
137. 6
138. John Jay
139. John Rutledge
140. Mr. President
141. Federal Hall
142. Boat
143. December 15, 1791
144. First
145. Fourth
146. Fifth
147. Rhode Island
148. Pennsylvania; eight
149. Two states
150. Vermont, Kentucky
151. Robert Livingston
152. 1 Cherry Street, New York
153. 53 years old
154. $25,000
155. $5,000
156. 57 years old
157. April 2, 1792
158. Philadelphia
159. The disme (dime) and the half disme
160. The copper half-cent
161. The $10 gold eagle
162. 1790
163. 3,929,214
164. Samuel Osgood
165. John Langdon
166. Three
167. New England states
168. Thursday, November 26, 1789

169. An "Act for Apportionment of Representatives"

The Presidency: Second Term

170. Federalist
171. 132 votes
172. 77 votes
173. Philadelphia
174. 135 words
175. Senate Chamber, Federal Hall
176. William Cushing
177. March 4, 1793
178. Pierre L'Enfant
179. Washington, D.C.
180. Tennessee
181. Miami Indians
182. Great Britain
183. They did not want to pay taxes on their whiskey stills
184. General Lighthorse Harry Lee
185. The *Philadelphia Daily Advertiser*
186. September 19, 1796 (some sources say September 18)
187. Alexander Hamilton and John Jay
188. The son of the Marquis de Lafayette and his tutor

Retirement and Death

189. Lieutenant General and Commander of all the Armies of the United States
190. 2 years and 285 days
191. December 14, 1799
192. 67 years old
193. December 18, 1799
194. In the family vault at Mount Vernon, Virginia
195. Some type of upper respiratory infection. Sources say pneumonia, quinsy, and influenza.
196. Bloodletting; a potion of vinegar, molasses, and butter
197. Dr. James Craik
198. To have taken his own pulse

199. Three doctors including Dr. Craik; his wife, Martha; his secretary, Tobias Lear; and a house slave named Christopher
200. "I die hard, but I am not afraid to go. It is well."

Art and Artists

201. Emanuel Leutze
202. Gilbert Stuart
203. William T. Trego
204. Only statue for which Washington posed
205. In the Virginia Capitol in Richmond
206. Colonel of the Virginia Militia
207. All painted portraits of George Washington

Places and Memorials

208. New York and New Jersey
209. 2800 feet
210. Mount Vernon Ladies Association, organized by Ann Pamela Cunningham of South Carolina. They bought the mansion in 1853.
211. The Capitol
212. Cambridge, Massachusetts
213. Washington took command of the Continental Army there
214. Washington gave the school a gift of stock valued at $50,000.
215. 555' 5⅛"
216. 55' 1⅛"
217. $1,187,710.31
218. Obelisk
219. 15' thick
220. 18" thick
221. Maryland Marble
222. 55 feet
223. 898 steps
224. July 4, 1848
225. August 17, 1880
226. December 6, 1884
227. February 21, 1885
228. 31 counties
229. A portrait of Washington in a circle, ringed with the words, "The Seal of the State of Washington 1889."

230. Millard Fillmore
231. 42nd State
232. November 11, 1889
233. George Washington, Thomas Jefferson, Abraham Lincoln, and Theodore Roosevelt
234. The Black Hills of South Dakota
235. Gutzon Borglum

Stamps and Coins

236. July 1, 1847
237. Ten cent black
238. The quarter
239. 1932; to mark the 200th anniversary of his birth
240. The dollar bill

Odds and Ends

241. John A. Washington Jr., the great-great nephew of the President
242. John Quincy Adams
243. Parson Mason Weems
244. George Gordon, Lord Byron
245. Like the Roman patriot, he too left his farm to save his country

Quotations By and About

246. The Marquis de Lafayette, November 15, 1781

247. First Inaugural Address, April 30, 1789
248. Farewell Address, September 1796
249. Daniel Webster on the completion of the Bunker Hill Monument, June 17, 1843
250. Henry Lee ("Lighthorse Harry")

Questions for "A Tribute to George Washington"

Family Relations

1. What was the name of George Washington's father?
2. What was the name of George Washington's mother?
3. What was the name of his father's first wife?
4. What was the date of George Washington's birth?
5. How many children did George Washington's mother have?
6. How many half brothers and sisters did he have?
7. How old was George Washington when his father died?
8. How old was his mother when she died?
9. How tall was George Washington?
10. With whom did George Washington stay as much as possible after his father died?
11. Name the county and the colony in which George Washington was born.
12. What was the name of George Washington's youngest brother and what were the dates of his birth and death?
13. Give the full name of George Washington's wife.
14. How old was he when he got married?
15. How old was George Washington's wife when they got married?
16. Give the name of the first husband of George Washington's wife.
17. How many children did his wife have by her first marriage?
18. Give the names of George Washington's stepchildren who were alive at the time of his marriage.
19. How many children did George Washington have?
20. Who were Eleanor "Nellie" Parke Custis and George Washington Parke Custis?
21. When was George Washington's wife born?
22. Where was his wife born?
23. What occupation was shared by both George Washington's father and his father-in-law?
24. In what year was George Washington's mother born?
25. In what year was George Washington's father born?
26. Name the date on which the marriage of George Washington's parents took place.
27. What disease killed Lawrence Washington?
28. What disease did George Washington contract while in Barbados in 1751?
29. What was the name of George Washington's plantation home?
30. What was the name of George Washington's father-in-law?
31. What was the name of George Washington's mother-in-law?
32. What was George Washington's religion?
33. Name the date on which George Washington's marriage took place and the county and colony where it was held.
34. Was George Washington older or younger than his wife?
35. Name the date on which George Washington's wife died.

36. How old was George Washington's wife when she died?
37. What is the name of George Washington's English ancestral home?
38. What is Ferry Farm?
39. On what river was Ferry Farm located?
40. Who was Anne Fairfax?
41. What was the later name of Epsewasson?
*42. Who was Sally Fairfax and what may she have been to George Washington?
*43. What information can you find about the kind of relationship George Washington had with his mother?
*44. When George Washington turned 21, he could choose the date he wanted for his birthday—February 11 or 22. Why?
45. Who were George Washington's godfathers at his baptism?
46. Who was George Washington's godmother at his baptism?
47. How old was George Washington's father when he died?
48. What color was George Washington's hair under his wig?
49. What color eyes did George Washington have?

Education

*50. According to one account, how did George Washington learn to read and write?
51. What was his favorite subject in school?
*52. What can you find out about George Washington's spelling?
53. What stopped him from joining the Royal Navy?
54. Where did George Washington's stepbrothers go to school?

55. For how many years did George Washington actually attend school?
*56. How do you account for the brevity of his schooling?

First Occupation

57. Where did George Washington get his first surveying instruments?
58. Who taught him about the trade of surveying?
59. How old was he when he became a surveyor?
60. His first surveying job was serving as an assistant on what expedition?
*61. Which town in Northern Virginia did he assist in laying out?
*62. At what college did he take a surveying course that led to his taking the licensing examination, which he passed?
63. For which county did he become the official surveyor?
64. How old was he when he became an official surveyor for a county?
65. What was his annual salary as the county surveyor?

Early Military Career

66. What was George Washington's first military appointment? Name the date on which it occurred and the rank that he held.
67. In 1753, George Washington volunteered to carry an ultimatum from Royal Governor Dinwiddie to whom? To what place?
68. What role did Christopher Gist serve on Washington's first military expedition?

69. Who was Half-King?
70. On what date did Washington give Governor Dinwiddie the reply to his ultimatum?
71. As a result of his first military expedition, Washington recommended that a fort be built. At which site did he suggest that the fort be built and what is the current name of the fort?
72. As a result of his first military expedition, Washington was promoted to what position?
73. In 1754, the French seized the fort that Washington had recommended be built. What did they name it?
74. What happened to Fort Necessity?
75. Who built Fort Necessity?
76. Where was Fort Necessity located?
77. After his return from Fort Necessity, what did Washington do with his military commission?
78. What job did Washington hold under General Braddock in 1755?
79. What were the dates of the French and Indian War?
80. After "Braddock's Defeat," Governor Dinwiddie gave Washington a new job and a new rank. What were they?
81. Who was General Braddock's successor?
82. In what year did Washington resign his military commission for the second and last time?

Plantation Life

83. What was the main crop of Mount Vernon?

84. What new crop did Washington introduce on his plantation?

85. How good a farmer was George Washington?

86. Mount Vernon overlooks what river?

87. What was the House of Burgesses?

88. When was Washington first elected to the House of Burgesses?

89. Name other famous members of the House of Burgesses.

*90. What kind of knowledge did Washington derive from his long service in the House of Burgesses?

91. How many years did Washington actually serve in the House of Burgesses?

92. What cash crop did Mount Vernon get from the Potomac River?

93. Approximately how many acres did Mount Vernon consist of?

The Revolution

94. How many delegates did Virginia send to the First Continental Congress?

95. When was the First Continental Congress held?

96. Where was the First Continental Congress held?

97. When did the Second Continental Congress meet?

98. What famous battles took place just before the Second Continental Congress met?

99. Who nominated Washington to be Commander-in-Chief of the Army of the United Colonies?

100. How much was Washington paid as Commander-in-Chief?

101. On what date was Washington elected Commander-in-Chief?

102. Where did Washington assume command of the Continental Army?

103. On what date did he assume formal command of the Continental Army?

104. Who was the King of England at the time of the Revolution?

105. Who was Lord North?

106. Who was the Queen of England at the time of the Revolution?

107. When did Washington cross the Delaware River?

108. What two battles did he fight after crossing the Delaware River?

109. Which group of soldiers did Washington attack on December 26, 1776?

110. Where did Washington establish winter headquarters in January of 1777?

111. What did Washington's army do in Valley Forge?

112. What were the conditions like at Valley Forge?

113. What was Baron von Steuben's role at Valley Forge?

114. What British general surrendered his troops in 1777 at Saratoga?

115. What famous Frenchman served in the Colonial Army?

116. What fort did Benedict Arnold betray?

117. What was the name of the British officer who was involved in Benedict Arnold's plot and what happened to him?

118. What happened to Benedict Arnold?

119. Who surrendered at Yorktown?

120. What was the date of the surrender at Yorktown?

121. What did this surrender at Yorktown mark?

122. Where was the peace treaty between Great Britain and the United States signed?

123. When was the peace treaty signed?

124. What did George Washington do at Fraunces' Tavern in New York?

125. When did Washington surrender his commission as Commander-in-Chief to Congress?

126. Who was John Honeyman?

127. What information did Honeyman give to Washington?

128. Who was the commander of the Hessian troops in Trenton?

The Presidency: First Term

129. How many electors voted in the first meeting of the Electoral College?

130. Who was elected as Vice President?

131. Who was the first Secretary of the Treasury?

132. Who was the first Secretary of War?

133. Who acted as Secretary of State until Thomas Jefferson assumed the office?

134. Who was the first Speaker of the House?

135. Where was George Washington inaugurated as President?

136. On what date did Washington take the oath of Office as President for the first time?

137. How many justices served on the first Supreme Court?

138. Who was the first Chief Justice of the United States?

*139. Which Justice of the Supreme Court was

nominated by Washington to become Chief Justice, but was rejected by the Senate?

140. Congress decided that George Washington should be called by what title?

141. What was the name of the building where Washington was inaugurated?

142. By what means of transportation did Washington arrive at the inaugural city?

143. When was the Bill of Rights ratified?

144. Which amendment in the Bill of Rights guarantees freedom of speech, freedom of the press, and freedom of religion?

145. Which amendment in the Bill of Rights guarantees that the police cannot invade a home without a search warrant?

146. Which amendment in the Bill of Rights does not allow the government to force a person to testify against himself or herself?

147. Which was the last of the original 13 colonies to ratify the Constitution?

148. Which state had the largest number of people signing the Constitution and how many signed?

149. After the original 13 states ratified the constitution, how many more were admitted during Washington's first term?

150. Name the states admitted during Washington's first term.

151. Who administered the oath of office to Washington at the first inauguration?

152. Where was the first Presidential mansion located? Give the street address.

153. How old was George Washington's Vice President at the first inauguration?

154. How much was George Washington paid as President?

155. How much was his Vice President paid?

156. How old was Washington when he was first inaugurated?

157. On what date was the U.S. Mint established?

158. In what city was the U.S. Mint established?

159. What were the first two coins issued by the U.S. Mint?

160. Which coin made by the U.S. Mint had the lowest value?

161. Which coin authorized by the first Congress had the highest value?

162. In what year was the census begun?

163. According to the first U.S. census, how many people were living in the United States?

164. Who was the first Postmaster General of the United States?

165. Who was the first President pro tempore of the senate?

166. For how many sessions did the first Congress sit?

*167. Where did Washington travel during the first Presidential tour that lasted from October 15 to November 13, 1789?

168. What date did Washington proclaim as Thanksgiving?

169. What was the first bill vetoed by a President?

The Presidency: Second Term

170. What was George Washington's political party?

171. How many electoral votes did Washington receive for a second term?

172. How many electoral votes did John Adams receive in the second election?

173. In what city was Washington inaugurated for a second term?

*174. George Washington's second Inaugural Address was the shortest ever given by a President. How many words did it consist of?

175. What was the name of the room and building where Washington took his second oath of office?

176. Who administered the second oath of office to Washington?

177. On what date was Washington sworn in for his second term?

178. Who was the architect of the Federal City?

179. What is the name by which we now know the Federal City?

180. What state was admitted during Washington's second term?

181. Who did General Mad Anthony Wayne defeat on August 20, 1794?

182. With what nation did the U.S. sign "Jay's Treaty"?

*183. Why did Pennsylvania farmers organize the Whiskey Rebellion?

184. Which general did Washington appoint to put down the Whiskey Rebellion?

185. Which newspaper printed Washington's "Farewell Address"?

186. When was Washington's "Farewell Address" published?

187. To whom did Washington send copies of his "Farewell Address"?

*188. Who accompanied the Washingtons to Mount Vernon when they left at the end of his second Presidential term?

Retirement and Death

*189. To what rank and title did President Adams appoint George Washington?

190. How long did Washington live after he retired from the Presidency?

191. What is the date of George Washington's death?

192. How old was George Washington when he died?

193. On what date was George Washington buried?

194. Where is George Washington buried?

195. What did George Washington die of?

*196. List some of the treatments that were used to try to save his life.

*197. Give the name of the doctor who treated Washington on his deathbed?

*198. What was the last thing that George Washington was reported to have done?

*199. Name some of the people present at his deathbed.

200. What were Washington's last words?

Art and Artists

201. Which artist painted "Washington Crossing the Delaware"?

*202. Which artist painted what is now the national official portrait of Washington (the one appearing on paper money)?

203. Which artist painted "The Winter at Valley Forge"?

*204. What distinction is held by the statue of Washington done by Jean Houdon?

*205. Where can Jean Houdon's statue of Washington be found today?

206. Charles Wilson Peale painted Washington in 1772. What uniform is he wearing in the portrait?

207. What do Gilbert Stuart, Charles Wilson Peale, and James Sharpless have in common?

Places and Memorials

208. What two states are connected by the George Washington Bridge?

209. What is the span of the George Washington Bridge?

210. Who is responsible for maintaining and preserving Mount Vernon today?

211. For what building in the nation's capital did Washington lay the cornerstone?

212. Where did the Washington Elm stand?

213. What happened under the Washington Elm?

*214. Why did the college now known as Washington and Lee University change its name from Liberty Hall Academy to Washington Academy?

215. How high is the Washington Monument?

216. How wide is each side of the base of the Washington Monument?

217. How much did it cost to build the Washington Monument?

218. What is the term used to describe the shape of the Washington Monument?

219. How thick are the walls of the Washington Monument at the bottom?

220. How thick are the walls of the Washington Monument at the top?

221. What material was used to cover the outer stone of the Washington Monument?

222. How high is the small pyramid on top of the Washington Monument?

223. How many steps lead to the top of the Washington Monument?

224. When was the cornerstone laid for the Washington Monument?

225. When did work actually begin on the Washington Monument?

226. When was the Washington Monument completed?

227. When was the Washington Monument dedicated?

*228. How many counties in the United States are named for George Washington?

229. What does the seal of the State of Washington look like?

230. What President created the Territory of Washington, which was later to become a state?

231. When Washington was admitted to the United States, it became the ____ state. (Give its number.)

232. Name the date on which Washington was admitted as a state.

233. Which Presidents are pictured on Mount Rushmore?

234. Where is Mount Rushmore located?

235. Who was the man selected by Congress to sculpt Mount Rushmore?

Stamps and Coins

236. Washington was the first U.S. President to appear on a U.S. postage stamp. When was it issued?

237. What was the denomination of the stamp on which Washington appeared?

238. Which U.S. coin shows a picture of Washington's head?

239. When and why was the coin with Washington's head issued?

240. On what denomination of paper money does Washington's picture appear?

Odds and Ends

241. The last private owner of Mount Vernon was a distant relative of Washington. What was his name?

*242. Which President named his first-born (b. 1801) after George Washington?

243. Who invented the story about George Washington and the cherry tree?

244. Who called Washington "Cincinnatus of the West"?

*245. Why was Washington called the "Cincinnatus of the West"?

Quotations By and About

246. To whom did Washington write, "Without a decisive Naval force we can do nothing definitive"?

247. When did Washington talk about "preservation of the sacred fire of liberty"?

248. When did Washington state, "The basis for our political system is the right of the people to make and to alter their constitutions of government"?

249. Who said, "America has furnished to the world the character of Washington . . ."?

250. Who referred to Washington as "first in war, first in peace, and first in the hearts of his countrymen"?

NOTE: Activities marked with * are more difficult.

PART
THREE

Bulletin Boards

Please note that the following bulletin boards originally appeared in various issues of *The School Librarian's Workshop* by Library Learning Resources, Inc., Box 87, Berkeley Heights, New Jersey 07922. © by Hilda K. Weisburg and Ruth Toor.

DID YOU FORGET THESE?

all grades—coordinates with Chapters 1 and 10

A cheerful elephant can be used to welcome students with a friendly reminder in September or after a long holiday. If you want to be more positive, substitute the phrase "Do You Remember These?" This bulletin board works well for most grade levels if suitable modifications in the library phrases are made.

To add to the effect, use rolled cellophane tape to attach real peanuts around the bulletin board. Keep a supply of peanuts handy; hungry nibblers will soon pick the board clean. Use the bulletin board as a springboard for a review of library organization and, for younger students, award peanuts for correct answers.

Materials:

    construction paper in assorted colors, including yellow, pink, and tan

    marking pen

    scissors

    overhead or opaque projector

    paste or stapler

    (*optional*) cellophane tape and peanuts

Preparation:

1. Cover the bulletin board with yellow construction paper.

2. Use the overhead or opaque projector to enlarge and trace the elephant onto pink construction paper. (Color choices are only suggestions.) For a 48" × 36" display, the elephant should have a body approximately 22½" wide with a head that is 15" wide and 12" high.

3. Use a marking pen to fill in details on the elephant.

4. Cut out the elephant and attach it to the bulletin board. *Do not attach the trunk.*

5. Trace the letters or draw your own on tan construction paper. Capital letters should be approximately 6" high.

6. Draw peanut shapes around the words and cut them out. The peanuts should be between 8" and 9" wide.

7. Attach the peanuts to the bulletin board. Fasten the "Forget" peanut to the elephant's trunk and affix both to the bulletin board.

8. Cut peanut shapes from assorted colors of construction paper and print words associated with the media center. Use any of the following terms or choose ones that are more appropriate to your situation:

Fiction	Circulation Desk
Nonfiction	Encyclopedias
Reference	Dictionaries
Atlas	Card Catalog
Dewey Decimal System	Call Number

For middle and junior high students include more sophisticated terms such as:

Readers' Guide
Almanac
Facts on File

9. Paste the peanut shapes onto the bulletin board. If you want, attach real peanuts, too.

APRIL SHOWERS

all grades—coordinates with Chapters 1 and 2

A spring theme, filled with bright colors and fanciful creatures, characterizes the bulletin board shown here. Any bulletin board or activity should have some educational purpose, and this one is appropriate for bringing gardening, flowers, and small animals to the attention of students. Meanwhile, the pastel colors and whimsical cartoons will bring an early spring into your classroom.

Materials:

1 sheet of 22" × 28" yellow posterboard
light green kraft paper
construction paper in white, dark green, light brown, pink, and yellow
marking pens in black, blue, red, and green
rubber cement
scissors

Preparation:

1. Cut a sheet of dark green construction paper into a right triangle. The short leg of the triangle is 7", and the long leg is 12". The hypotenuse is a wavy line. (See the illustration here.)

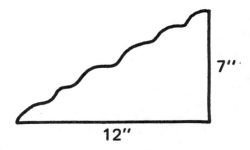

2. Paste the dark green triangle along the right-hand side of the posterboard with the right angle 5½" from the bottom edge of the board.

3. Cut a 28" wide sheet of light green kraft paper. The height should descend from 10" on one side to 7" on the other in a gently rolling line.

4. Paste the kraft paper onto the posterboard with the 10" height on the left. The paper will cover the bottom of the dark green triangle.

5. On white construction paper, print "April Showers . . ." in 2″ high letters with a blue marking pen. Use the marking pen to outline a large cloud around the words. Cut out the cloud and paste it onto the posterboard.

6. On white construction paper, print "Discover seeds and plants, see 580s" in ¾″ high letters with a blue marking pen. Use the marking pen to make a cloud around the words. Cut out the cloud and paste it onto the posterboard.

7. On light brown construction paper, draw a large mushroom and cut it out. The cap measures 10½″ at the widest and is about 3½″ high. The stem is 1″ wide and 4″ high.

8. Outline the mushroom with a black marking pen. Use the marking pen to draw gills on the underside of the mushroom, to shade the stem, and to print ". . . bring mushrooms and flowers" in ¾″ high letters.

9. Paste the mushroom onto the kraft paper and the posterboard. The center of the stem is 13″ from the left side of the posterboard. The base of the stem is 8″ from the bottom.

10. Use dark green construction paper to cut out the stem and leaves of the flower. The stem is 10½″ high.

11. Cut the full blossom and the bud from pink construction paper. Use a red or black marking pen to outline the petals. The blossom measures 3½″ × 1½″; the bud is about ¾″ long.

12. Paste the blossom and bud onto the stem and paste the entire flower onto the bulletin board. The bottom of the stem is 1½″ from the left side and 1¼″ from the bottom.

13. Print "Get your garden growing, see 635" and "Find nature in your back-yard, see 574" on pink construction paper with a black or red marking pen. The letters are 1″ high. Draw a 6″ wide cloud around each group of words, cut out the clouds, and paste them onto the bulletin board.

14. Draw about six small mushrooms on light brown construction paper. Outline them with a black marking pen. You can add dots to some of the mushrooms for variety.

15. Draw the frog (2″ high) and the worm (4″ long) on dark green construction paper. Outline them and fill in the details with a black marking pen.

16. Draw the bird (3½″ high) on yellow construction paper with a black marking pen.

17. Draw the bumblebee (1½″ wide) on yellow construction paper with a black marking pen. Cut it out and paste it onto the large mushroom. Draw the feet and antennae with a black marking pen after the bee is pasted in place.

18. Draw the snail (2¼″ high) and the butterfly (5″ high) on pink construction paper with a black or red marking pen.

19. Cut out the mushrooms, frog, worm, bird, snail, and butterfly. Paste them onto the bulletin board.

20. Use a black marking pen to draw the ant at the bottom of the bulletin board.

21. Use dark green and black marking pens to draw blades of grass where the stems of the mushrooms and flowers are pasted onto the bulletin board.

MAY MAGIC

grades 4–8—coordinates with Chapters 1 and 2

Spring makes beautiful magic. Fill a bulletin board with the soft shades of spring and highlight books on magic. Students will have no difficulty locating the books after this. For fun, assign the "Unmagicked Book Report" in Part Four, and "Magic in the Air" in Part Two.

Materials:

> yellow construction paper
>
> construction paper in pink, light green, dark green, light blue, violet, and gray
>
> purple, black, and brown marking pens
>
> white chalk or white paper
>
> bandana, handkerchief, or a piece of material
>
> paste
>
> stapler
>
> scissors
>
> overhead or opaque projector
>
> (*optional*) green marking pen, playing cards, play money

Preparation:

1. Cover the bulletin board with yellow construction paper.
2. Use the overhead or opaque projector to trace the rabbit onto pink construction paper. Use a black marker to make an outline; to fill in the eyes, nose, and whiskers; to shade the figure; and to make the lines of the ears. The rabbit should be at least 22″ high.
3. Color the tooth with white chalk or paste white paper in the appropriate spot.
4. Cut the suit from light green construction paper and paste it onto the rabbit. Be sure the right paw shows. Or, instead of using paper, you could color the suit with a green marking pen.
5. Cut a bow tie from dark green construction paper or color it with a black marking pen.
6. Attach the rabbit to the right-hand side of the bulletin board.
7. Attach a bandana, handkerchief, or piece of material to the rabbit's paw.
8. Lift the bandana and print the word "Magic" with a purple marking pen. If the word cannot be seen through the material, add the direction "lift up" with an arrow pointing to the bandana.
9. Use the overhead or opaque projector to trace the table (without the pitcher or glass) onto light blue construction paper. The table should be at least 10½″ high and 14″ at the widest point. Use a black marking pen to outline and indicate the folds. Cut out the shape.
10. Color the legs with a brown or black marking pen.

11. Use a black marking pen to print the Dewey numbers onto the tablecloth. Attach the table to the bulletin board.

12. Trace the pitcher onto purple construction paper and the glass onto gray construction paper. Cut them out and paste them onto the table.

13. Trace the hat onto light green construction paper. It should be at least 18″ across the brim and about 12″ high.

14. Using a black marking pen, shade the interior of the hat and write the directions for the subject headings.

15. Cut a slit in the brim so you can insert the letter "M," and attach the brim to the bulletin board.

16. Cut each of the three letters from different colors of construction paper such as pink, violet, and blue. Make the letters bold, about 8″ high, but do not be concerned about making them exactly even.

17. Attach the letters to each other and slide the leg of the "M" into the hat. Attach the completed word to the bulletin board.

OPTIONAL: If there is room, attach fanned-out playing cards in a few places. Play money can also be added.

INFLATE YOUR VOCABULARY
grades 3–6—coordinates with Chapter 3

Children love to play with long words. Encourage or stimulate this interest with a bulletin board that will provide a good introduction to looking up unusual words in the dictionary.

Materials:

1 sheet 22″ × 28″ colored posterboard

4 balloons

ball of lightweight yarn or string

cellophane tape

rubber cement

stapler

9″ × 12″ sheets of construction paper in various colors

fine-tip marking pen

1 sheet of white construction paper

medium-tip marking pen

scissors

3″ × 5″ index card

(*optional*) crayons or colored marking pens

list of 14 words from the dictionary or the following list:
    absterge (ab sterj´) verb—to wipe off
    bombastic (bom bas´tik) adj.—inflated
    carcharodon (kär kar´ ə don) noun—large man-eating tropical shark
    dhow (dou) noun—ship with triangular sails

eulogium (yü lō′ jē əm) noun—praise

googol (gü′ gol) noun—the number one followed by one hundred zeros

imbricate (im′brə kāt) verb—to overlap (as tiles or shingles)

klompen (klom′pən) noun—wooden shoes worn by the Dutch

natator (nā ta′ ter) noun—a swimmer

plenitudinous (plen′ ə tu′ də nəs) adj.—stout

somnambulate (som nam ′byə lāt) verb—to walk in your sleep

troglodyte (trog′lə dīt) noun—cave man

vicinal (vis′ə nəl) adj.—neighboring, near

waggery (wag′ər ē) noun—joking, clowning

Source: *World Book Dictionary* (Field Enterprises)

Preparation:

1. Write four of the words from your list on the four balloons (one word on each balloon) with a fine-tip marking pen.

2. Blow up the balloons, knot them, and attach long strands of yarn to them.

3. Cut out the letters for the word "Inflate" from different colored construction paper. The letters should be 4″ high.

4. Choose any word from your list. Write the word in capital letters with a marking pen on a sheet of colored construction paper. Below the word, in smaller letters, write the pronunciation, the part of speech, and the meaning. Draw a balloon shape around what you have written and cut out the balloon.

5. Repeat step 4 with each word on the list. Use different colors of construction paper.

6. Staple a long piece of yarn to each balloon cutout. The yarn can be trimmed later.

7. Draw or trace the cartoon figure holding the dictionary on white construction paper and cut it out. You may color the figure with crayons if you want.

8. Print or type the source of the pronunciations and definitions on the 3″ × 5″ index card.

9. To assemble the bulletin board:

   a. Position and paste the cartoon figure on the posterboard. Do not paste down the raised arm.

   b. Roll pieces of cellophane tape and attach the pieces to the backs of the inflated balloons. Attach the balloons to the top of the posterboard.

   c. Catch the four pieces of yarn behind the cartoon figure's upraised arm and staple the yarn to the posterboard. Cover the staples with the figure's hand.

   d. Use a marking pen to print "Your Vocabulary" and "Use the Dictionary" on the posterboard.

   e. Position the letters for the word "Inflate" and paste them onto the posterboard.

   f. Staple the construction paper balloons to the sides of the posterboard.

   g. Trim excess yarn.

   h. Attach the 3″ × 5″ card to the bottom of the posterboard.

In the Card Catalog
See
MAGIC, TRICKS,
OCCULT SCIENCES,
HALLUCINATIONS,
AND ILLUSIONS

On the shelves look for
793.8
and
133.4

MAGIC

INFLATE Your Vocabulary

Use the Dictionary

Notator
eulogium
googol
bombastic
plenitudinous
vicinal
waggery

notator
googol
Vicinal
dhow

somnambulate
imbricate
absterge
Klompen
Troglodyte
carcharodon
dhow

DICTIONARY

Definitions & Pronunciations from World Book Dictionary

269

DEVELOP YOUR WORD POWER
grades 3-6—coordinates with Chapter 3

This bulletin board will encourage students to use the dictionary and discover that many words in our language have several definitions which dramatically change the meaning of the word. The bulletin board provides several samples. If you want more than the number of barbells illustrated for your bulletin board, you can add these words:

ABOUT— 1. aimlessly
2. toward a reverse direction

BEAT— 1. to defeat
2. to excel

BLAZE— 1. bright light
2. white spot in the face of a horse

BRUSH— 1. brief encounter
2. dense growth of bushes

CAPE— 1. sleeveless garment
2. point of land projecting into the sea

CASE— 1. specific instance
2. container

CLEAVE—1. to split or separate
2. to cling to

CLUB— 1. heavy stick
2. group organized for a common purpose

COB— 1. core of an ear of corn
2. male swan

DEED— 1. an act
2. document showing property ownership

HAIL— 1. to precipitate pellets of ice
2. to salute

WIRE— 1. telegram
2. finish line at a racetrack

WEAR— 1. to be clothed in
2. to fatigue

Materials:

construction paper in yellow, gray, green, white, or brown

colored chalk

scissors

opaque projector

X-acto® knife

stapler

Preparation:

1. Cover the bulletin board with yellow construction paper.
2. Use the opaque projector to trace the strong man onto white or brown construction paper.
3. Cut out the figure and fill in the details of hair and costume with colored chalk.
4. Use the X-acto® knife to cut around the fingers of the strong man and attach him to the bulletin board.
5. Cut pairs of assorted size circles from gray construction paper.

6. Cut bars to attach to the weights from white or light green construction paper.

7. Assemble the largest weight, the one being lifted by the strong man. Fill in the word and its two definitions, insert under the fingers of the figure, and attach.

8. Assemble the other barbells and add the words to the bars and the definitions to the weights. Attach to the bulletin board.

9. Use the opaque projector to trace letters (or make your own) onto green construction paper. Cut them out and attach.

IT'S NOT WHETHER YOU WIN OR LOSE . . .
grades 3-6—coordinates with Chapter 3

Help students appreciate the richness of the English language with this sports bulletin board. Students tend to be limited in their choices of words and often seem not to hear or see the variety of terms available to succinctly and colorfully describe a subject or event. You can use this bulletin board to introduce them to a thesaurus and/or a dictionary of synonyms and antonyms.

As a further development, suggest looking at the sports pages to see how many ways sports writers say "win" or "lose." More thesaurus work can be done if you use team names to extend the winning/losing metaphor. For example: The Flames *burned* their rivals. (They won.) The Flames were *snuffed out* last night. (They lost.)

NOTE: If your school is not filled with soccer enthusiasts, you can make an even simpler bulletin board using baskets and a basketball, or goal posts and a football.

Materials:

   green construction paper

   white construction paper

   black marking pen

   stapler

   opaque projector

   (*optional*) netting material (see your art teacher)

Preparation:

1. Cover the bulletin board with green construction paper.

2. Staple netting material onto the bulletin board or use the opaque projector to draw the net.

3. Use the opaque projector and lightly outline the frame of the goal.

4. Cut white construction paper into strips that are the same length and width as the penciled-in outline. Attach them to the bulletin board, completing the goal.

5. Trace the soccer ball onto white construction paper and cut it out. Use a black marking pen to fill in the black pentagons. (To make the ball look really

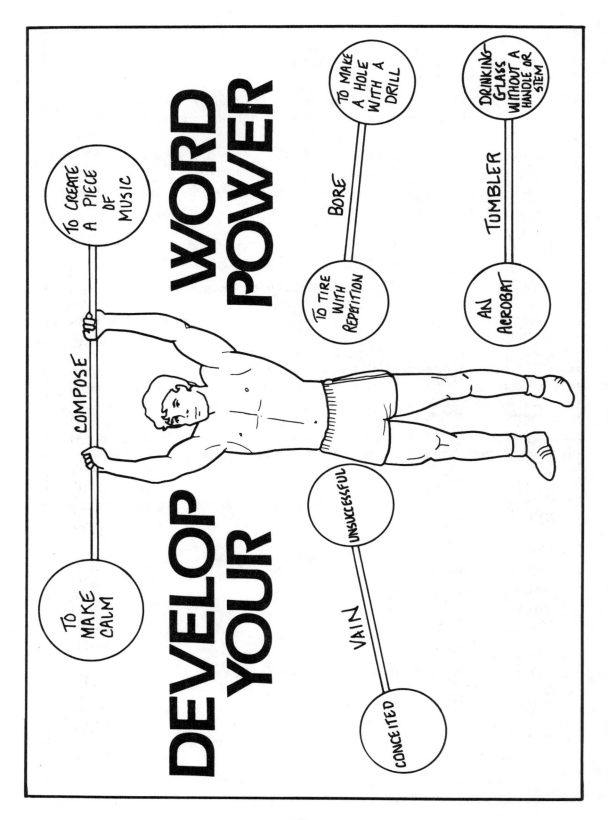

It's Not Whether You Win Or Lose

...It's How You Use The Term

LOSE
WAS DEFEATED
FORFEITED
LET SLIP
WAS SUBDUED
MINUS
WAS THWARTED
WAS FOILED
FAILED
WAS ROUTED

WIN
CONQUER
TRIUMPH
BEAT
MASTER
SUCCEED
ACHIEVE
SURPASS
VANQUISH

round, be sure to include the white highlights shown in the illustration.) Attach to the bulletin board.

6. Cut out the letters "It's not whether you win or lose" from white construction paper and attach.

7. For the two lists, cut out irregular rectangles from white construction paper. Print the terms and attach.

TALKING ABOUT WEATHER
grades 4–8—coordinates with Chapter 3

This bulletin board takes a lightly humorous look at winter while encouraging students to turn to two basic reference tools—the dictionary and the thesaurus—to enrich their vocabularies. If you want, you can add the note "Check dictionaries for the meaning of underlined words and a thesaurus to find more wintry words" to the bottom of the bulletin board.

Although it looks complicated, this bulletin board can be put up quickly with the help of an opaque projector. If you prefer a less crowded look, separate the parts over a larger area.

Materials:

    aluminum foil
    white construction paper
    marking pens in assorted colors including black
    blue construction paper
    scissors
    stapler
    opaque projector

Preparation:

1. Cover the bulletin board with aluminum foil.

2. Use the opaque projector to trace the figures onto the white construction paper.

3. Fill in the figures using colored marking pens of your choice.

4. Cut out the figures and attach.

5. Print cartoon bubbles and sentences on white paper. Underline the word to be looked up. Cut out and mount.

6. Cut out letters for "Talking About Weather" from blue construction paper and attach.

7. Cut out the "chilly" shapes from either blue or white construction paper.

8. Fill in the shapes with words from a thesaurus that are associated with cold weather and attach.

9. Be sure to have dictionaries and several thesauruses available for students to check.

10. Encourage students to locate more words in a thesaurus and add them to the bulletin board.

TALKING ABOUT WEATHER

VARIATION: If you are pressed for time, cut out books instead of figures. Put the words on the outside of the book and either a sentence or a definition on the inside of the book. Students can add more "books" to make the bulletin board grow.

UP, UP, AND AWAY
grades 4–8—coordinates with Chapter 4

In March when the wind blows or any time you want a lift, prepare this bulletin board, which was created by Patricia L. Fazekas (Art Specialist for the Sayreville Public Schools, Sayreville, New Jersey).

Only three questions are shown in the illustration but you can add as many clouds as you like. Students can find answers in encyclopedias or books on ballooning.

Materials:

construction paper in blue, white, gray, and black

yellow posterboard

black yarn

red tissue paper

fish net or similar netting made from yarn

cardboard scraps

stapler

marking pens

scissors

Preparation:

1. Cover the bulletin board with deep blue construction paper.
2. Cut several large clouds from white paper. Print your questions on the clouds and staple them to the background.
3. Outline the edges of the clouds that overlap with a black marking pen.
4. Cut an oval for the balloon in two halves from yellow posterboard.
5. Cover the upper half of the oval with fish net, bringing the excess around to the back of the shape and taping it in place.
6. Score and fold strips of cardboard scraps and staple them to the back of each of the two balloon halves. These will make the balloon stand away from the board.
7. Cut the passenger section of the balloon from gray paper and staple it to the board.
8. Connect the top half of the balloon with netting to the passenger section below.
9. Swag yarn along the edge of the balloon bucket.
10. Form sandbags with stuffed tissue paper and staple them to the balloon bucket.

11. Cut birds and figures in silhouette from black paper and staple in place.
12. Cut lettering from white paper and staple to the board.

Answers to Questions Shown on Board:

1. When ballast is thrown over the side the balloon becomes lighter and rises. Just before landing some ballast is thrown out to avoid a hard landing.
2. Although hydrogen is lighter, it is highly explosive and burns easily, while coal gas is not as light as helium.
3. At Annonay, France on June 5, 1783, Jacques Etienne and Joseph Michel Montgolfier launched the first balloon using a smoke-filled cloth bag.

PROMOTE PERIODICALS

grades 3–up—coordinates with Chaper 7

Put the spotlight on the variety of magazines available in the media center and the many exciting things that can be found between their covers.

Begin with this bulletin board and let your imagination spur you to further creative ways of using periodicals. Magazines are a great tool to use with slow and underachieving students because articles are generally short and are accompanied by illustrations. You might want to assign the book report "A New Idea: Magazine Reports" in Part Four.

Materials:

    construction paper in light and dark shades

    scissors

    opaque projector

    white construction paper

    fine-tip marking pen

    paste

Preparation:

1. Cover the bulletin board with dark construction paper.
2. Cut a large rectangle from light-colored construction paper to represent the magazine cover.
3. Use the opaque projector to trace the child shown in the illustration.
4. Use a fine-tip marking pen to letter the masthead on light-colored construction paper. Do your own or trace from the illustration.
5. Add the words "Short Stories," "Games," "Facts," "Pictures," and "Fun" in the appropriate spots.
6. Copy the titles shown (or select other titles of interest to your students) onto white construction paper.
7. Paste the magazine titles onto the bulletin board.

young miss

penny power

NATIONAL GEOGRAPHIC
world

For a change...
TRY A
MAGAZINE

SHORT STORIES
GAMES
FACTS
PICTURES
FUN

Odyssey

Dynamite

BOYS'
LIFE

Cricket

250+ YEARS OF U.S. HISTORY

grades 5-8—coordinates with Chapter 8

This bulletin board can be used as part of the usual observation of George Washington's birth each February, and with "250 Questions About George Washington" in Part Two. Involve your students in updating the board each year. Not only will they improve their reference skills, but they will also gain a deeper awareness of how the United States has changed over the years.

Materials:

    construction paper in red, white, and blue
    black marking pen
    scissors
    stapler
    opaque projector

Preparation:

1. Cover the middle section of the bulletin board with blue construction paper and cover the two flanking sides with red construction paper.

2. Cut 12 strips of white construction paper to make the stripes and attach them to the board.

3. Use an opaque projector to trace the picture of George Washington and his signature onto white construction paper. If you prefer not to draw, use one of the multi-colored posters of Washington that are commercially available. Attach the portrait to the board.

4. Using the marking pen, go over the signature as well as the portrait if you are using the one illustrated.

5. Cut from white construction paper the numbers and letters to spell out "250+ Years of U.S. History" and attach them to the board; then cut from blue construction paper numbers for each of the 50-year intervals (and any additional years) and attach them to the board.

6. If you have room place 13 white stars down each side of the center blue panel.

7. Under the dates place pictures or written descriptions of important events in the history of the United States. Find your own information about major happenings or choose from the partial list below. Here are some book sources you can check:

Carruth, Gortin, and Associates, *The Encyclopedia of American Facts and Dates*, 6th ed., Crowell, 1972.

Kane, Joseph Nathan, *Famous First Facts*, 4th ed., H.W. Wilson Co., 1981.

Morris, Richard B., ed. *Encyclopedia of American History,* Bicentennial edition. Harper, 1976.

250+ Years of U.S. History

1732
1782
1832
1882
1932
1982

Washington

Partial Listing of U.S. Historical Facts

1732

- George Washington is born (February 22).
- James Edward Oglethorpe is given a charter to found Georgia, the thirteenth colony (June 9).
- The craze for white stockings instead of colored hose (begun around 1730) continues. It won't end until the close of the century.
- The first guide book to America is published.

1782

- Peace talks have been in progress since the Revolutionary War ended on October 19, 1781.
- Harvard Medical School is two years old.
- Noah Webster's famous blue-covered *Speller* is introduced.
- Martin Van Buren is born. He will be the first president to have been born a U.S. citizen.

1832

- Andrew Jackson is President of the U.S.
- A major cholera epidemic sweeps the country.
- "America" was introduced at services in Boston, Massachusetts on July 4, 1831.
- *Swiss Family Robinson* by Johann Rudolph Wyss is published in the U.S.

THE PAST DECADES

grades 5–8—coordinates with Chapter 8

Use everyone's interest in nostalgia to construct a bulletin board, which will be cluttered with an assortment of incidents that occurred in the three decades reviewed. If you like, continue the strip to include the 1980s and let students draw on their memories or check reference sources.

Materials:

> construction paper in yellow, gray, brown, white, blue, green, and other assorted colors
>
> paste
>
> stapler
>
> scissors
>
> brown marking pen
>
> opaque projector

Preparation:

1. Cover the bulletin board with yellow construction paper.

2. Use a brown marking pen to draw the hourglass. Even though its center will be covered, make a complete glass; it will help you to make the shape correctly.

3. Trim sheets of contrasting shades of construction paper to form a band that runs from the top right-hand corner to the bottom left-hand side. Use the brown marking pen to outline the top and bottom and to camouflage any rough edges.

4. Staple the band to the bulletin board. Be sure it covers the center of the hourglass, but allows the sand (brown construction paper) in both halves of the hourglass to be seen.

5. Using the brown marking pen or strips of construction paper, divide the band into three equal areas.

6. Cut labels from white construction paper and write the dates of the decades with the brown marking pen. Paste them onto the correct sections of the banner.

7. Cut the letters to spell "The Past Decades" from brown construction paper.

    NOTE: You can leave the bulletin board at this stage for a day or two. It gives you a chance to prepare subsequent additions under less pressure and stimulates student interest.

8. Use the opaque projector to make the rock singer, the two maps, the spaceship, and the shark. For best results make the drawings on white paper, then paste them onto colored construction paper, outline them with the marking pen, and add them to the bulletin board.

9. Write out a block asking students to add to the bulletin board and paste it on the bottom right-hand corner.

    NOTE: Stop here for another day or two. Items located by students should be added as soon as possible. While it is not necessary to have an illustration for each fact, it looks better if you do.

10. Whether the students contribute or not, continue adding to the bulletin board every other day until it is full. If you should get a large response from students, cover the walls of the classroom with the three decades.

FLOWERY THOUGHTS

grades 5–8—coordinates with Chapter 8

Make a garden grow on your bulletin board and encourage the use of *Bartlett's Familiar Quotations* and field guides. The entry words for *Bartlett's* can be "garden," "rose," or other names of flowers. When the quotation is general, attach it to the fanciful blooms. Illustrations of real flowers (roses, daisies, violets) should be used when the quotation is specific.

Have students find more quotations and prepare their own flowers for the board. If they don't know how a particular flower looks, or if they find it is too difficult to draw, pull out field guides or other sources that include flower illustrations. Then with an overhead or opaque projector students can add another flowery thought to the garden.

Materials:

> construction paper in light blue, gray, green, yellow, pink
> white drawing paper
> marking pens
> chalk
> scissors
> paste
> stapler

Preparation:

1. Cover the bulletin board with light blue construction paper.
2. Select quotations and determine the real flowers you need. If you choose any with a rose, violet, or daisy, use an opaque or overhead projector to trace the illustration onto white drawing paper. Color the flowers, stems, and leaves with marking pens. (For the daisy, use gray construction paper and white chalk.)
3. Attach flowers to the bulletin board.
4. Cut "grass" from green construction paper. Print the quotation and the source and attach them to the base of the flower stem.
5. To make the fanciful blossoms use the illustration here to trace a set of five petals for each flower from yellow or pink construction paper.
6. Cut out the petals and staple them together at the center.

OUTSIDE

7. Cut a circle from the same or a contrasting color construction paper and paste onto the center of the flower.
8. Curl the petals into interesting shapes to create a three-dimensional look and staple them to the bulletin board.
9. Cut a stem and leaves from green construction paper, attaching this to the flower and the bulletin board.
10. Repeat step 4 for the fanciful flowers.
11. Trace the words "Flowery Thoughts" onto the board using a colored marking pen of your choice.

VARIATION: You might want to write the quotation in the grass on a swirl of paper and attach it as was done with the rose in the illustration.

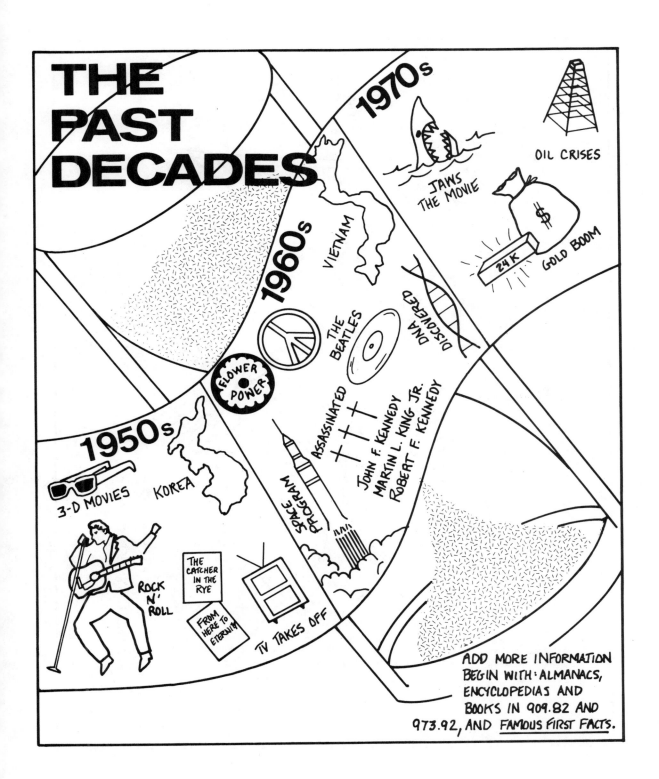

Flowery Thoughts

"ROUGH WINDS
DO SHAKE
THE DARLING
BUDS OF MAY.
AND SUMMERS
LEASE HATH
ALL TOO
SHORT A
DATE."

SHAKESPEARE:
"SONNET 18"

"YOU ARE
VIOLETS WITH
WIND
ABOVE THEM."

EZRA POUND—
"A GIRL"

"MEADOWS
TRIM, WITH DAISIES
PIED,...."

MILTON—"L' ALLEGRO"

"O, MY LUVE IS LIKE A RED, RED ROSE."
ROBERT BURNS—JOHNSON'S MUSICAL MUSEUM

"MAY, WITH ALLE
THY FLOURES AND THY
GRENE, WELCOME BE
THOU, FAIRE, FRESSHE MAY."

CHAUCER—"CANTERBURY TALES—
THE KNIGHTS TALE."

HIGHLIGHTING REFERENCE TOOLS
grades 5–8—coordinates with Chapter 10

A bulletin board on reference tools serves to remind everyone that there is more to reference than just encyclopedias, and may be the springboard to a teaching unit. The display shown here involves many steps, but since the tools are cut out of construction paper there is a cartoon-like quality and strict accuracy is not necessary. Dimensions are given but they are meant primarily as guidelines.

Materials:

> 18″ × 24″ oaktag or light-colored posterboard
>
> construction paper in these colors: 1 tan piece about 20″ long, 2 gray pieces 8½″ × 11″, 1 black piece 8½″ × 11″, 2 or 3 assorted light-colored pieces 8½″ × 11″, and assorted dark-colored pieces 8½″ × 11″
>
> marking pens in black and brown
>
> pencil
>
> paste
>
> scissors

Preparation:

The Board

1. Cut tan construction paper to make the board. It measures 2¼″ wide at the top and widens to 7¼″ at the bottom with a thickness of ¾″. The length along the diagonal is 18½″.

2. To letter "Learn to Use Them," draw a faint line with a pencil from the midpoint of the top of the board to the midpoint of the bottom, and center the letters along the line. The "L" is ½″ high, the "M" is 1½″ high. (NOTE: To heighten the effect, use brown marking pen to make wood-like grain in the board.)

3. Cut a straight line 1¼″ into the board, about where the "T" from the word "to" is positioned. The saw will go in here.

The Saw

1. Use the full 8½″ width of a piece of gray construction paper for the top of the saw.

2. Cut a diagonal line, beginning 4″ from the top on the left side to ½″ from the top on the right side.

3. Make small triangular cuts into the diagonal to form the saw teeth. (A pair of pinking shears would be helpful.)

4. Cut dark construction paper to form a handle 4″ along the top and approximately 4½″ high.

5. Paste the handle over the blade. Leave about 1″ of the blade showing at the bottom.

6. Draw bolts on the handle with a black marking pen.

The Awl

1. Cut the head of the awl from tan or dark construction paper. The head is 1″ at the widest part and 1¼″ high.
2. Use a black marking pen to make lines suggesting shape.
3. Cut a piece of construction paper about 2¾″ long and ¼″ wide at the top, tapering to a point.
4. Paste the awl head to cover ¼″ of the black construction paper.

The Hammer

1. Cut the head of the hammer from dark construction paper. The head measures 2¼″ across.
2. Cut the claw or use a black marking pen to indicate it.
3. Cut tan construction paper to make the handle, about 3¼″ long.
4. Paste the hammer head to cover ¼″ of the tan handle.

The Screwdriver

1. Use dark construction paper to cut the handle 2¼″ long and 1″ at the widest point.
2. Cut a blade 3¼″ long from gray construction paper. The blade is tapered at the top.
3. Either paste the screwdriver handle over ¼″ of the blade or cut a slit near the tip of the handle to fit the blade in.
4. Use a black marking pen to draw ridges in the handle.

The Electric Drill

1. Cut black construction paper in a thin strip 2″ long for the drill bit.
2. Cut gray construction paper for the body of the drill, 3½″ along the top and 2½″ down the side.
3. Use a black marking pen to make ridges.
4. Paste the drill body over the top ¼″ of the drill bit.
5. Cut a thin strip of black construction paper for wire and widen your cut to form the "plug."
6. Paste the end of the wire without the plug to the drill body.

The Pliers

1. Cut dark construction paper to make pliers 6″ long.
2. With a black marking pen draw bolts and other lines as shown in the illustration.

The Hand Drill

1. Cut gray construction paper for the hand drill. Total height is 6½″, cap is 1¾″ wide and ⅞″ high. The open space between the top and bottom sections is 1½″ high. The drill bit is 1½″.
2. Use a black marking pen to fill in lines on the cap, barrel, and cross-hatched area, marking diagonal lines to indicate the spiral of the drill bit.

REFERENCE TOOLS

READERS' GUIDE

INDEX

ATLAS

ALMANAC

REFERENCE

ENCYCLOPEDIA

DICTIONARY

To Complete the Display

1. Cut light construction paper into three geometric and three irregular shapes. Use a black marking pen to print the names of the reference tools.

2. Paste the wooden board onto the oaktag.

3. Position and paste the other carpentry tools and the reference tool labels. (NOTE: You can carefully twist the construction paper wire of the electric drill for a more natural effect.)

4. Print "Reference Tools" with the black marking pen in letters 1½″ high. If you prefer, cut the letters from tan construction paper and use the marking pen to make a wood-like grain.

BOOK ENDS

grades 4–8—a reading motivator

People often select books by reading the first sentences. Yet all books eventually come to an end and many authors close with lines that haunt readers' thoughts long after the book has been returned to the library. One of the best examples of an ending that lasts is E. B. White's for *Charlotte's Web*. It is shown on the open book of this bulletin board, which is designed to tempt readers with books that have intriguing endings. You should, of course, find your own examples.

The directions are for a three-dimensional bulletin board and may appear complicated. Actually, if you follow along step by step the preparation is simple, though time consuming.

If you are short of time you can streamline the board without the three-dimensional effect by tracing the books onto white construction paper and coloring them with marking pens. In this case, paste the typed sheet behind the books before attaching them to the bulletin board.

As a companion activity to the display assign the "Book End Book Report" in Part Four.

Materials:

construction paper in dark green, red, brown, yellow, tan, and light green

paste

stapler

white paper

marking pen

(*optional*) pressure-sensitive labels

Preparation:

1. Select books from your school's media center that have interesting last lines.

2. Make "sets of books" by folding pieces of construction paper in different colors into book shapes. Allow for a front and back cover as well as for at least a 1″ spine.

3. Print the author and title of the books you have chosen for their endings onto

your construction paper books. If the paper is too dark, use pressure-sensitive labels.

4. Cut book ends from red and dark green construction paper. Fold along the top dotted line as shown in the illustration here. You will fold along the second dotted line later in the directions.

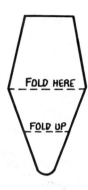

5. Paste the top part of the book end above the fold to the "front cover" of one of the "books" you have labeled. The bottom of the "book" now rests along the fold line.

6. Staple the "back cover" of that book to the "front cover" of a second, unlabeled book preferably of a different size.

7. Turn up the tongue of the book end along the second fold line (see the illustration here) and staple it to the back of the first book and the front of the second. This makes the "set of books" more sturdy.

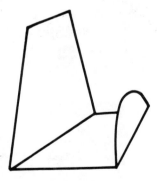

8. Repeat the process for as many sets as you want for your bulletin board.

9. Make some opened books as well. These are pasted to the book ends.

10. Print or type the last sentences of the books on paper appropriate to the size of the construction paper books you have made. Staple them to the inside of the book at interesting angles as shown. For the open book design, cut the page to size before typing and then paste it onto the book.

11. Now cover the bulletin board with light green construction paper.

12. Staple the back covers of the book sets to the bulletin board. Angle the books slightly. This will allow you to staple other parts of the sets to the board.

13. Cut out the letters from brown construction paper. You may find it easier to cut them as one single block.

14. Cut book ends that "hold" the letters from dark green construction paper. Paste the "B" and "S" onto the book ends.

15. Attach all the other letters to the bulletin board.

CURL UP WITH A BOOK

all grades

When the colder weather begins, or any time at all, think cozy comfortable thoughts and encourage your students to snuggle up with a book as they do in this book-centered pajama party bulletin board designed and executed by Barbara Goldkopf (Sayreville Public Schools, Sayreville, New Jersey). If you have a good reading list you can post it next to the bulletin board or use examples of old book reports instead. Use the illustration here as a cover for your list.

Materials:

      construction paper in light blue, yellow, and dark blue

      white drawing paper

      stars

      fine-tip and wide-tip black marking pens

additional marking pens

paste

scissors

Preparation:

1. Cover the bulletin board with light blue construction paper.
2. Cut an oval from white drawing paper.
3. Cut a pie-shaped wedge from light blue construction paper. Paste the wedge onto the left-hand corner of the oval.
4. Cut the window seat from yellow construction paper. The seat should be about one-third the height of the background sky.
   - If you use an opaque or overhead projector to copy the bulletin board shown here you can draw both the girl and window seat at the same time. Otherwise, draw the girl separately and paste her onto the window seat.
   - Color the girl and the trim on the seat with marking pens and paste these pieces onto the oval.
5. Cut the curtain from dark blue construction paper. The curtain should divide the oval in half lengthwise and come two-thirds of the way down the oval. Use a black marking pen to indicate the folds of the curtain. Paste the curtain onto the oval.
6. Cut a freehand yellow moon and paste it onto the sky.
7. On white drawing paper trace and cut out the two seated girls. For the girl who is lying down, use a red marking pen to color stripes on her pajamas. Give her brown hair and a red bow. Paste her onto the oval at the foot of the window seat. Use a marking pen to draw an oval rug around her.
8. Cut the lamp shade from yellow construction paper and paste it onto the oval. Cut the lamp base from dark blue construction paper and paste it onto the oval. Use a black marking pen to add the chain and to draw the effect of light being cast.
9. Color the face of the girl in front with a black marking pen. Use red or yellow felt marking pens for her nightgown and paste her onto the oval. Draw the sleeping bag beneath the girl using any color you want.
10. Use leftover scraps of construction paper to cut out assorted books, including those being read by the girls, and paste them on.
11. Paste a few stars around the moon.
12. Cut casual-looking letters to spell "Curl Up with a Book" from black construction paper. Do not measure the letters. Try for a relaxed look.
13. Paste the oval onto the bulletin board. Outline the oval with a wide black marking pen. Paste the letters around the oval. If there is too much background around the oval paste additional stars near the letters.

A Special Note:

TEN-STEP BULLETIN BOARDS—
THE OVERHEAD PROJECTOR AND YOU

Do you feel pressured by a blank bulletin board, little time, and no artistic talent? Believe it or not, you can turn out impressive-looking bulletin boards even without artistic talent and with a minimum of effort. All you need is an overhead projector, some acetate sheets, assorted colors of transparency markers (fine-tips are best), and selections from a book of bulletin board ideas.

Step 1—Cover the bulletin board with construction paper.

Step 2—Looking at the illustration of the bulletin board you plan to make, select a large figure that must be drawn.

Step 3—Decide how large you want that figure to be. How many inches high or how many inches wide?

Step 4—Take a sheet of acetate and several colors of fine-tip transparency markers and trace the figure.

Step 5—Take construction paper or other material onto which the figure is to be drawn and make light marks to indicate the height or width you decided on in Step 3.

Step 6—Lightly tape the paper to the wall at a convenient height.

Step 7—Place the transparency on the overhead projector and position and focus it so that the projected image approximates the dimensions you want. (You may need to move the construction paper a little, or put the projector on the floor.)

Step 8—Trace over the figure being projected onto the paper with pencil or felt markers (*not* transparency pens). To check for missed lines, turn off the projector.

Step 9—When the drawing is completed remove the paper from the wall, cut out the figure, and attach it to the bulletin board.

Step 10—Repeat steps for the remaining items and letters until the bulletin board is complete.

Many teachers and library media specialists have used the opaque projector for similar purposes, but the overhead is far more suited to this task for several reasons. The room need not be darkened, so you can prepare the bulletin board while students are working. Because the original work is never on the projector, it is not subject to heat damage. Since you trace onto acetate, you can streamline the drawing as you go along, eliminating details you find too difficult. Even bulletin boards that are designed to be three-dimensional can be translated into a quick, flat version this way.

Your first attempts will probably be copies of suggested bulletin boards, but once you see how simple it is, you will be limited only by your imagination. Need a tree for a bulletin board? Find one you like in a book or magazine and trace it onto acetate. The possibilities are endless!

PART
FOUR

Book Reports

THE SUPERNATURAL

grades 4–6—coordinates with Chapters 1 and 2

October book reports always seem to be ghost stories or mysteries, so that a mad rush of students soon exhausts this material in the media center and the public library.

Advance preparation on your part will allow students to choose a book that appeals to them, rather than to take what is left. No one wants to eliminate the occult as a theme for October, but you can avoid the problem by broadening the topic.

The range of subjects for this activity can be enhanced by including supernatural elements in folklore or investigations into parapsychology. Students can read about the history of magic or do book reports on famous magicians. Short story collections about cats, black or otherwise, could be made acceptable as well. Students in the upper elementary grades can be introduced to mythology by reading about monsters from ancient myths. Almost any section of the collection can be utilized to obtain material relevant to the topic.

If possible, take your class to the media center so you can guide them in their selections.

Once students have chosen their books, plan a creative presentation that gets your room decorated as well. Instead of the formal report or the ever-popular diorama, suggest they try something new—such as bat, ghost, or pumpkin mobiles. Templates can be made on posterboard and students can use them to cut the shapes from construction paper. If students prefer still different shapes they are free to use their own imaginations. The templates are only for those who want to use them.

The book reports can be written on a series of 3″ × 5″ cards. The unruled side of the *last* card should have the author and title. If possible, the call number should be included. The cards are then suspended by strings from the ghost, bat, or pumpkin. (See the illustration.) The students then tie another piece of string to the head of the ghost, bat, or pumpkin, and hang the reports in the classroom or the hall.

SPORTS

grades 5–8—coordinates with Chapters 1, 2, and 7

It is always a challenge to find an original approach to book reports. To stimulate interest, suggest doing the old tried-and-true sports book report with a few new twists that have appeal and add to library skills experiences. Selections can be made from either the fiction or nonfiction collection, thus reminding students how libraries are arranged.

When they write their reports students will, of course, indicate whether the book is factual or not. But in either case the format of the report will be like that of a magazine article. Biography and fiction lend themselves to interviewing techniques. Other nonfiction works can be written about in straight reports.

Because this assignment requires more creativity than the traditional book report it is best to anticipate that students will need help in getting started. After the class has been told what must be done and after they have made their selections, several follow-up lessons should be planned to avoid student panic as the due date nears.

A few typical sports magazines should be brought to class. The key elements brought up in the discussion about them can be listed on a ditto sheet so each student will have a copy when writing the book report. Words and phrases used to describe such repetitious items as wins and losses can be listed on a chart.

The differences between reporting on a sport and interviewing a sports figure should be discussed. For example, explain that in an interview there is no need to write "and then he said." The reporter can put just his or her name followed by a colon to indicate the interviewer's questions and then in another paragraph write the player's name followed by a colon to indicate the answer.

Reports can include history, records, highlights, humor, or whatever was in the book. Sections can be set off with a brief heading describing what is to follow, thus imitating the bold-faced type of a magazine article.

To have students practice their library skills have each book report conclude with a two- or three-book bibliography on the sport for recommended future reading. Students must include one fiction and one nonfiction suggestion. For some sports, this may prove difficult. If so, students could name an alternate unusual sport in their bibliography.

So much work goes into these book reports that they deserve to be put on display. A bulletin board in the hall outside the class is ideal. Have students give their "sports magazine" a name and let them prepare the masthead for the bulletin board.

During or after class an "editorial board" can meet to organize the reports. They may choose to group them by sport or by format (interview, straight report) and then prepare a table of contents. An editorial describing the assignment can be written and a cover designed.

Instead of collecting all the reports under one cover, it should appear (for the purpose of display) as though the magazine were cut up into separate pages. Just be sure it reads from left to right with the cover being at the extreme left followed logically by the contents, editorial, and other elements. Be sure the editorial staff gets credit.

Artistic students may draw sports scenes to illustrate the articles. Additional pictures may be cut from old magazines. Some students may become so inspired that they may decide to include other items like a crossword puzzle or a sports quiz.

Just because the assignment began as a book report does not mean it must be confined to that framework. Doing the extra activities will require the further use of library skills, thus allowing students to become proficient at gathering information.

Enrichment Activities

Phyllis Newman (reading teacher at the Harry S. Truman School in Sayreville, New Jersey) uses some further ideas to enrich the book report. She has students make lists of sports terms found in their books and requires them to check the dictionary for the definitions of all the unfamiliar ones.

The students are also challenged to devise a completely new game—giving all the rules, terminology, and equipment needed. These rules can be displayed in the hallway or media center for all the students to see, or they can be offered to the physical education teacher to see if the new games will really work.

THE CARD CATALOG

grades 3–6—coordinates with Chapter 2

Book reports have always been the traditional method of requiring students to read on a regular basis, but Beverly Zinze (a teacher at the Harry S. Truman School in Sayreville, New Jersey) wanted to do something more with the activity. The following is her account of how her students became involved in a most unusual series of book reports:

My combined third and fourth grade class had just completed a six-week unit on library skills, and I talked with the library media specialist who handled the instruction. With her help on technical matters I was able to assign a series of book reports that met the original criterion, introduced students to new subject areas, reinforced their library skills, and had them asking for more.

Sears—A Guide to Book Reports

Students were allowed to choose subjects for their first book reports from a preselected list. The library media specialist and I sat down with Sears List of Subject Headings *and made up a list of about twenty subjects that she knew were well represented in the card catalog and that I thought would be of interest to my students. This was my first introduction to* Sears.

The students picked any subject they liked, or, if nothing appealed to them, they could check with the library media specialist and come up with another subject. I distributed the form listing the subject and all necessary information (on page 302) and brought my class to the media center. They used the card catalog to compile a list of at least three books on their subject. The form helped them stay organized and it was easy for me to check. After their lists were completed students had to locate the books on the shelves. Using techniques explained earlier in the year they evaluated the books as to level of difficulty and personal interest and chose one for a book report. I approved their choices before they were permitted to check out the books.

Some students tried to pick books that were too easy or too difficult. Occasionally, their choices were poor because the titles under their original subject were not appealing, or, when they made their list from the card catalog the subject was so large that they inadvertently selected books on the wrong level. In all these cases the problems were resolved by rechecking the card catalog, and, when necessary, talking with the library media specialist and changing to another subject.

As the class proceeded it was easy to help students who were having difficulty at any stage on a one-to-one basis. This allowed me to see where their reasoning had led them astray. The whole class was successful in finding books that interested them and left the media center anxious to move on to the next part of the assignment.

Instead of having the class summarize the books, those who read fiction titles had to describe the setting, the main character, and three events. At first, students had trouble trying to figure out the setting. I spent a lot of time helping them find the clues that tell readers whether a story is modern, historic, or futuristic; in an urban, rural, or suburban setting. The time was well used, as students became aware that many messages are included within a story and they must learn to be alert for them. Students who read nonfiction had to explain what made their selection a good book (examples are illustrations and lots of definitions) and three facts they learned.

The covers for their book reports were to be in the form of a subject card, including the call number, the subject (in capital letters), author, title, publisher, place of publication, date, and number of pages. I was amazed at the number of students who became so enthusiastic about their books that they returned to their original list and continued to read more on the subject they had selected.

The Second Report

The author book report was designed following the success of the subject book report. To begin, the library media specialist gave me a list of 25 authors represented in the collection with at least two and preferably three or more books, all suitable for students at my grade level. She gave me the approximate reading level for each of these authors and a word or two indicating the subjects they wrote about. Some authors, like Beverly Cleary, cover a wide range as they write for several reading levels.

I assigned the authors based on my knowledge of students' abilities. We went to the media center again and the students turned to the card catalog. They used their evaluation techniques and forms to select one book from their lists which I then approved.

The cover of this book report was an author card. The contents of the report included main character and setting. Few students needed much help in determining setting. An additional question was, "Did you enjoy this author? Why or why not?" I felt that this question was necessary since I had assigned the author. Several students liked their books so much that they checked out more titles by the same author.

Name _____

Subject _____

Call Number	Author	Title	Pages

The Only One Left

Student enthusiasm was so high after these two book reports that a title book report seemed obvious. I prepared a list using the favorite books the students had read, plus some additional suggestions by the library media specialist and gave each student a strip of paper with a title on it.

At the media center students looked up their titles in the card catalog to find the call number and author. Despite the previous library instruction some had difficulty, most often when the title began with "A," "An," or "The," but again the one-to-one help I was able to give solved problems rapidly.

For variation, the cover had to contain the title card, the author card, and one possible subject card for their book. In order to do the last part students had to learn how to read the tracings on the bottom of the catalog cards.

The content of the report included setting, main character, and three events. By now, the class was quite confident with those requirements. I asked them to list five new words they had found, copying the sentence in which the word had appeared, underlining it, and then defining it. I thought more than five would prove to be a chore and would not be done as carefully. Not only did this encourage dictionary skills, but most students also tried to find the five hardest words.

Afterthoughts

The level of student work and their enthusiasm was so high I am looking forward to repeating the series next year. I plan to make one change—assigning the subject book report last. The search for subjects in the card catalog gave students the most trouble, and I think it will be easier for them this way.

The class learned a lot and enjoyed doing their book reports as well. I cannot remember ever having a class with so many students who were interested in reading. I am convinced it is because they had so many opportunities for choice. I was not prepared, however, for the one student who asked me after finishing the third book report, "When are we going to do book reports?" She was having so much fun, she didn't believe it was the real thing!

ANIMALS

grades 4–8—coordinates with Chapter 2

Subjects for book reports are frequently selected because there are enough materials in those areas. Students get more out of reports when the assignment is structured so that it expands on and reinforces library skills and also sharpens analytical skills.

Animal books are a perfect choice to meet these multiple objectives. There is never a problem finding enough titles. Every media center has a large assortment. The topic interests a high percentage of students throughout all grades. Whether you use this with a class of fourth graders or with an eighth grade class, the structure of the report will be the same. The differences lie in the reading levels of the books selected and in the sophistication of the student responses. For the lower grades, you may prefer to select the titles and then have students choose among them.

In any case, take the opportunity to discuss with the class the subject entries in the card catalog that will lead them to various animal books. This is a good time for them to appreciate when the subject heading ANIMALS—FICTION is used, and when the name of the animal followed by—FICTION is the heading. With the increased use of commercial processing, many media centers have cards under specific animals when there are only one or two entries under the heading, and this concept should be explained to students.

Developing Analytical Skills

After students have made their selections, discuss the nature of animal stories. The fact that a book is about horses does not mean that its format is the same as that of other horse stories. Once a book is classified by type, further analysis generally stops. Few students or teachers consider the various structures within a genre. Stimulate students' awareness of distinctions within a type by presenting the following subcategories:

1. A fictionalized account that is nonetheless an accurate picture of the life of an animal.

2. A story of the relationship between a person and an animal. The animal does not talk, nor are its thoughts explained, but the animal plays an important role in the life of the person.

3. A story of the relationship between a person and an animal where the animal has human characteristics.

4. A story that centers completely around animal life. Human beings play a negligible role. The animals have human personalities while retaining certain physical characteristics of their species.

Give examples of the four categories to help students understand the distinctions. *Dupper* by Betty Baker (Greenwillow, 1976) falls into the first category. The classic animal tales such as *Lassie Come Home* by Eric Knight (Holt, 1940) belong to the second category. *Charlotte's Web* by E. B. White (Harper, 1952) is an example of the third category. In that story, Fern is very involved with Charlotte and Wilbur, who are constrained by their animal problems but also exhibit human characteristics. Jean Van Leeuwen's *The Great Christmas Kidnapping Caper* (Dial, 1975) is typical of the fourth category; although Marvin the Magnificent and his cohorts are bent on rescuing Macy's Santa Claus, the human beings are peripheral characters. Read selections from the four books to the class and have the students assign them to their proper categories.

When students write their book reports, one section should require them to determine in which category their animal book belongs. Analyzing information is not a skill learned overnight. To teach the ability to appraise material from several approaches, you must make analysis a regular, integral part of what the student is studying. This particular exercise is simple, but it provides a first step, requiring students to stop and think. As you become aware of analysis as a needed skill, you will be continuing to integrate it into future activities.

Follow up this book report with a nonfiction assignment on animal books. Students should be able to point out where the fictional account includes accurate information and where the author's imagination takes over. This is a particularly successful exercise if you have completed a unit on fact and fiction.

MOOD AND EMOTION

grades 5–8—coordinates with Chapter 3

One of the primary aims of a book report should be to guide students into becoming critical and aware readers. Merely asking them to recite the plot or event to explain the theme does not require students to apply their own reasoning to what the author has set before them.

Students enjoy books about problems faced by their contemporaries. You can use this interest as a springboard for a book report on mood and emotion that makes your students think.

Phyllis Newman (reading teacher at the Harry S. Truman School in Sayreville, New Jersey) introduces the book report to her fifth and sixth grade students by presenting them with a selection from one of their reading textbooks that illustrates a tranquil setting that is disturbed by the onset of a storm. The students analyze the adjectives chosen by the author to reinforce the two contrasting moods. Older students can look for additional techniques used, such as alliteration and assonance.

Now the students are alert to the presence of mood in literature, Mrs. Newman reads several picture books such as *The Quarreling Book* by Charlotte Zolotow (Harper, 1963), *We Never Get to Do Anything* by Martha Alexander (Dial, 1970), *Noisy Nora* by Rosemary Wells (Dial, 1973), and *Hug Me* by Patti Stren (Harper, 1977).

Because the books are so simple, the students find it easy to isolate the mood words. If you are in a middle or junior high school, try *Gertrude Kloppenberg (Private)* by Ruth Hooker (Abingdon Press, 1970) or ask your library media specialist to arrange an inter-library loan from the elementary schools.

While the introductory phase is going on, prepare a large classroom collection on such topics as death, divorce, mental handicaps, old age, and weight. You can locate titles in these categories using the card catalog or check for suggestions in *The Bookfinder* by Sharon S. Dreyer (American Guidance, two volumes). Put the books in bins, boxes, or whatever is available. Attach labels to the front of the boxes to show the different categories.

Now assign the book report. Students choose from those books you have already gathered. Hand out a form such as the one shown on page 307. They all must answer the first questions and then answer the ones listed under the category of the book they have chosen.

The book report is presented as a booklet, complete with cover. Students also prepare the mobile described after the eighth question. While this may be omitted for grades seven and eight, it does make a colorful display in the classroom and hall.

A NEW IDEA: MAGAZINE REPORTS

grades 4–8—coordinates with Chapter 7

Sometimes getting back to a routine after a holiday break or vacation is difficult. Perhaps a new idea might restimulate creative thinking and generate enthusiasm. Instead of assigning book reports, assign magazine reports. (The "Promote Periodicals" bulletin board in Part Three can accompany this assignment.) In addition to offering them a change of pace, students benefit by working with non-book information sources. Some will be introduced to a new area of the media center; others who regularly read one or two magazines will learn of other titles. Slow readers love this assignment because it requires comparatively little reading. All students will gain as they learn to use periodicals.

Borrow an assortment of back issues keeping in mind the interest level of the group you teach. In most situations, the entire collection can be used. If you are in an elementary school remember to include periodicals that are below the reading level of the class for students who have reading difficulties.

Ask students who read magazines regularly to tell you their favorites. Write their answers on the chalkboard. Divide their responses into two groups—those titles that are nonfiction and those that include fiction and nonfiction articles.

After you have obtained enough answers, stop to see if the class can determine why you placed a particular magazine in one column or the other. At this time review the methods by which the class can determine whether an article is fiction or nonfiction.

Distribute among the students the magazines you have selected and tell them to turn to the table of contents. (Students will use these magazines only during the explanation. Later, they will make their own selections for the magazine report.)

The headings in the table of contents should help students determine which articles are fiction and which are nonfiction.

Point out that most magazines have regular features. Few of these are acceptable articles for this assignment. Letters to the Editor, the Editorial Statement, puzzle pages, and other such material are interesting to the general reader but cannot be included in the framework of the magazine report. However, some periodicals such as *Natural History* have articles on special topics by regular contributors. These can be used.

Before students select their magazines explain how they are expected to write their report. Ask the class to read four articles (the number may be increased at your discretion) from at least two magazines. One of the articles must be fiction and two must be nonfiction. It is also wise to establish the minimum number of pages that an article can have. For younger children two pages may be enough because magazines for their reading level rarely have long articles.

Tell the students to summarize each article in two paragraphs. Then ask them to explain in a separate essay why the article was included in the magazine. Warn them that it is not enough to say that a sports article belongs in *Sports Illustrated*. They must observe that the average reader of that magazine is a sports spectator, not a player. The articles are not concerned with how to improve one's play, but rather with how to observe the finer points of a game.

The final form of the book report can be presented in one of two ways: each article can be listed at the end of the report, giving students a chance to apply skills at writing the proper bibliographic citation for periodicals; or the articles can be listed according to the form used in the *Readers' Guide to Periodical Literature*. To do this, they will have to locate the volume number and know how to interpret a listing in that book.

MOOD AND EMOTION BOOK REPORT

1. What is the prevailing mood (happiness, sadness, etc.) of your book?

2. What is the problem the character faces?

3. How does the character deal with the problem?

4. Does the character solve the problem alone, with friends, or with an adult?

5. Is the solution a positive one, or at the end of the book is the character still left to face it?

6. How would you deal with the problem?

7. Find five adjectives that would describe the mood of the book. Try to be as specific as you can.

8. Does loneliness play a part in the book? How?

    Make a large bubble, cloud, or sun to represent the mood of your book. On one side, paste the paper with the answers to the questions. On the other side, list the adjectives. Be creative in your display.

Expanding the Unit

Students can follow up their reports by taking a closer look at magazines. For instance, they can learn why library media specialists call magazines "periodicals." They can also extend their analytic abilities by looking at the type of advertising in the magazines. Questions for this study can include the following:

- How do advertisers capitalize on the readers for which the magazine is meant?
- How does the number of advertising pages compare to the total number of pages?
- Why do some magazines have no advertising? Does this affect their subscription cost?

As students answer these questions, they gain further insights into how the unwary consumer can be manipulated, and they learn that it is wise to be observant.

THE PLAY'S THE THING

grades 5–8—coordinates with Chapter 2

Phyllis Newman (reading teacher at the Harry S. Truman School in Sayreville, New Jersey) tries to give her fifth and sixth grade students a broad range of experiences, both for their enjoyment and for improving their skills. The following is her description of a book report that gave students experience in new areas and stimulated their creativity as well:

Although the students are familiar with poetry and long and short works of fiction and nonfiction, I discovered a great weakness in their comprehension of plays. Whenever a play appeared in the basal reader, students became easily confused because of the different format. I felt that this difficulty could become a springboard for a whole new area of study, and it did. Students learned how to analyze and better understand a play and a whole new world opened up for them. Their interest kept skyrocketing, and the unit kept on expanding with fantastic results.

We began by studying a few short plays from our basals as well as some others which were duplicated so that each student could have a copy. The class learned about the different aspects of playwriting such as dialogue, stage directions, scenes, setting, narration, and characters. A vocabulary of theater words was developed. Stories were compared to plays and their similarities and differences were noted.

Students took turns acting out the plays to further their understanding. They became aware of stage directions, learning that they are written in italics. By reading the dialogue and following directions, they learned to understand the playwright's meaning. After finding the main idea and the details, they soon realized the similarities between a play and a book.

Instead of ending the activity here, it was carried a step further. Our school library media specialist helped me develop a "Play Book Report."

We gathered up all the "play" magazines as well as any books containing plays. Anthologies of plays are listed in the card catalog. Those that appear in magazines can be located using a periodical index. Students had three weeks in

Name _____

Class _____

Date due _____

PLAY BOOK REPORT

A play is a story written to be presented as a dramatic performance. A play is written in a special form so that the actors know what they are supposed to say and do. Important elements in a play are *characters, scenes, settings,* and *dialogue.* You should also be aware of *stage directions, props* you will need, and what the *production crew* does as you read your play.

Be prepared to give an oral summary of your play, including main idea, important characters, and setting.

Choose one of the following:

1. Pick one scene from your play and prepare a puppet show to dramatize it.

2. Write a different ending for your play. Include setting, stage directions, dialogue. Prepare a puppet show to dramatize it.

3. Your play has ended. Write out the next scene that would take place if it had continued. Include setting, stage directions, dialogue. Prepare a puppet show to dramatize it.

Make your puppets out of paper towel rolls, socks, tongue depressors, straws, and so forth.

You might want to use the space below to make some sketches of your puppets.

which to prepare at home for a class presentation to include a brief oral summary of the play, giving the main idea, setting, and important characters. They were also asked to construct a simple puppet stage and puppets. I made a sample using a carton and straws with faces for the puppets.

There were three choices for the puppet show, planned so that students could perform satisfactorily at their own level. (See the worksheet on page 309 for the exact requirements.) *The easiest was simply to act out a scene from the play. Before this could be done the context of the scene had to be explained to the audience. A second choice was to write a new ending for the play. A third alternative was to add on another scene. These two activities had to be written up in play form using stage directions, italics, narration, etc.*

The results were exciting. The sample stage and puppets I had made looked like the work of a three-year-old compared to what the students made. They performed their scenes in front of their class and evoked great enjoyment and admiration from fellow classmates. I thought the work was so spectacular that a week later all the stages and puppets were displayed in the media center and students gave special performances to all first and second grade classes.

And Still More

The unit continued. We set up a learning center called "The Show Must Go On" in the classroom. Those students who had developed a real interest in plays and the theater were placed in this center for further independent study. They did research on such things as the history of the theater, architecture, famous theaters, types of productions, performers, lighting and sound, makeup, costumes, and set design. As a final activity, some students designed sets, costumes, and masks, experimented with theatrical makeup, and wrote original plays.

What began as an attempt to improve reading comprehension in one area blossomed into a whole course of study that proved truly valuable to everyone. Not only did students overcome their weaknesses; they developed new strengths in oral and written expression as well as new interests to pursue.

POETRY

grades 5–8—coordinates with Chapter 9

An ideal assignment during or after a classroom poetry unit is a poetry book report. Materials to report on include the works of a single poet, or works on a single theme, although any poetry book would be acceptable.

Prepare a list of questions students should answer in their reports. Some sample questions include the following:

1. What is the poet's name?
2. What are the dates of his or her birth and death?
3. What is the poet's nationality?
4. How many poems are included in the book, or is the book one long poem?
5. On the average, how long are the poems?
6. Do the poems rhyme? (If this report is given to students in grade six or above there could be a question about the rhyme scheme as well.)

7. What seems to be the favorite subject matter of the poet? Give an example.

8. Which poem or section of a poem did you like best? Give an example.

9. Is this the first poetry book you have read? If yes, did you like or dislike it? Explain. If no, compare this to the one or ones you have read.

When the subject is poetry, oral reports are best since the sound of the language will be emphasized. If there isn't enough time, students can tape their reports and hand in the cassette for you to hear.

If your students have never taped book reports before, they may be surprised to discover that taped reports are more difficult to do than written ones. Try to reserve a quiet area for students to use when taping their reports. Be available to offer technical guidance, and remind the students to speak slowly and to know in advance what they are going to say.

At this age, few students are capable of speaking from an outline; therefore, prepared notes are essential. Hesitations in speech are very pronounced on tape. One bonus of this lesson is that students learn to speak more clearly.

MAKING FULL USE OF BIOGRAPHIES

grades 5–8—coordinates with Chapter 9

Biographies are one category of literature that teachers most commonly assign as topics for book reports. Their flowing narratives not only make them an excellent introduction to nonfiction, they also make them easy to compare and contrast with fiction.

Because biographies are such a natural subject for book reports, they are not always used for other purposes. For instance, they could be used as a means of expanding the understanding of other times and customs. Instead of allowing a book report on biographies to be just another homework assignment, make it the beginning of a mini-unit on changing times.

The objectives of the unit will enable students to:

• visualize which famous people were contemporaries

• show that they are familiar with major historical events, as well as common occurrences

• extract meaningful information from biographies.

Furthermore, as students complete the unit they will construct a labeled and illustrated time line.

Young children do not have a good understanding of the past. Events that took place a year ago seem to them to be ancient history. Although this incorrect sense of time gradually lessens as they grow older, it is present throughout most of their school years.

The problem is compounded by the teaching of history, which is done by presenting it in neat packages. As a result, a junior high school student may understand that George Washington was a historical figure to Abraham Lincoln, but may not realize that Queen Victoria was a contemporary of Lincoln. By combining a book report with the unit, an awareness of the past will quickly be developed, and a frame of reference that will make learning easier will be provided.

As soon as you decide to assign a biography book report consider the available resources and the length of the reports.

First, you should decide on the range of the assignment. For instance, you can limit the biographies to people who lived in a specific century or country. It is always best if the assignment complements other areas of study.

A limit may be placed on the assignment by the amount of space available to display the time line. For a fully developed unit, the corridor outside the classroom is probably the best place to exhibit the time line. Once you know where to put it, you or some of the students can begin to construct the time line, which should be divided by bold vertical lines as shown in this illustration.

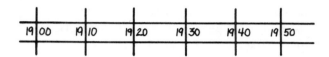

Care must be taken, particularly if students are involved in this early preparation, to make sure that all the segments are of equal length.

A guide sheet that lists what kind of information the students should extract from their reading should be handed out when the assignment is given. For example, the guide sheet may contain the following:

Author:

Title:

Subject's full name:

Dates:

1. List major events in the subject's life.
2. Note any reference in the biography to the following:
   a. clothing (describe)
   b. transportation
   c. world events

Additional categories such as inventions, artists, musicians, disasters (earthquakes, floods, shipwrecks) can be added to the book report or assigned as a group project.

Each student need not locate information in all of the selected categories. Although the students must examine their chosen biographies for all descriptions of or references to the categories listed on the guide sheet, they will work in groups to create their part of the display. If, for example, the transportation group does not have enough information, they alone will have to do further research.

After students have read one biography they can use the *Index to Young Readers' Collective Biographies* and add to the time line information about other people who were contemporaries of the subject of their biography. You might even limit this book report just to collective biographies. Require students to read 125 to 200 pages, just as they would for a full-length biography, but this way they will read about the lives of a number of different people.

Descriptions of the different categories of the reports will have to be written on separate pages so that each group that is working on a category can use them to start their research. For example, there should be one page for clothing, another for transportation, and so on. (The pages should be labeled with the proper dates on top.) Once the reports are graded, the sheets can be distributed to the groups.

Because you are the first to see all the biography book reports, you can control the amount of research each group has to do. Give a slower group less to look up, making them responsible for just displaying the names and dates of the subjects. A brighter group can be given more to research.

The success of the time line and the supporting research will depend on whether the information is presented in a visually meaningful way. To create a vivid picture, have the dates of a person's life represented by a bar cut to fit the scale of the time line. (See the illustration here.)

A color code can be used so that the bars representing the lives of Americans are one color and those representing the lives of Europeans, Africans, and Asians are other colors. The dates of single events, such as disasters or inventions, can be written inside large stars. These, too, can be color-coded. Sections on transportation and clothing should include pictures as well as descriptions. (Remind students that just as automobile designs change over the years, so did those of carriages.)

For easy reference the time line can be divided according to the various categories. The idea is to get the message across as clearly as possible. (See the illustration on page 314 for an example of a completed time line.)

As always, an evaluation must be conducted to determine whether the objectives of the unit have been met. Simply monitoring the progress that the students have made in the classroom and in the media center is one way of making sure that the students are on the right track. If any difficulties are discovered, they can be corrected by offering additional instruction.

A writing assignment can be used to make a final evaluation. Have students choose a year on the time line during which they would have liked to live as an adult, a teenager, or a child. After using the time line to make notes, they are to describe a typical day in that year.

In their descriptions they are to include as much information as possible about the lives of the people of that day. The simplest way to accomplish this assignment is to begin by writing about the morning and progressing to evening by describing the ritual of dressing, reading a newspaper, or overhearing an adult conversation, going to work or school, and so on. They can, of course, refer

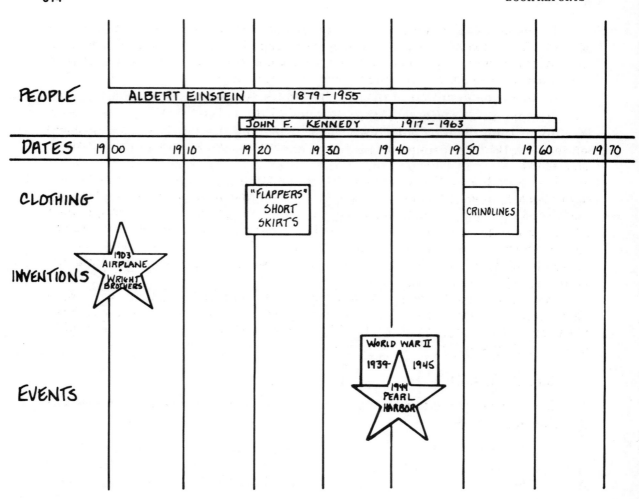

to historical events that took place before the day they are describing; they cannot describe those that took place after.

The resulting paper will show how much students have learned about the sequence of history. As an extra benefit, many students will continue to read biographies, not only to learn about the life of the subject, but also to appreciate the lifestyle of the times.

"PRESENT"ING

grades 4–6—motivates reading

The week before Christmas and all through the school halls, eager students are anticipating their hauls! Of course, not all their thoughts are mercenary; the spirit of the season also means students are concerned about the gifts they are giving to others. What they are *not* thinking about is school work. Nevertheless, teachers must get work done. You can save your sanity with this book report which is perfectly attuned to the prevailing mood.

The completed report is a holiday-wrapped gift for an important character in the book that the student read. The box may contain drawings of the item, miniatures, or the real thing.

To explain the requirements, a completed sample gift box should be displayed. The fictional character who is receiving the gift should be familiar to most of the students. If you read full-length works regularly to the class, choose one of these titles for the sample. Otherwise, select a popular work, perhaps one that has been made into a movie or adapted for television.

Give a copy of the worksheet (on page 317) to each student. It is necessary to explain to students what is meant by "analyze the character." The process becomes simpler as you use the following example to walk the students through the report.

For Annabel in *Freaky Friday* by Mary Rodgers, for example, some students might choose cosmetics for use when Annabel becomes her mother, or marshmallows (her favorite food). Other more thoughtful presents might be a notebook and pens to continue her writing, toothpaste to keep her now braces-free teeth shining, and a book (non-existent) on "How to Impress a Boyfriend." More gift ideas will quickly be suggested, but be sure all presents are explained as to why they are appropriate.

With the introduction complete and books selected, students can begin thinking of presents while they are reading. It may seem unnecessary to have worksheets for a simple assignment, but when students have directions readily available they seem to do a better job.

To Make the Gift Box

Cut a sheet of oaktag so that it can be folded into a box as shown in this illustration.

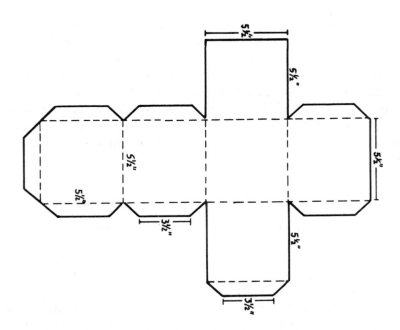

Students are to trace the outline to make their own gift boxes. Wrapping paper is cut to the same size and pasted onto the oaktag. When properly folded, the present is already gaily wrapped and waiting to be filled with the gift items.

Complete the package with a gift tag. A sample is shown here.

```
From _____
              (student's name)

To   _____
             (character's name)

In   _____
                  (title)

By   _____
                 (author)
```

Then hang the presents from the ceiling or display on the windowsills for a holiday decoration that joyously announces that books bring good cheer.

BOOKMARK BOOK REPORTS
grades 3-6—motivates reading

Make a book report into a bulletin board. Have your students express the main idea of the book they have read in one simple illustration that can be turned into a bookmark. The ones shown on page 318 were designed by several students of Paulette DiMeola (sixth grade teacher at the Eisenhower School in Sayreville, New Jersey). The two bookmarks that do not have the titles written on them are for *The Great Christmas Kidnapping Caper* by Jean Van Leeuwen and *The Toothpaste Millionaire* by Jean Merrill.

If you want to make the bulletin board in addition to the bookmarks, you will need the following:

scissors

aluminum foil

red and green construction paper

bookmarks

stapler

Cover the bulletin board with aluminum foil. Cut out large stars from red and green construction paper and attach to the bulletin board. Attach a bookmark to each star. Cut out the letters from construction paper and attach.

GIFT BOX FOR YOUR FAVORITE CHARACTER

Due _____

1. Read your book.

2. Pick one character and do an analysis of him or her:

   a. physical traits (age, appearance, male or female)
   b. personality traits
   c. likes and dislikes (hobbies, talents)
   d. time and place

   Write this information in complete sentences on index cards.

3. Plan a gift box for your character. What things would you like to give the character based on what you learned about him or her? Make sure the items are appropriate for the time and place of the story.

4. Make the gifts out of construction paper, cardboard, wood, etc., or find the actual items.

5. Make a greeting card for your character. Tell the character why you are giving him or her the gifts you chose. (Optional: Do the card in verse.)

6. Use the pattern to make a gaily decorated gift box and place the items in the box.

7. Complete the package with a gift tag.

BOOK END BOOK REPORTS

grades 5–8—motivates reading

Book reports can be used to help students develop critical thinking skills. At least one question in the report should require some analytic reading.

Fiction books are the most commonly assigned topics because students find them easiest. Teachers, on the other hand, are often hard-pressed to find another approach to make the report different from previous ones.

One solution that also makes students think is to spin off book reports from the "Book Ends" bulletin board in Part Three. A book comes to an end for a reason. The plot has been resolved and generally all loose ends have been tied up. Although not all books have endings as thought-provoking as those on the bulletin board, they still relate to the story.

An added bonus that you will appreciate is that it is extremely difficult to answer the questions without having read the entire book.

Questions for Book End Book Reports

Have students copy the last three sentences of their book. (They may use more than three sentences if it is necessary for clarity.) Then they are to answer the following questions:

1. Who is speaking or what is being described?
2. How do these sentences relate to the plot?
3. Why does the author end the book at this point?
4. What do you think happens after the book ends?

UN-MAGICKED BOOK REPORTS

grades 6–8—motivates reading

One of the major objectives of education is to encourage students to develop a love of reading. More poetically, this can be described as "helping students discover the magic and wonder of books" or "finding the magic of reading." Here is a way to take the magic *out* of reading!

Unlike regular book reports, whose primary purpose is to encourage reading, this book report is designed to develop analytical skills and to stimulate creative responses. When assigning them you will need to be patient and understanding since students might find them difficult and frustrating at first.

The basic procedure is outlined here: (1) Read a folk story or fairy tale in which magic plays a significant role. (2) Have the students describe the influence that magic has on the plot. (3) Ask them to rewrite the story but to *eliminate* the magic and to *substitute* it with other causes, conditions, occurrences, and so forth, so that their stories will arrive at the same conclusion.

It is always best to give students a more detailed explanation, such as the one that follows.

You may need help in selecting the books, since the card catalog does not contain an entry that satisfies the requirements of this assignment. (The entry MAGIC—FICTION does not contain the kinds of books you will need.) Therefore, work your way through the 398.2 collection, pulling out as many appropriate titles as you can find. Do not ignore the large anthologies. Students will not need to read the entire volume; reading just one or two of the collected tales will be sufficient.

Try to have more books than there are students. The extras will allow them to have a choice.

Choose one story, preferably a short one, that you can use to demonstrate the procedure to the class. *The Funny Little Woman* by Arlene Mosel (Dutton, 1972) is a good choice, but there are many others. If possible, take the class to the media center or public library and seat them near the folk tale collection. This area is convenient because if some students prefer to use books that you did not select they will be near the proper section. You will be able to assist them and still be able to work with those browsing through the books on the table.

Once the students have settled down briefly introduce the assignment, quickly explaining that they are to select books for their next book report and that the topic of the report is called "The Un-Magic of Folk Tales."

Explain that they must think carefully before they begin to actually write this book report. Tell them that to help them along you will do one book report together.

Before beginning the story ask the students to pay particular attention to the instances of magic in the tale. If you read *The Funny Little Woman*, tell the class that magic is present at the beginning, in the middle, and at the end of the story. Ask the students to list all the instances of magic and record their answers on a chalkboard or transparency. Write all their responses on the left-hand side of the board or transparency.

When the students cannot name any more instances of magic, have them restate the conclusion. For *The Funny Little Woman*, the conclusion should be expressed something like this: "With the help of her magic paddle and with her talent for making rice dumplings, the little woman went into business and became the richest woman in Japan."

Now comes the difficult part—transforming all the instances of magic into possible occurrences. Accept highly improbable explanations. For *The Funny Little Woman*, one class decided that instead of the dumpling falling through a crack, a prince traveling in disguise comes upon the hut and tastes the excellent dumplings. The little woman is then seized by the prince, instead of by the Oni, and is compelled to provide him with dumplings daily. No magic paddle is needed. The woman is given a complete kitchen staff to help her speed up her work.

Although the woman again must escape her captor, there are not any Oni having the power to hold water in their mouths. The class explained that the little woman kills the prince by poisoning the dumplings. Since she is not a fool, she not only takes as many valuables from him as she can put into a cart, but she also takes a good supply of kitchen utensils and her trusty kitchen staff.

The conclusion the class arrived at was the same as the one in the original tale—but it was arrived at without including any instances of magic. (The class merely had to substitute the phrase "large group of workers and the money to get things started" for the words "magic paddle.")

Record the instances of reality fabricated by the students next to the instances of magic they substitute. Although all the magical happenings will be eliminated, it is not necessary to account for each instance of magic. In *The Funny*

Little Woman, for example, the talking statues of Jizo had no realistic counter-part in the new tale because it would not fit in this version.

The students must carefully be told about the kind of analysis they must make; otherwise, their rewrites might be too broad. For example, at first the class explained the woman's accumulation of wealth in *The Funny Little Woman* by simply saying that she wins a lottery, causing her to become the richest woman in Japan.

Such an explanation is not acceptable because it does not deal with the woman's cooking skill or her magic paddle. Although it may have been more acceptable if the class had added that the woman was able to buy with her lottery money a rice field from which she procured the ingredients to make dumplings, the explanation radically changes the cause for the story's action, which is the woman's ability to make dumplings. The final version written by the class deals better with the plot of the story.

After the students understand what must be done, give them time to make their selections. You should be prepared to deal with tensions that the students may have because of the assignment. Although anxiety is to be expected any time something new is required, you can anticipate that this report will upset the students more than most assignments.

Calm the students' fears by telling them they will be given a worksheet that will help them and that will spell out all the requirements of the assignment. This sheet should outline the story as it was outlined on the transparency or on the chalkboard. The left-hand column should list the magical elements and the right-hand column should list the revisions.

It might be wise to give sixth graders a second sheet that can be filled in. (See the worksheet on page 322.) Such a form will allow them to retell in a few sentences the story they have read and will allow them to separate all the instances of magic. Provide space on the right side of this sheet so that students can make their alterations by section. The complete story can then be rewritten by properly connecting the events so the whole tale makes sense.

So much work goes into this book report that you might want to display the results. A good idea is to decorate a bulletin board with a magician or wizard on one side, a computer or robot on the other, and to hang the reports between the figures.

FORM FOR UN-MAGICKED BOOK REPORTS

Sample: *The Funny Little Woman*

The Original

1. The funny little woman makes great rice dumplings. A dumpling falls into a hole under her hut. She follows it and is captured by the wicked Oni.

2. The Oni give the woman a magic paddle to speed the cooking of rice. She is to make rice dumplings for all the Oni.

*   *   *

The woman takes the paddle and escapes in a boat. The Oni drink the water leaving the boat high and dry. When the woman falls in the mud, they laugh and the water falls out of their mouths. She gets back into the boat and gets away.

3. With the help of her magic paddle and her talent for making rice dumplings, the little woman goes into business and becomes the richest woman in all Japan.

Without Magic

1. The funny little woman makes great rice dumplings. An evil prince, traveling in disguise, comes to her hut, tastes a dumpling, and kidnaps the woman.

2. The prince sets the woman to work in the kitchen of his great household. She has a large staff and the latest in kitchen utensils to help her make dumplings daily.

*   *   *

She puts poison in the dumplings and it kills the prince. She flees, taking as many treasures as can fit into a cart. She also takes her well-trained staff and her kitchen utensils.

3. With the help of her large staff of workers, the money to get things started, and her talent for making rice dumplings, the little woman goes into business and becomes the richest woman in all Japan.

Now do the same with your book. Use another sheet of paper if necessary.

Author _____   Call Number [   ]

Title _____

The Original

1.

2.

3.

Without Magic

1.

2.

3.

GLOSSARY

Annotation. A brief description of the contents of a work found on catalog cards.

Author Card. A type of catalog card in which the author's name (last name first) appears on the top line.

Book Card. The card used to identify the person who has borrowed a book.

Book Pocket. Holds the book card and/or the date the book is due.

Call Number. Identifies a particular book's location. Consists of letters or letters and numbers, and is found on the book's spine, its card and pocket, and its catalog cards.

Collation. A brief line on the catalog card giving a technical description of the book including number of pages, illustrations or maps, and title of series.

Collective Biography. A single work encompassing the lives of more than one person, grouped by a theme such as presidents or tennis stars.

Continuous Revision. A practice followed by most encyclopedia publishers under which a predetermined portion of the work is updated annually to keep it current without the need to issue a totally new edition.

Cutter Number. A system of using numbers in place of all but the first letter of the author's last name to reduce the number of characters in the call number while permitting detailed filing.

Dewey Decimal Classification System. Commonly called the Dewey Decimal System, devised by Melvil Dewey, and used by most school and public libraries, it divides all areas of knowledge into ten sections or "hundreds," subdividing extensively within each section to define a subject.

Divided Catalog. A card catalog divided into two or three sections in which subject cards are *always* filed in a separate alphabet and author and title cards are sometimes separated. In contrast to a *unified* card catalog in which all three types of cards are interfiled.

Entries. The term for an encyclopedia article or a dictionary definition. (See also "Main Entry.")

Library of Congress Classification System. A system of classification using letters and numbers more extensive and complex than the Dewey Decimal System. Generally found in academic and special libraries.

Main Entry. The word or words being defined in a dictionary.

Main Entry Card. The basic catalog card from which all other cards are constructed, commonly the author card, but occasionally an organization or title appears on the top line when authorship cannot be determined.

Media. A term encompassing all methods of communication, commonly applied to print and nonprint materials.

Periodicals. Almost synonymous with the word "magazines."

Software. Programs played or shown on audio-visual machines such as filmstrips, records, cassettes, transparencies, and computer programs.

Spine Label. The label attached to the spine of a book giving its call number.

Subject Card. A type of catalog card in which the subject (all in capital letters) appears on the top line, filed under the first letter of that subject.

Title Card. A type of catalog card in which the title appears on the top line, filed under the first letter of the title except when the first word of the title is "A," "An," or "The."

Tracings. Information found at the bottom of the catalog card naming all the other entries for that particular book in the catalog.

Trays. The drawers in which catalog cards are kept.

Vertical File. A pamphlet and/or picture file alphabetically arranged by subject, generally kept in a file cabinet and used to provide current and ephemeral information.

INDEX